The Anatomy & Development of the
FORMULA FORD
RACE CAR

Steve Nickless

Motorbooks International
Publishers & Wholesalers

First published in 1993 by Motorbooks International Publishers & Wholesalers, PO Box 2, 729 Prospect Avenue, Osceola, WI 54020 USA

Motorbooks International books are also available at discounts in bulk quantity for industrial or sales-promotional use. For details write to Special Sales Manager at the Publisher's address

Library of Congress Cataloging-in-Publication Data

Nickless, Steve.
 Anatomy & development of Formula Ford race cars/Steve Nickless.
  p. cm.
 Includes index.
 ISBN 0-87938-807-2
 1. Automobiles, Racing– –History. 2. Automobiles, Racing– –Design and construction. 3. Ford automobile– –History. 4. Automobile racing– –History. I. Title. II. Title: Anatomy and development of Formula Ford race cars.
 TL236.N53   1993
 629.228– –dc20   93-19422

On the front cover: One of the most famous of all Formula Ford cars, *Magic Merlyn* (a Merlyn Mark 11), which was driven by Emerson Fittipaldi, Jody Scheckter, and Colin Vandervell in the late 1960s and early 1970s. It has since been immaculately restored. *Gary Gold*

On the back cover: Nelson Ledges, 1976: SCCA National action in the glory years of Formula Ford, which featured a variety of manufacturers, healthy fields, and star drivers. One the front row here were Canadian Jon McKnight (Crossle #03) and perennial FF champion Dave Weitzenhof (Zink #67). *Randy Unsbee*

Printed and bound in the United States of America

Contents

Preface

Had production of this book not been delayed for over 12 months by a change of publishers, it would have emerged a pessimistic tome indeed, an obituary for Formula Ford, dead of neglect at 25.

Instead, it arrives on your bookshelf (thank you very much!) as something else—less a requiem for the dead than a semi-serious nostalgic ditty collection.

In the spring of '92, see, the original publisher put this 25th Anniversary of FF book on hold. So in March and April, when I would have been hard at the computer, I was puttering around instead, looking at pictures and not doing much else.

Suddenly it was the spring of '93, and as well as a new contract from Motorbooks International, there were some pleasant new thoughts about FF to enjoy. And so: Instead of a straight-ahead obit written in one long blast—birth, life, death, condolences to racing's next of kin—this book got stretched out over a year and became a verbal collage of fragments not strung together until the very last minute.

It's probably not as good a *book* for being so disjointed. But it's a more honest review of Formula Ford 1600's first 25 years, colored not by sadness that the class is gone but by wonder that it was so good for so long.

The difference between '92 and '93 was:

• A splendid battle between Van Diemen and Reynard (and a trio of young drivers) in the '92 Rapid Fit-sponsored British Open FF Championship—just like the old days!

• A spectacularly exciting FF Festival featuring several stars of tomorrow and a number of diverse and competitive chassis—just like the old days!

• A keen interest from the important engine tuners in Ford's announcement of the new Zeta engine—not at all like the lukewarm reception given the overhead-cam 2-liter Pinto engine.

Clearly, the Formula Ford we who grew up with it remember, is dead. The racing class using its name and wearing its clothes today is no longer the 'only obvious choice' for a young driver with F1 aspirations, and that was what set the real FF apart, forget the fingerprints and dental work.

But unlike the late '80s FF imposter, this '90s one isn't bad. Experiencing the explosive popularity of club FF and vintage FF in the U.S.; enjoying the winter-long EuroSwift vs. Van Diemen "Battle of the Sales Managers and Fastest Laps" with the new Zeta four; seeing the first pictures of Wiet Huidekoper's new Vector (which may or may not be the Swift of the '90s, but certainly looks the part!) ... all those things have released a flood of adrenaline.

It's the adrenaline I used to finally get this book done—just like the old days!

Formula Ford is dead. Long live Formula Ford.

Steve Nickless
Huntington Beach, Calif.
April 1993

Prologue

In hindsight, Formula Ford's drawn out '63-'67 birth looks like something of a haphazard affair. But in fact, both in its conception and in its rules genesis, Formula Ford probably sprang to life in as orderly a manner as is possible in motor racing.

It was only *after* FF kicked off that all hell broke loose.

Conceived by a racing school proprietor, Formula Ford's original mandate was to fill a void in 'race driver education': There were no inexpensive single-seat racing cars at the time offering performance and mystique enough to satisfy all the would-be Graham Hills. And the schools were going broke trying to run hoary old Formula Juniors and out-of-favor F3 cars.

'Formula Ford' mated an attractive and contemporary-looking (if marginally outdated) F3 chassis to a reliable near-stock Ford Cortina GT 1500cc engine and radial street tires—a simple concept which emerged as a brilliant idea when guys like Sterling Moss and Denny Hulme and Graham Hill drove one and found it was a lot of fun.

In fact, Formula Ford was such a brilliant idea it flourished quickly and soon left behind the sheltered race driving school environment which spawned it. Its legacy was spurned as chassis builders all over the world saw the opportunity to peddle their wares in large volume, and jumped in with both feet.

Before too long, engine tuners and tire makers and aftermarket parts companies of every description joined them, all of them selling FF and its advantages.

The Ford Motor Company, specifically Competition Manager Henry Taylor and then-Director of Public Affairs Walter Hayes, was quick to see merit in the concept and give its blessing—yet another marketing master stroke by Hayes who put the Ford badge on the Cosworth DFV Formula 1 cam covers in '68 for a ridiculously small amount of money!

Certainly, Ford helped fuel the swell of interest. But more powerful than any of the firms with something to sell—more powerful even the involvement of the Ford Motor Co.—was the drivers' immediate support for this new class. It was love at first sight: Racing cars which sold complete for £1,000 (that low price was originally written into the rules!) and offered a performance envelope very close to Formula 3 (which at the time featured highly stressed 1000cc production-based racing engines and expensive race tires).

The schools ran their training programs and their better students then raced out in public with their new Formula Fords, and the groundswell gained momentum at a terrific rate: There were only four manufacturers represented on the grid of the first, standalone FF race in July 1967; less than a year later there were 12 different makes on the grid for the mid-March '68 Formula 1 Race of Champions FF supporting race. Twenty-five years later, an unofficial tally shows that over 150 firms have built at least one FF prototype.

More important in the overall scheme of things, though, and more to crux of the matter: It is reasonable to assume that over 6,000 FF chassis have been sold since 1967 and that something like *30,000 men and women* have raced these cars.

Much more than a stepping-stome class, therefore, Formula Ford is a phenomenon. Indeed, vintage FF racing just now appearing will be a 'can't miss,' for all the old virtues are preserved: relative low cost, ease of maintenance, parts availability (generally, if not specifically) and a huge measure of fun.

Formula Ford became increasingly complex (and therefore expensive) as it matured and as cars like the ADF and Lola T-340 and Quest and Swift DB-1 altered perceptions about what a 'Formula Ford' should be. But long before the first one of those arrived, FF's foundation was comfortably secure.

And now FF is 25, and grown way beyond the scope of a single volume. With apologies, then, for all the many good stories ignored, names overlooked and crucial facts missed, the author humbly submits this ...

1

Pre-History (1961-1966)

THE 1-LITER FORMULA 3 which emerged in 1964 from the shadow of a struggling Formula Junior would produce the most consistently thrilling wheel-to-wheel racing ever seen in Europe for the next half-dozen years. But, despite the best efforts of the international rules makers, F3's shining light was dampened by an affliction shared with its FJr predecessor: cost vs. reliability.

The raucous Cosworth- and Holbay-tuned Ford-based four-cylinder screamers favored in this new F3 were a joy to the ears, but the noise of their impressive output numbers came at a relatively high price.

In an earlier age, the cost of an engine would hardly have mattered; motor racing had always been a rich man's game. But by the early 1960s, the sport's explosive appeal and a creeping worldwide affluence brought a new generation of young people who wanted to take part—in unprecedented numbers.

In fact, John Frankenheimer's 1966 feature film *Grand Prix* rode a tidal wave of Walter Mitty wishfulness like nothing seen before ... or since.

A key tributary in the floodwaters of mid-'60s driver supply was the "Race Driver School." Several of these appeared in the late '50s and early '60s. Among the most notable (because they appeared in England, the sport's motherland): Geoffrey Clarke's Motor Racing Stables based (initially) at Finmere Airfield near Silverstone and later at Brands Hatch; and former Formula Junior/F3 driver Jim Russell's Racing Driver School, based at Snetterton.

If F3 racing's appeal was the seed, then these racing schools were the soil for Formula Ford, a racing class upon which a new age of motor racing was built.

Formula Ford photos to open a Formula Ford history book? Well ... no. Instead, 1-liter Formula 3 which, because of its spectacular intensity and cost, would be FF's catalyst. (LEFT, ABOVE) Silverstone '66. (LEFT) Castle Combe '67.

Pompous words, "new age of motor racing." But this class, Formula Ford, launched literally thousands of careers (drivers, mechanics, constructors, traders and, yes, even journalists) as it delivered upon a promise it proved almost impossible for rival "low cost" formulae to meet: For a quarter of a century now, it has been possible in FF to achieve *some* level of notoriety beyond the boundaries of the class itself.

There never were any guarantees, of course, and many more thousands were probably turned away from racing careers. But it was the numbers that set FF apart and the silent promise-that-wasn't that made Formula Ford fun.

The Schools' Problem

Formula Ford's origins remain contentious, but there's no question that all this fun began at the racing schools which, in the early 1960s, shared a common complaint. The Jim Russell School, Motor Racing Stables, and others initially featured "proper" single-seat FJr/F3-like machines from world class constructors like Cooper and Lotus—cars in which the aspiring Formula 1 star could not only learn his (or her, but then as now it was mostly "his") craft but look the part.

Trouble was, the schools—even with record numbers of customers pounding to their doors—had their hands full trying to keep from going broke. Blame their fiscal insecurity on the cost of Dunlop racing tires and the 1.1-liter Coventry-Climax FJ and later sleeved versions of the same oversquare Ford Anglia 105E engine featured in the 1-liter Formula 3.

By 1966, a ready-to-race F3 car cost nearly £3,000 and racing tires another £80 a set. And they were finicky to boot, the Cosworth MAE66 engine, for instance—production block, single 40 DCOE Weber carburetor et al—producing 100hp at 9500rpm.

"We were using Coventry-Climax engines (which) were very, very expensive, and the boys kept

Suggestions for a 'one marque' race.

Type of vehicles: T.R.4's or Spitfires (standard trim).

Number required: Minimum 12 – maximum 20 (plus 2 reserves).

Selection of drivers: By invitation – 6 or 8 most promising
                       drivers from the Jim Russell Racing
                       Drivers School plus 6 or 8 from
                       Motor Racing Stables.

Venue: Brands Hatch or Snetterton (ideally one race at
        both) with possibly a final elsewhere).

Race organisation: To be included within framework of
                    a B.R.S.C.C. meeting (Club or National).

Prize; 100 guineas – or a pot to be won every season (like
        the Ashes) .... or a T.R.4 !

Drivers choice of car: To be drawn by lot – immediately
                        prior to practice.

Preparation: By your own works – mechanics to ensure all
              cars are as near identical as possible in
              performance, tyre pressures etc.

Prior familiarisation with vehicles: One car to be made
              available to each organisation on loan for
              a fortnight prior to race to enable drivers
              to familiarise themselves with type of
              vehicle.

...   .

blowing 'em up!" explains Geoff Clarke, who opened his own school in 1959 after coming away disappointed from a program run by Cooper.

But, as the crush of students wanted to learn in a proper racing car, neither Clarke nor primary competitor Jim Russell (whose school opened even earlier, in 1957) had much choice. The boys kept blowing them up while both Clarke and Russell looked hungrily for an FJr/F3 alternative.

Several interested journalists have tried to cut through the chaff, but there remains too much controversy and too little on record to put a precise date on the "birth" of Formula Ford. What evidence there is narrows the time frame to a two-year period 1963-'64. In that time, radial tires were first introduced in Europe. And in that time, MRS, in desperate seach of reliability, began exploring the option of fitting standard engines and standard road tires (radials) to the school's spaceframe single-seaters.

John Tomlinson, a mechanical engineer and would-be racing driver who helped out at MRS in the early years—"trading labour for lapping time"—recalls ferrying a British Leyland four-cylinder out of a junked Austin A35 up to Finmere in the trunk of his street car for one such trial.

(A scene-setting aside: The "boot" of Tomlinson's Renault Dauphine played a significant role in MRS history. Living southwest of London, he used to swing by the Yeoman Credit F1 team garages frequently to pick up cast-off Dunlop racing tires on his way to Finmere in Buckinghamshire, the steady supply courtesy of Yeoman driver Stirling Moss who was a director of Motor Racing Stables.)

Important news for MRS was a Nov. 1963 move to the emerging Brands Hatch circuit. The tough winter of '62-'63 had seriously damaged Finmere's runways, and Clarke took the big plunge—his first business experience with John Webb, Managing Director of Motor Circuit Developments which ran Brands Hatch and three other British tracks. There was a lot of excitement at Brands that winter: The dramatic Kent circuit southwest of London would host the British GP for the first time in 1964 after major construction work brought up to GP length in 1960.

In the course of moving his school's base of operations, Clarke remembers, the MRS mechanics refitted two of the school's Lotus FJ chassis—probably 20s or 22s—to Clarke's orders, installing in each a stock 1498cc Ford pushrod engine as featured in the recently introduced Cortina GT sedan.

THE LEYLAND MOTOR CORPORATION
LIMITED
BERKELEY SQUARE HOUSE BERKELEY SQUARE
LONDON, W.1
TELEPHONE GROSVENOR 6050 TELEX NO. 22498 TELEGRAPHIC ADDRESS LEYMOTORS LONDON TELEX

YOUR REF

OUR REF

G. D. Clarke, Esq.,
Motor Racing Stables Ltd.,
International Racing School,
Brands Hatch Circuit,
Nr. Fawkham,
Kent.   1st December, 1964

Dear Geoffrey,

I thank you for your letter of November 16th
concerning the possible organisation of a 'one Marque'
race.

I will discuss this with our competitions department
and let you know what we decide as soon as possible.

Yours sincerely,

K. B. HOPKINS
Group Public Relations Officer

(OPPOSITE PAGE) Clarke had a terrific idea shortly after settling Motor Racing Stables in at Brands Hatch, and fired off a two-page letter to The Leyland Motor Corp. This time (LEFT), Clarke was rebuffed. But as the MRS boss continued to wrestle with this "one-marque" concept, another Formula Ford seed was sown.

Tomlinson was one of those mechanics and today he recalls the school picking the Cortina over the similar BMC four because it had five main bearings vs. four and was therefore sturdier.

"It was a very good move," recalls Tomlinson, who left the Brands Hatch School operation in 1987 to produce the SkidMaster car control instructional device. "The 1000cc engines we (MRS) had originally were very highly stressed—high revving and cammy. And students weren't always very good at reading tachs. I remember going to Finmere four consecutive Saturdays in about 1961 to do my laps. On three occasions, the engine expired or the car got bent before I got in it. The fourth time, I said to Geoff, 'If I mend that, can I have my laps?'"

The 1500 Cortina, with its sensational reliability and horsepower output fairly close to "F3 proper" proved a resounding success in the school. And the earliest experiments with radial tires bore fruit as well: The students of the day didn't care that these weren't racing engines or racing tires, just that the cars were equal and that at the end of the day, they could answer the question, "Who's quickest?"

These discoveries were fuel for the ambitious and promotion-minded Clarke, who had a lot of ideas. One

came to light in a proposal to the Leyland Motor Corp. in Nov. 1964 for a "one-marque" race. Clarke's concept was a match race, a select group of his students vs. a similar group from the Russell School to be held at Brands Hatch or Snetterton (or, ideally, in qualifying round format at both). The cars would be identically prepared Triumph TR4s or Spitfires, a driver's race mount drawn by lot prior to the start.

Leyland declined, but dreams of one-marque races were there in Clarke's winter '66 hotel bar conversation with Webb which author Nick Brittan says (in his *The Formula Ford Book*, ©1977, Patrick Stephens Limited) marked the real beginning of Formula Ford. (More about that in chapter two.)

Alternatives eclipsed

As the early '60s became the middle '60s out in the "real world" away from the schools, as the gap between the bottom rung and Formula 1 grew with the new 3-liter engine formula, and as F3 blossomed, "low-cost motor racing" popped up all over the place.

Among the more interesting newcomers were Formula Vee and Formula IV. A single-seater class hatched by American Hubert Brundage in 1959, Vees

Invented in Italy in about 1966, Formula IV featured fairly straightforward spaceframe chassis and motorcycle engines from Bultaco, Ducati and others. It initially attracted as much attention in England as Formula Vee.

featured near-stock, air-cooled Volkswagen 1200 and 1300cc engines. With unprecedented levels of support from the manufacturer, Vee gained important toeholds in the U.S. and on the European continent.

Formula IV, meanwhile, was apparently invented in Italy (a 250cc Ducati-powered machine built by karting wizards Tecno being the first example), but the idea quickly emigrated, finding a handful of enthusiastic disciples in other countries.

Neither FV nor F4 (it looks funny if you abbreviate it "FIV"), about which much was written in 1966, would catch fire in England—for a variety of reasons. One, of course, involved their technical attributes: The Vee curse was an upright fan shroud and torsion bar front suspension that virtually decreed the cars be hideously ugly. Formula IV's handicap was the auto racing fraternity's general lack of familiarity with (or sympathy for) motorcycle engines.

Another reason for their failure to catch on—in the U.K. at least—was that, for the fledgling racer on a budget, there were already an extraordinary number of small-bore club racing classes (many of them decidedly, er...offbeat). Fledgling clubman's class and monoposto groups were both defensive and aggressive.

But surely the most significant reason why those and other formulae failed to make it big in the center of the motor racing world's universe was the amazing early success of a class that was not even named when Vee and IV first arrived. Formula Ford would not only blot out their sun, but eclipse almost everything else. But, in the winter of '66-'67, who knew?

Nick Brittan tries a Vixen F4. Remember that name ("Brittan," not "Vixen"): The racer, author and promoter is a key figure in FF folklore.

With heavy Volkswagen support, interest in Formula Vee skyrocketed on the European continent (ABOVE, a typically large field at the Nurburgring in 1967) and in the U.S. But, though it debuted in England just two weeks before FF, it never caught on big there—too much fun, perhaps, for a country which takes its motor racing so seriously!

The father of Formula Ford

GEOFFREY CLARKE WAS proprietor of Motor Racing Stables, a race driver school based at Brands Hatch in the '60s and '70s which set new standards of driver training excellence. Today, MRS is no more and Clarke himself is retired. Unlike his contemporary, Jim Russell, Clarke speaks bitterly, sometimes angrily, about many of his experiences—especially those involving John Webb, Managing Director of Motor Circuit Developments which ran Brands Hatch and three other British circuits at the time when MRS—and FF—first flourished.

Clarke, though—living in peace in Canterbury, Kent—did consent to a series of telephone interviews in early 1992, and then provided not only a wealth of school material but also priceless copies of newspaper clippings. Here are some excerpts of what were a few free-wheeling and fascinating long-distance calls...

AUTHOR I'm finally beginning to pull together the pieces of Formula Ford's history. But a very key part of the story I'm still missing is yours ...

GEOFFREY CLARKE Well, that's very flattering.

AUTHOR (MCD's) John Webb is generally given the credit for inventing the Formula Ford class. And I suppose, as regards it becoming a successful, standalone class, the facts seem to point to that being true. But the premise seems to have emerged from your activities at Motor Racing Stables in the early '60s.

CLARKE That's right. You've got most of your facts right. John Webb took a lot of the credit when he didn't actually deserve it.

AUTHOR Well, help me complete the puzzle. The story begins at Motor Racing Stables, the racing school which you opened in 1959?

CLARKE That's right.

AUTHOR What was your background leading up to wanting to have a racing school?

CLARKE I'd gone down to Brands Hatch in 1957, and saw the Cooper racing school—that's what motivated me: I decided they weren't doing it properly. I didn't approve of what they were doing.

I was trying to find out, back then, whether I'd got what it takes to become a racing driver myself. Eventually, I went away and hired an airfield from the British Air Ministry ...

AUTHOR The abandoned WWII airfield at Finmere?

CLARKE That's right. I turned the control tower into a clubhouse and the old fire station building into a racing workshop. That was in 1959.

We moved the school to Brands Hatch in 1963, but it was at Finmere that Formula Ford was first created. That's where we first put a standard engine in (and road tires on) a single seater.

AUTHOR The school used Formula Juniors in the beginning, didn't it?

CLARKE No, not Formula Juniors. Lotus and Cooper...oh, I can get all those details out for you later. (We were using) Coventry-Climax engines (which) were very, very expensive and the boys kept blowing 'em up! And in those days, Dunlop Green Spots, Red Spots and Yellow Spots were the racing tires and they were also very, very expensive.

But what I found was that the boys who wanted to do this, they didn't really mind how expensive the cars or engines were; they just wanted to go and battle against themselves, answer the question: "Who was quickest?"

And we found, by putting standard tires and standard engines in, that while the lap times were raised, the differences in tenths of a second between the drivers were just as significant.

All in all, it was a less expensive way into the sport.

AUTHOR Were you worried that using these standard bits might hurt the school's reputation as a *racing* school, might hurt sales?

CLARKE No, quite the reverse. Consider the damage to our reputation, you know—not to mention the cars—because the boys were blowing the engines left, right and center!

The Coventry-Climax engines were far too much: We used to wreck one a week (through) overrevving. We put limiters on to stop the revs, but it wasn't enough.

That was 1959-60. In '60 or '61, we started playing about with the principle of standard engines and standard tires. And when we got to Brands Hatch—mind you, I'd been working hard building the school up—I decided we really had an opportunity to establish a new formula for the "poor man." Not technically a "poor man"—I didn't like that phrase. But a formula where all the cars were equal and the difference would be purely on driver ability.

The theory was—my theory was—if you fit all the cars with standard engines, standard tires, standard gearbox, you would then find the good drivers. You'd single out the excellent drivers from the merely average or above average.

Are you with me?

AUTHOR I am indeed. Are you saying the racing cars of the time were so expensive that a winnowing process wasn't happening?

CLARKE That's right! And a lot of people were being kept out of the sport because it was too expensive.

AUTHOR Sounds very familiar, in fact...

CLARKE A lot of people will take the credit, Steve, because the thing was a success. It didn't particularly bother me, actually, because I knew who'd done it.

I financed it—I bought the first 16 cars, ordered the first 50 from Colin Chapman at Lotus. And it all went from there. Jim (Russell), he could see it was going to go and he got some Formula

Fords, too. It was good for him, good for me—and very good for the sport.

AUTHOR The first "Formula Fords" as such were the two Lotus 20's you had cleaned up prior to the move to Brands ?

CLARKE Yes, I think they could be claimed as such. They weren't called Formula Fords then, of course.

AUTHOR Where did the name come from?

CLARKE I (eventually) decided I was going to build a fleet of cars and let the boys race between themselves—all in identical cars, which was my aim. As the racing school grew more successful, I could afford to think a little bigger, begin to think about building my own fleet of single-seaters, but with the standard engines and the standard tires.

I planned to announce this to the motor racing world at the (Dec. '66) Racing Car Show at Olympia: "Here you go boys, come on in." I'd already gotten very excited.

(John) Webb (who ran Brands Hatch) and I had been conversing and had gone through a number of names. And eventually we decided to put it to Ford: "Would they like to come in? Give us a few engines? Do they want this to be known as Formula Ford?"

I don't know how many engines we asked for; not many actually—a dozen, maybe 20 engines ... I can't remember. Webb rushed off to get Henry Taylor's and Walter Hayes' blessing. And there was no hesitation; the decision was made and back to us in a couple of hours. They said 'Yes!' straightaway.

Remember, the small car thing then was Formula Vee, Formula Volkswagen—nasty little bug-like things with Volkswagen engines in them.

AUTHOR And also, in England at the time, they were trying to sell Formula IV—single-seaters with motorcycle engines.

CLARKE Oh, hopeless, hopeless ... yes, yes, yes. It all comes back to me. (Formula IV), though, had a much better turned-out car altogether than Formula Vee; (F4's) were proper racing cars compared to the others.

AUTHOR Back to a story in Nick Brittan's *The Formula Ford Book*, that you and John Webb went for a couple of drinks at a hotel bar before the Racing Car Show opened, and that's where the idea was born...

CLARKE The idea of Formula Ford?

AUTHOR The idea of Formula Ford. But it's pretty clear from what you say that the idea came long before.

Had you, at the time of this pre-show meeting with Webb, already contemplated placing a big chassis order with Colin Chapman?

CLARKE Oh no...well, I may have done. I'm not sure; I'll have a look in my scrapbook. No, at this show, I was announcing to the world, "Come and race this car at our school!"—that sort of thing—and I can't remember the precise order of events. It was, after all, God knows *how* many years ago!

(ABOVE) The first ever stand-alone Formula Ford race, Brands Hatch, England, July 2, 1967. (RIGHT) The first purpose-built Formula Ford was the Lotus 51. This one was owned by Joseph Lowrey.

2

Roots (1967)

Geoffrey Clarke, his MRS school flourishing since the move to Brands Hatch thanks to its reliable new Cortina-powered cars and some terrific instructors including Tony Lanfranchi, came to the Racing Car Show at Olympia Hall on a mission.

Clarke had decided to build a fleet of cars and, as he says, "let the boys race between themselves—all in identical cars, which was my aim.

"I planned to announce this to the motor racing world at the '66 Racing Car Show," Clarke goes on. "'Here you go boys, come on in.' I'd already gotten very excited."

Clarke had kept MRS' landlord John Webb—Managing Director of the Grovewood-owned Motor Circuit Developments, which controlled four of Britain's leading circuits including Brands Hatch—appraised of all this, of course. These ambitious plans were, Clarke remembers, a central topic of discussion as the two sat talking in the cocktail lounge of London's Royal Garden Hotel after helping to set up stands at the nearby show hall.

At some point in that conversation, another thought burst forth, quickly embellished: If these standard-engined, road tire-equipped, MRS single-seaters were perfectly suited to a healthy racing school's needs, then why wouldn't they be good enough for anyone/everyone else?

And since they've got Ford engines, why shouldn't we call them "Formula Ford"?

And why not get Ford to pay for the privilege?

Webb, says Clarke, was on the phone the very next day to Ford Competition Manager Henry Taylor, who talked things over in turn with his boss, Walter Hayes. Ultimately, quickly, Ford agreed to provide Clarke and MRS with 50 Cortina GT engines at a mere £50 apiece—£15 cheaper than their retail £65—and to lend their support to the "Formula Ford" moniker.

Clarke recalls that the whole negotiation and approval process took something on the order of hours.

"I don't think there were any telexes or any consultations with the States, although there may have been. I doubt it," Clarke notes.

Oh, how much simpler it was in those days to act upon grand ideas...

Off and Running

The hard-charging Webb was soon off and running, contacting first the RAC's Competition Director Dean Delamont to get an official rule-writing process in motion; then BRSCC Executive Secretary Nicholas Syrett to see about some additional race dates (Webb had already committed the Grovewood circuits, including Brands Hatch); and then the media.

On Friday, Feb. 12, 1967, Ford announced the class to the world, and very suddenly, Formula Ford was in the news.

'Ford Launch a New Racing Car' read one Saturday morning newspaper headline. "The Ford Motor Company is to launch a single-seater racing car called the Formula Ford—to encourage more young people to race. The price of the car will be less than £1,000. It

MCD Managing Director (and FF instigator) John Webb.

will be introduced on Britain's racing circuits this year. A series of 40 races has been planned for this type of car."

"A standard Cortina GT engine with extra baffles in the sump to reduce oil surge under race conditions will be the sole power unit permitted. The gearbox must be taken from a standard Group 2 production saloon with no more than four forward speeds," read another article headlined 'Formula Ford car on racing circuits.' "The first batch is under construction by Motor Racing Stables, of Brands Hatch, using standard Lotus 31 spaceframe chassis equipped with Ford components. However, any similar single-seater tubular chassis which are Ford equipped will qualify under the new regulations."

The "less than £1,000" number was a wonderful marketing angle hit upon by Clarke and Webb, and eventually written into the first generation of the rules. The initial reaction, though, was not all positive: The English racing weekly *Autosport* issued a warning in a February 16, 1967, edition editorial: "FF could certainly provide fairly low-cost single-seater racing, but *Autosport* sincerely hopes that no promoter will jump into the category too hurriedly, otherwise it could be killed stone dead, with few starters and, even more disastrous, too few finishers. Far better to wait until fairly large fields are assured, otherwise it could quite easily suffer the fate of other formulae which never really got off the ground."

Formula Ford won swift political approval, though sometimes for curious reasons. On the list of FF supporters was the colorful Nick Syrett, Executive Secretary of the BRSCC. "I had gone to the U.S. in February to serve as steward for the Daytona 24 Hour and Sebring 12 Hour sports car races," Syrett recalls, "and at Daytona I saw one of those interminable Formula Vee races. I wasn't for Formula Ford, especially. But I was dead set on FV not happening in England. It was the *noise* those things made as much as anything else, like geese farting through grass ..."

Public and media fears reflecting FF's "commercial" (rather than purely sporting) origins were quickly forgotten—or, more aptly, the arguments were machine-gunned out of existence by Clarke who had some rather ... er, *strong* opinions of his own. The class received the RAC's blessing rather quickly, rules were published in May and, after a formal debut in July, the grids filled even faster, soon rewarding the august organizing body and the far-seeing race promoters with full fields of cars.

A Full Fleet

Where exactly did all the cars come from?

Clarke, like Webb, had wasted no time. In February, he saw interest in his "school fleet" concept explode following Ford's pledge of support—claiming as early as February that he had orders for 50 cars—and he rejoiced in the large supply of engines at such a bargain price.

He needed a chassis. As stated in the original press announcement from Ford, MRS' original goal was to produce cars itself—Lotus 31 copies or the like. But 50 cars was a very tall order.

One afternoon, Webb and Clarke went together to ask fledgling constructor Bruce McLaren to build them. But, after giving it some real thought, the New Zealander declined the commission.

In March, the dynamic duo had a far more successful audience with Colin Chapman. The Lotus boss was quite amenable, and quickly agreed to have production race car subsidiary Lotus Components provide 50 cars in two batches of 25 for under £1000 each, granting MRS exclusive sales rights.

There was just one teeny, tiny, stipulation: The cars had to use Renault gearboxes.

This was a clever and truly inspirational way for Chapman to meet some of the PR obligations he'd accepted in tying up all the Lotus Europa loose ends.

(LEFT) The RAC's Dean Delamont played an important role in putting together the rules which assured FF's immediate credibility.

(FAR LEFT) Gregarious BRSCC Executive Secretary Nicholas Syrett, an important early ally of the class.

The Rules: Mk. 1

The Royal Automobile Club, U.K. motorsports' governing body, wasted little time in responding to everyone's needs for Formula Ford technical regulations. Formally approached in February, the RAC's Dean Delamont and his staff wasted little time, and rules appeared in May—straightforward stuff, really, except for that "£1,000 per car" clause so necessary to early PR efforts and immediately contentious.

The following is the article which laid it all out first, reprinted from the May '67 issue of the *RAC Motor Sport Bulletin*.

Single Seaters encouraged

Enthusiasm for the idea of moderately priced single seater racing cars continues unabated. Whilst the efforts of the Volkswagen Company have spread Formula Vee across the United States and through most of Europe—over 150 entries were submitted for a race at Nurburgring—Great Britain has lagged behind. Now the Ford Motor Company has entered the arena with the backing of Grovewood Circuits for a Formula Ford. Built around the idea of using the Ford Cortina GT engine, the price limit is £1,000 per car.

Clubs who promote events at Grovewood Circuits are all being asked to consider staging races for these cars, and already the B.R.S.C.C. is drafting a programme of events for 1967 and 1968.

There should be no shortage of cars because Motor Racing Stables already have a fleet of 12, used for their racing school at Brands Hatch, and will expand this to over 20. The M.R.S. cars are of Lotus construction, but it is known that the other prominent racing car manufacturers, including Brabham, and private builders have only been awaiting precise details of the Formula before putting cars into construction.

Formula Ford has now been agreed by the R.A.C. as follows:—

1. Type of Car—This Formula is only open to single seat cars with open coach work as defined by the F.I.A. for Formula 1, 2 and 3 and complying with R.A.C Vehicle Regulations.

2. Engine and Ancillaries—Standard normal specification Cortina GT engine. All standard parts to be used with the exception of the air cleaner (which may be removed and substituted by a 'trumpet'), carburettor jets, spark plugs, exhaust manifold, oil

sump and pump ('dry sump' is allowed). Re-boring is permitted using production pistons to a limit of .015. The only modification allowed is balancing and polishing, but the compression ratio must not exceed 9.5:1 (total combustion space to be not less than 44.2 c.c. per cylinder). The dimensions of all moving parts must be within standard Ford production tolerances.

3. Electrical Equipment—Standard dynamo and starter to be retained in working order. Diameter of dynamo drive pulley free.

4. Cooling—Radiator, fan and water pump free.

5. Gearbox—Not more than four forward speeds and one reverse (which must be operable from the driving seat) but otherwise free.

6. Flywheel—Standard Cortina GT.

7. Clutch—Free including attachment to flywheel.

8. Drive—Rear-wheel drive only, final drive ratio free, but torque biasing differential not allowed.

9. Steering Gear—Free.

10. Wheels—Only steel disc type with a maximum rim width of 5½ ins.

11. Brakes—Only standard parts from any homologated Group II car/s allowed, except for drums or discs and linings.

12. Fuel pump—Free.

13. Chassis—Of tubular construction with no stress-bearing panels except bulkheads and undertray, but the curvature of the undertray must be limited to a maximum of 1 in. Tubes may transport liquids if required.

14. Body—Free within limits of 1.

15. Fuel tanks—Free.

16. Suspension and Running gear—Free except that all parts are of steel except springs, hub adaptors, rear hub carriers and bearing bushes the materials of which are free.

17. Shock Absorbers—Free.

18. Tyres—Racing tyres not allowed—otherwise free within standard production retail range as specified in Section 1 of R.A.C. Tyre Regulations.

19. Weight—Minimum weight of 400 kgs. (881.6 lbs.).

20. Cost—Not to exceed £1,000 retail complete in running order.

21. Eligibility—No driver who has competed in an International Formula 1 or Formula 2 race may participate.

The Jim Russell School quickly followed Motor Racing Stables in adopting Formula Ford. (This is one of the most over-used photos in motor racing—it's surely been included with every history of FF book and article ever written! That's Jim Russell himself pointing at the far left. His brother-in-law Ralph Firman is second from the left in the group of four standing by the truck.)

The Renault-powered Lotus coupe had debuted just months before, in Dec. '66.

Unfortunately, this one condition would prove to be a mistake for Lotus, and would eventually lead to the unraveling of Motor Racing Stables' prominence in the FF world it created.

To Clarke at the time, though, Chapman's terms seemed quite acceptable. The arrangement hammered out would give Clarke 25 complete, ready-to-run, school cars for a final cost of £850 complete, and let him sell 25 more for £1000 each to the early recruits of this promising new class.

To pay for the order, Clarke used his ownership share in the school as collateral on a note—another reasoned decision which ultimately proved costly.

Chapman had just the car for MRS and Formula Ford: The '64 Lotus 31 was an unsuccessful space-frame Formula 3 chassis built for the first year of the new 1-liter formula, a hastily penned derivative of the '62 type 22 Formula Jr. which was itself a clone of the slippery '61 type 20 FJ. The 31 had languished, developed by Jim Russell as a school car but nothing more as Lotus Components' own F3 endeavors focused on the monocoque 27.

With Clarke's deposit check in hand, the 31 jigs were quickly pulled down from the rafters and work begun on the Lotus 51—the very first purpose-built Formula Ford, Renault gearbox, Triumph Herald front uprights, steel wheels, Firestone radial tires and all...

The date was April '67. The die, as the say, was cast.

Frantic Activity

Here, rival racing school boss Jim Russell picks up the narrative: "When I returned from *Grand Prix*—I worked on that motion picture for seven months, built

Snetterton in June: "Proper" Formula Fords from the Jim Russell school take part in a Formula Libre event. JR himself provides some last-minute inspiration.

all the cars which were Lotus Formula Juniors, you know, and trained all the stars—I heard about this Formula Ford. And when I was ultimately approached by Webb on the subject, I said 'I think it's fantastic.'"

Russell, who, coincidentally, had last raced in a Lotus 31 in 1964, spoke to Chapman about Formula Ford cars for his own school at the big Easter Meeting at Snetterton. But, with a 50-car order from Clarke already in his pocket, Colin insisted upon the same size order from Russell. Jim would commit to only what he knew he could afford—he only wanted 10 cars at first—and so said goodbye and crossed the paddock to Jack Brabham's transporter.

The Ron Tauranac-designed Brabham chassis were then on top in F3 and converting them to FF spec would not be a big deal. Jack gave Russell's FF project very serious consideration before deciding, a month later, that his firm's production plate was full.

"When it transpired that Colin wouldn't do it and Brabham couldn't do it," says Russell, "I approached Allan Taylor, in Birmingham, who built the Alexis car. We decided to jointly produce a car we would call the Russell-Alexis.

"I felt very strongly that the car should have a Hewland gearbox, but of course the rules were out by then and the price could be no higher than £1,000 complete. That was a problem.

"Ultimately, of course, we did it: We sold the Russell-Alexis for £999—with a Hewland 'box."

There could not have been much profit there ...

The Russell-Alexis prototype would not be ready until August. In the meantime, Russell converted several of his school's Lotus 31 chassis to FF specification. In late April, a trio of proper Formula Fords entered by the Jim Russell School competed for the first time, in the Formula Libre class, at Snetterton.

Answering the critics

Not everything written and said about Formula Ford following its Feb. '67 introduction was positive. Indeed, MRS boss Geoffrey Clarke's name became a staple in the letters sections of the various auto racing publications over the next few months answering FF's critics. This is from *Motoring News*:

Formula Ford

To reply to various points of criticism made last week in connection with Formula Ford I would enumerate as follows:—

1. Criticism is levelled because of the number of cheap formulae which have been introduced. It is precisely because these previous cheaper formulae have proved ineffective, uninteresting and relatively slow that Formula Ford is being promoted.

2. It is alleged it will not be a cheap formula. As far as speed related to cost is concerned, what is wrong with 56.5s round Brands short circuit at £990 compared with 53.5s (for Formula 3) at £2,500? A cost/speed ratio of about £500 per second. Admittedly, the 56.5 was achieved on racing tyres and it is still under discussion whether, because of the supply position allied to the cost, it would not be better to allow standard radials. This would slow lap times by about two seconds per lap but at least everyone could then get tyres.

3. Criticism is levelled on the grounds that the Formula is untried. The critic is obviously not aware that prototypes have been subject to considerable and strenuous testing for well over a year. Agreed, races have not yet been run but then a start has to be made somewhere.

4. Criticism is levelled by Mr. Tiedeman—who, lest it has escaped notice is Secretary of the newly R.A.C. approved Monoposto Racing Club—(and who is the same gentleman who is asking the R.A.C. in its wisdom not to allow Formula Ford) ... I must respond by asking how the Monoposto Club can possibly hope to cater for the many dozens of drivers who would like to compete in single-seater racing. There are just not that number of cars available which conform to the Monoposto

CONTINUED ON PAGE 21

The First (Proper) Race: BARC Brands Hatch, July 2, 1967

Although Jim Russell hosted one or two FF-only events in his Snetterton Championship series (the Jim Russell Racing Driver School was a recognized "club" under the RAC umbrella), the race given historical credit for being the first "proper" (standalone) Formula Ford event took place on Sunday, July 2, 1967, on the 1.24-mile Brands Hatch short course, the fourth race on the BARC Trophy Races slate.

The preliminary entry list showed 20 cars: 10 MRS Lotus 51s, five JRRDS Lotus 31s, a trio of cars from the Lydden Racing School (two refettled Brabhams and a Piper), and one front-engined Mallock U2 clubmans car. Seventeen cars posted qualifying times, but only 14 took the green flag—and then the number was 13 as Simon Sherman's third-row qualifying MRS Lotus snapped its Renault gearbox quill shaft on the line.

Pole winner George Lewis (MRS 51) led the first lap but spun at Paddock Bend, leaving ex-serviceman Ray Allen to lead the rest of the way unchallenged in another MRS machine.

Russell Lotus 31s driven by Malcolm Payne, Claude Bourgoignie and Malcolm Fletcher finishing in a knot 5.8 sec. behind, with two more MRS drivers (Peter Wardle and Edmund Patrick) in tow.

A rather quiet beginning—truly, the calm before the storm.

RESULTS: RACE #4/BARC TROPHY RACES
BRANDS HATCH (1.24 miles), KENT, ENGLAND
JULY 2, 1967 (WEATHER: Overcast)

1. Ray Allen (#94 MRS Lotus 51), 10 laps, 10:04.4, 73.86mph; 2. Malcolm Payne (#103 JRRDS Lotus 31), 10:10.2; 3. Claude Bourgoignie (#105 JRRDS Lotus 31), 10:10.8; 4. Malcolm Fletcher (#104 JRRDS Lotus 31), 10:12.0; 5. Peter Wardle (#98 MRS Lotus 51); 6. Edmund Patrick (#95 MRS Lotus 51), 10:13.4; 7. John Day (#107 JRRDS Lotus 31); 8. unknown; 9. unknown; 10. unknown; 11. unknown; 12. P. Grainger (#101 MRS Lotus 51); 13. George Lewis (#100 MRS Lotus 51), DNF, 1 lap, accident; 14. S. Sherman (#92 MRS Lotus 51), DNS, 0 laps, quill shaft.

RACE FASTEST LAP: Allen, 0:59.0, 75.66mph

The PR firm Gordon Bruce Associates came up with this wonderful idea on the occasion of FF's 25th Anniversary: '92 Rapid Fit Open FF Champ Jamie Spence (Swift SC92) poses with '67 Brands Hatch winner Ray Allen (Lotus 51) It's not the same old Lotus, of course, nor the right colors or number. But what a great idea!).

The months of April, May and June were tremendously exciting as Clarke, Webb and Ford's PR department got Formula Ford bags of publicity—some bad, most of it good. Denny Hulme drove the MRS Lotus 31 prototype in early April and enjoyed the experience. All the magazines and newspapers sent reporters to drive the car, and all wrote favorable articles. In

In June, just two weeks before the first standalone FF race was scheduled to be held at Brands Hatch, the great Stirling Moss, a director of MRS, returned to a single-seat cockpit to try out one of the first Lotus 51s at a very public "test session" in the rain.

Needless to say, cameras whirred and pencils scratched.

"Despite Moss' connection with MRS, who have sole selling rights for the Lotus 51, his enthusiasm was patently genuine," wrote one of the newspaper reporters on the scene.

"Asked how it compared with the Formula Vee cars, his answer was brief and to the point: 'No comparison. It (the FF) has bags of torque. The others are fun cars; this is a small racing car. It's got real suspension.' "

Marketing Wars

With surprisingly little fanfare, the first Formula Ford race took place at Brands Hatch on July 2, 1967 (see the sidebar opposite). Lotus won the first battle with their cars (31s and 51s) filling the grid, but Jim Russell went on to win the first-year marketing war. The more-modern Russell-Alexis was immediately more competitive, winning on its Aug. 19 debut in the hands of rapid Belgian Claude Bourgoignie.

Fitted with a Hewland Mk VI gearbox, the Russell-Alexis cars had two advantages right off the

---

Answering the critics (cont.)

CONTINUED FROM PAGE 19
requirements. Also, whilst there is a plan to make Formula Ford racing available to the driver who cannot afford his own car, there is presumably no similar plan by the Monoposto people to provide a similar service.

5. Criticism of Formula Ford is also made on the extraordinary assumption that because the origin is commercial, with commercial interests behind it, the best interests of the sport will not be served. ... This type of accusation is constantly being levelled by armchair critics against organisations which make a significant contribution towards the sport in spite of the commercial motivations. If one were to carry this specious argument to its logical conclusion then the best interests of the sport already are not being served because the fuel companies, the tyre companies, the racing car manufacturers, the engine builders, the tuning equipment and accessory manufacturers, the circuit promoters, the motor sport journals, the championship sponsors to say nothing of the Formula I and Formula II drivers themselves are not acting in the best interests of the sport simply because their interest is professionally and commercially motivated. What a nasty, sordid, wicked world it is. All these dreadful people with their nasty commercial interests all trying to make money out of *our* pure sport of motor racing.

It is time people ... woke up to the fact that the days of Brooklands, the Bentley Boys and all that was most excellent and non-profit making *in those days* are over.

Motor sport today is a fast growing and highly commercial business. Whilst this may be regretted by the small hardcore of true blue enthusiasts who hark back to the old days, together with a large number of people who resent successful commercial enterprise in any form, the fact remains that it is only the drive behind the commercial interest that will lead on to a better and more efficient sport as a whole. Motor racing is one of the few sports in which this country leads the world. This certainly was not achieved by a woolly minded, muddle-headed, non-profit-making approach. - **G. Clarke, Motor Racing Stables**

Ford PR goes to work on the Formula Ford concept circa 1968. The original 1500cc Cortina GT engine gave way to the 1600cc crossflow unit that year, but the reliability and "functionality" of both took the FF class a long way.

bat: The Hewlands were 1) much more reliable than the fragile Renault boxes and 2) had changeable ratios. Before Chapman personally wooed Russell back into the Lotus fold in 1968, 54 Russell-Alexis chassis had been sold.

MRS, meanwhile, saw outside sales of the Renault-gearbox 51s dry up virtually overnight. Deeply in debt financing the first 25 cars, MRS never took delivery of the second batch and never fully recovered though the school continued to prosper at Brands Hatch and Mallory Park, and an increasingly bitter Clarke kept things afloat well into the '70s.

Motor Racing Stables would eventually be absorbed into the Grovewood fold and emerge, without its founder, as the Brands Hatch School. In the late '70s, Geoffrey Clarke left the FF scene forever—a quiet retreat for an entrepreneur to whom the class owes much.

Formula Ford, meanwhile, blossomed—no, *exploded*. In August '67, World Champion Graham Hill drove both a Formula Vee and a Formula Ford for *The Sunday Times* and, while being politic, left little doubt about which machine he preferred: "This (the FF) is obviously a refined, sophisticated, race-bred car rather than a racing machine made out of passenger car bits," Hill said.

He agreed that "the Vee was more of a 'fun car' and the Ford more of a serious stepping stone to faster machinery for the youngster determined to break into motor racing."

Over the winter months, conversation swirled around the class' use of radial tires with most of the conclusions in favor of their use. "We did some checking and found out that at the school, the rate of spins and accidents actually went down after the switch to radials," said the BRSCC's Nick Syrett. Until then little known in Europe, Firestone F100s emerged on top of MRS school back-to-back tests and the American tiremaker would be an important FF supporter.

The Prophet

Once the new Formula Ford class started gaining momentum, the £1,000 price ceiling in the first-generation FF rules picked up the center-of-controversy gauntlet originally worn by the question: "Do we need another low-cost formula?"

This rule caused a real stir, and much was made of it in '67-'68. Few discussions were as reasoned, though—and fewer still would prove as prophetic—as these points penned weeks before FF formally debuted by John Miles.

Miles, the intelligent and thoughtful Englishman who would partner Jochen Rindt at Gold Leaf Team Lotus during the 1970 Grand Prix season, was a front-running Formula 3 driver when he penned the following commentary, excerpted from one of his popular "On The Racing Scene" columns in the English *Car and Car Conversions* magazine:

During last month I have been doing some testing on the new Lotus 51 Formula Ford. Of all the new cheap single seater formulae—(including) Formula IV, Formula Vee and Monoposto—Formula Ford is obviously most likely to succeed, for it utilises an available motor (Cortina G.T.), tin wheels, and road tyres, and a car is supposed to cost less than £1,000.

The rules as they stand at the moment, however, would appear not to be strict enough. (They state) amongst other things that the engine must be bog standard, but say nothing about 'blueprinting'. That is to say, taking the engines apart and building them to the manufacturer's spec.

The average standard G.T. engine produces something like 65 h.p. but, if it's not put together by a "rock ape" (and has) things like straight con-rods, parallel crank and camshaft tunnels, and bores that are at right angles to the crankshaft axis, it might produce something like the advertised 85 nags.

But then, of course, who can tell the difference between a 32 oz. contact breaker spring and the standard product, or a set of Terry's Extra Strong valve springs apart from the standard gear? Dry sumping is allowed adding another £50 or so to the cost. Shot peened rods and crank would be hard to detect also. Whilst these things in themselves are not expensive, once one man has done it, everybody has to do it to keep up, and so, to a lesser extent than F3, costs could still spiral.

Let's take a man who wants to win in Formula Ford. The engine costs around £120 with all ancillaries. We can then reckon £20 for brake testing, £100 for 'blueprinting' and fitting of dry sump gear, £50 for the dry sump gear itself, and £200 for the Hewland gearbox—a Renault can be used but the winners will have Hewlands for sure—so already we have spent half the imaginary £1,000 and we haven't even got a car yet!

The fact that one has to use steel wheels and road tyres does not stop chassis development taking place and again costs must rise.

In spite of all this, I think the Formula is a first class idea and bound to succeed. The speeds these cars will do may surprise people—early development cars are already doing 58s round Brands and 1:50s round Snetterton. To give you some idea of how quick this is, Roger Taylor's 1820 c.c. Anglia holds the Snetterton special Saloon car lap record at 1 min. 49.7 secs.   (Despite) the apparent pitfalls, the first two years of F/Ford will, I'm sure, provide ultra-close racing and a good apprenticeship for F3.

- **John Miles,** *Car and Car Conversions*

Twenty-five years later, how prophetic driver John Miles' words sound. Though Formula Ford succeeded beyond anyone's imagining, costs did indeed "spiral" quite ferociously.

3

Growth (1968-1972)

Lotus, and particularly Motor Racing Stables, lost out in the first roll of the FF chassis sales dice, but almost everyone else succeeded beyond their wildest imaginings over the first few years of Formula Ford's existence: All the schools, including MRS, flourished—Jim Russell's soon expanding to two other British circuits and to other countries including Canada and the U.S. At least a dozen chassis constructors joined the fray in 1967-'68 to challenge Lotus and Russell-Alexis. Many started right off selling cars in what were, for the day, astonishing quantities.

The component suppliers profited, too. Firestone watched sales of its F100 radial tire soar. Hewland wound its MkVI and later Mk8 (and even later Mk9) production line up to a pace that wouldn't slow for 20 years. Highly regarded frame builder Arch Motors saw its orders increase, as did companies like Specialised Mouldings, founded by David and Peter Jackson in '59, a trusted bodywork producer for the "big" firms—Brabham, Lotus, Lola and Cooper.

Oh, and let us not forget the Ford Motor Company which, for the cost of a £15 discount on 50 engines and the permission to use the Ford name, was profiting handsomely from all the publicity.

Ford replaced the original 1500cc engine in the Cortina GT with a new 1600cc crossflow four in mid-summer '67 which the RAC let into FF at the start of the '68 season. (Actually, an FF racer could have used a 1600 in '67, but would have had to put a "P" in front of his number and would not have been eligible for prize money. Apparently, no one did until the 1600cc-equipped Merlyn Mk11 prototype was loaned to Dan Hawes for a Boxing Day race.)

(LEFT, ABOVE) '68 protagonists Claude Bourgoignie (#14 Lotus 51) and Tim Schenken (#21 Merlyn Mk11) go head to head. (LEFT) Colin Vandervell scores another win for the ex-Emerson Fittipaldi "Magic Merlyn" in '69.

Not far into the '68 season, the RAC decided to formally allow engine blueprinting (i.e. balancing, polishing and assembly within the range of manufacturer tolerances) in under the class' price ceiling. All the serious FF competitors were having this done anyway. The service cost £125-£175 depending upon the tuner (Chris Steele, whose engines powered Tim Schenken's all-conquering Merlyn, charged £165), raising the unrealistic £1,000 price ceiling on FF to something like £1,200. This did nothing to slow the growth of the class, of course, but it did fuel another important industry: Many quality engine tuners got a big shot in the arm, while many newcomers got a start.

The industry bible *Autosport* kept its watchful editorial eye on this new FF game. In a May '68 issue, Part Two of a feature entitled 'Cheap Motor Racing: The single-seater formulae,' editor Simon Taylor observed:

"Let it be said that FF is the most professional of the cheap single-seater formulae, and the drivers who are doing the winning are the men who are in it because they want to get to the top in motor racing, and their funds do not allow them to start on a higher rung of the ladder.

"Thus FF is fiercely competitive—which is good for the formula, for apart from Schenken's usual superiority, the racing is close and exciting, which pleases the spectators—but the reward may be a sponsored drive in something faster."

Ah, yes: The biggest winners of all in 1968: Driver Tim Schenken who won 33 of 37 FF races, the Hayward brothers' Merlyn firm in Colchester which built his Mk11 (and later Mk11A) chassis, and Chris Steele who assembled his Cortina engine.

This partnership's success triggered the next step in Formula Ford's evolution, the Big One that really locked-in FF's future: In the very beginning (1967), FF served the schools and drivers at the bottom of their upward learning curve. But as FF evolved (1968 onwards), it became not a curve but a straight-up launch-

Formula Ford's first great champion

Timothy Theodore Schenken arrived in England with letters of introduction drafted by journalist Davis McKay, but he never used them. Born Sept. 26, 1943 in Gordon, Australia, he first raced an Austin A30 his father helped him buy when he left school. He was his country's Hillclimb Champion in '64, and equally competitive in Australian F2 with an aging Lotus 18 before sailing to the UK where he bought a Lotus 22 F3 car. He scored a few placings in '67, but that generally disastrous season ended in September with the car wrecked against a barrier at Crystal Palace.

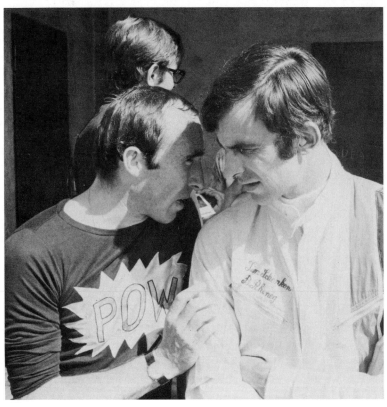

Schenken intended to rebuild the Lotus as an FF, but instead wound up driving the Ken Bass-owned Merlyn Mk11 prototype—and was utterly dominant during the '68 season. The tall, quiet-spoken Aussie reeled off an unparalleled string of victories in the 27-round Guards FF Championship, then stepped into a Sports Motors Brabham F3 at mid-season and immediately started winning British championship races with that. His efforts on the club racing scene would earn him the prestigious Grovewood Award.

More F3 followed in '69 (he won seven races) and F2 in '70, the same year he made his GP debut in Austria driving one of Frank Williams' star-crossed DeTomaso-Fords.

His success with Brabham chassis in F3 and F2 contributed to his getting an F1 seat alongside Graham Hill in '71, and his debut with the works team was marked by a race-long duel with, ironically, Howden Ganley's BRM at the Race of Champions ("ironic" because the two would be partners in Tiga Racing Cars just five years later). Tim's most memorable '71 result was a third-place finish in Austria after a stirring battle with Emerson Fittipaldi.

Learning that at the end of the year Ron Tauranac would be selling the Brabham F1 team to Bernie Ecclestone, Schenken left for Surtees.

"In hindsight," said Tim in a *Motoring News* interview, "that was a serious mistake."

His best result with the Surtees was a fifth-place finish in Argentina. Things were much happier for him in the Ferrari endurance team (he won twice co-driving with Ronnie Peterson) and in F2 with a Rondel Brabham (he won at Hockenheim).

At the end of '73, he turned down a number of offers awaiting the Rondel/Motul F1 car which materialized later as the Token but then was given to another ex-FF star, Tom Pryce. From 1975-'77, Schenken drove Georg Loos' Porsche 935s and overweight Group 2 factory-entered Jaguar sedans. His last official F1 drive came at Watkins Glen where he failed to qualify the perhaps best-forgotten Lotus 76.

Tiga Racing Cars came into being in 1976, Tim's focus the sales side while striving to create a successful F3 team. He left Tiga in the early '80s, though, moving his family to America where he stepped into a team management role with John Fitzpatrick's J. David-financed Southern California-based IMSA endurance racing team. When the latter's shaky financial empire crumbled, many innocents lost a lot of money; some lost all they had. Schenken, one of the nicest men to be found in motor racing, was badly singed.

He returned to his homeland where, as a principal at CAMS, the Confederation of Australian Motor Sport, he remains actively involved in the racing scene—the first and one of the greatest champions the FF world has ever seen.

With Chris Steele power, a Merlyn Mk11 chassis loaned by Ken Bass, and prep advice from Chas Beattie (the curious "four-box" logo on the nose is a "CBP"), Aussie Tim Schenken was all but unbeatable in 1968.

ing ramp to the stars—in perceived value if not always in reality.

It was certainly a ramp for Australian Schenken who won over two dozen Formula Ford races in 1968 en route to claiming the first significant British FF championship. Just two seasons later, Schenken made his Formula 1 debut in Austria, driving a DeTomaso-Ford for Frank Williams.

His was a meteoric climb, precipitated by success in Formula Ford. But even more of an impression in F1 was made during that '70 GP season by another ex-Merlyn FF driver, Emerson Fittipaldi, who debuted in a Lotus at Brands Hatch, two GPs before Schenken.

The brilliant young Brazilian made short work of Formula Ford: Finishing second between entrant Jim Russell's two quasi-works Lotuses in a European Championship race at Vallelunga, Italy, in 1969, he so impressed veteran Russell that when Fittipaldi dropped by the school a few days later to ask if he might drive for him, Jim refused!

"You're too good for FF," Russell remembers telling the quiet, 22-year-old South American. "Let's get an F3"—which they did, trading in Fittipaldi's Merlyn on a Lotus 59. (That particular Merlyn Mk11A, nicknamed "Magic," went on to launch the careers of Colin Vandervell and Jody Scheckter, and is now owned by Paul Pfanner, publisher of *Racer* maga-

zine—in far nicer shape today than it ever was when raced by that trio of hard-chargers!)

In 1970, Fittipaldi became the first FF graduate to win a Formula 1 Grand Prix. In 1972, he became the first FF grad to win the World Championship...

The JRRDS mechanic assigned the task of running Fittipaldi's Lotus F3 car, meanwhile, was the boss' brother-in-law, Ralph Firman. Three years later, with help from Tasmanian Ross Ambrose, Firman decided to step forward and build his own Formula Ford called the Van Diemen. The first obviously Lotus-inspired Van Diemen RF73 rolled out in May '73, and 20 years later, Firman is still at it. Having sold something over 2,000 chassis now, he can boast the record of being the most successful FF builder of all time.

How symmetrical: Russell-Firman-Fittipaldi-F1-FF-Schenken-Merlyn-Van Diemen ... a tidy chain of people and events.

Into the Fray

As word got around, Formula Ford spread like an out-of-control forest fire all across Europe (though not to France, curiously), the Scandinavian countries and Benelux nations. Handling some of the communication chores which sparked this growth was the Ford- and Firestone-sponsored Formula Ford Register

27

Jim Russell introduces his newly signed Formula 3 driver Emerson Fittipaldi.

founded by the BRSCC's Nick Syrett and the promotion-oriented Nick Brittan (see sidebar below).

Brittan's 1977 *The Formula Ford Book* chronicles in exciting detail the spread of enthusiasm, from school race in the spring of '67 to BRDC standalone race (July '67) to F1 Race of Champions supporting event (March '68) to first international event on the continent—the *Coupe de Belgique*, held at Zolder, Belgium on April 21, 1968 (at which, Brittan notes, "Lotus took five orders.").

Belgium hosting the first race outside England seems appropriate given the great success of JRRDS graduate Claude Bourgoignie. Unofficially FF champion in 1967 following a string of late-season wins in his Russell-Alexis, the young Belgian's record was second only to Schenken's in the 27-round Guards series.

Who was that masked man?

Today's Nick Brittan is the man responsible for the London-Sydney Marathon revival. If you caught him yesterday, he was the controversial columnist responsible for 'The Private Ear,' one of the most popular columns ever to appear in the hallowed pages of *Autosport*. He was an agent for many of the top names in the sport. And his name winds in and out of the Formula Ford story, not just as the author of the seminal *The Formula Ford Book* commissioned by Ford to celebrate the 10th anniversary of the class in 1977, but as a very influential figure in the class' rapid international expansion.

By the time he reached age 29 in 1966, Brittan had collected several karting championships and had spent the summer of '65 winning seven of 15 races in one of the most crowd-pleasing sedans of all time, the Ford Anglia "Green Bean." A publicist for the Good Relations PR agency, he founded his own company in '66 and soon had irons in several motor racing fires.

An extremely proficient driver, Brittan was involved with the launch of Formula Vee racing in England—he was a teammate of eventual race winner Jenny Nardin in the first English FV event in June '67. Later that year, with the backing of Ford and Firestone and in partnership with Nicholas Syrett, Executive Secretary of the BRSCC, he started the Formula Ford Register.

One thing led to another, and Brittan wound up not only putting together the first FF show outside Britain (at Zolder, Belgium, in April '68 where he also competed, finishing an impressive second in a factory Titan) but soon putting on a series of races, seven of which became the first European Championship (won by Crossle driver Gerry Birrell) in 1969. The FF Register was eventually disbanded as Brittan worked on a new entity, Formula Ford International, which managed the Johnson Wax-sponsored Euro Championship in 1970.

FFI, too, dissolved after accomplishing its goals and Brittan moved on into bigger game, his organizational and promotional influence felt for decades—and remembered.

Long before he was James Hunt, World Champion, and long even before he was "Hunt the Shunt" in F3, he was J. Hunt, dreamer and not particularly well-off Merlyn FF driver.

Bourgoignie had perhaps the best-sorted Lotus 51 as the '68 season wound down. Motor Racing Stables had given up the 51 sales franchise, and so did JRRDS sever its ties with Alexis late in the year when Colin Chapman took it upon himself to bring Russell back into the fold. Privateer Dave Walker thus claimed the honor of being the fastest Alexis driver in 1968—briefly, for the Australian was drafted into Russell's works Lotus team in '69—though another youngster, James Hunt, would gain some notoriety in a Russell-Alexis that summer.

At the top of the '68 heap were sales leader Merlyn, Lotus and a fading Alexis but there were other cars out there. Frank Williams' F3 mechanic Tony Trimmer turned a '67 F3 Brabham BT21 into a rapid FF; the gorgeous Titan FF turned a few heads; and Syd Fox had several good outings in a Pringett-Mistrale.

The big guns all fired late that summer with cars for '69: Lotus unveiled the wedge-shaped 61 while Crossle, Elden, Dulon, Hawke, and Royale—names that would feature prominently in years to come—all debuted FF models.

Sadly, FF racing claimed its first fatality that summer of '68 when 26-year-old Englishman Ron Riley hit the bank and rolled his two-month-old Merlyn at Silverstone's infamous Copse Corner. Seat belts, remember, were not *de rigeur* in Formula Ford until the next season.

In 1969, a Nick Brittan-led association called Formula Ford International (FFI) blossomed from the nucleus of the original FF Register, and hosted a fabulous seven-race European Championship with races in Belgium, England, Holland, Ireland, Italy, Sweden and Switzerland. Les Leston sponsored a second major English championship, and the class spread to the U.S. where it was finally recognized as a National class by the SCCA. This was truly a watershed year.

The early '70s (1970-1972) featured continued evolution of the front-radiator, outboard suspension spaceframe chassis ideal in Formula Ford pioneered in F3 the early '60s. Most of the cars still looked like mid-'60s F3 cars, too.

It was time for a change here, which would come in the form of suspension and aerodynamic advancements—but not yet.

What *was* going on technically was mostly invisible: advances in tire technology, for instance. In 1969, given a publicity boost by eventual champion Gerry Birrell, Avon Wide Safety cross-ply tires took over from the original Firestone F100s as "the" tire to have. Firestone, however, clawed back, unveiling its Torino Wide Oval in 1970 which dominated for several years until the arrival of a new Dunlop radial. (Indeed, Torinos survived well into the '70s as the intermediate tire of choice, even in America.)

The engine tuners were hard at it, too, and a battle equally as entertaining as the one among chassis manufacturers played out in rocker cover badges: Chris Steele got a boost from Schenken's success, but others like John Read (Holbay), Denny Rowland, Alan Wardropper (Scholar), David Minister, and many others engaged in a pitched battle of wits, not only with extracting as much horsepower as possible through careful assembly and dyno work but also in the area of at-the-track psychology: There is nothing so fragile as a race car driver's ego, and, in a class which shook down as hotly competitive as Formula Ford, it was *always* the engine tuner's fault ...

Beyond the continued geographic expansion of the class, there was one more noteworthy development in 1972: The invention of the Formula Ford Festival which would become the single most important FF1600 event in the world for the next two decades.

The late Ian Taylor won the first such event in 1972 driving a Dulon. The success of this event in the years to come was a phenomenon as important to drivers of the day—and to historians!—as the development of FF itself.

(ABOVE) Colin Vandervell drifts Magic Merlyn, working hard to fend off Bob Evans' Palliser and another competitor's Lotus 61 in 1970. (BELOW) Tim Brise's ex-Tony Brise Mk8 Elden gets away first at this damp '72 event.

(ABOVE) Much-admired Tom Pryce was killed in the South African GP in 1977. Seven years before, he was sliding Lolas. (BELOW) Lovingly restored late '60s Merlyn, Lotus and Alexis at Donington Park in '92.

Gary Johnson (Merlyn) and Dan Fowler (Beach) at Daytona International Speedway in '69.

Made *for* the U.S.A.

Before too long, the U.S. emerged as the single biggest market for FF outside England, though in the beginning—as it had been in England—FF was something of a tough sell.

The single-seater classes in American club racing had, at the time of FF's debut in England, just undergone reconstructive surgery at the hands of the Sports Car Club of America (SCCA). The old Formula Libre and Formula Junior had given way to a sensible new Formula A/B/C system with FB and FC roughly equivalent to the European Formulae 2 and 3, sharing, specifically, a relatively high cost.

At the bottom, there was Formula Vee which was thriving—a *huge* success in America.

"The reaction in the United States to the recent Formula Ford announcement has been most enthusiastic, and a prominent member of the SCCA Competition Board expressed to me the hope that it would replace Formula Vee in the SCCA programme in due course. 'The only trouble,' he said, 'is that we are primarily a members' club and Formula Vee has become so well established in America that a very large number of our members own these cars.'" Nick Syrett explained in a preliminary report on Formula Ford which appeared in the May '67 issue of *BRSCC News*.

Despite almost immediate pressure from members who followed the "trades" and understood FF's wonderful implications, the SCCA Competition Board and Board of Governors was in no position to respond instantly: They had recently made a commitment to the future of FA, FB and FC. And, given the whole-hearted support of Volkswagen of America—then the number-one distributor of imported vehicles by a whopping margin—they were understandably afraid to muck up the great thing they had going in Formula Vee.

Well into the '68 season, the SCCA's Jim Patterson wrote in *Sports Car* magazine: "At mid-season ... there has not been demonstrated interest (i.e. purchase and running of cars) to justify the establishment of a National Championship class for these (Formula Ford) cars. In November, the Competition Board will again take a hard look at the class and make a decision for the 1969 season. Meanwhile, of course, the cars can continue to run in Class B.

"At this point, it's still wait and see."

One of those to whom Formula Ford's advantages seemed particularly clear was engineer Jules Williams who bought a Lotus 51B (the '68 chassis featured some

The first (proper) U.S. race: Willow Springs, March 23, 1969

The first SCCA National of the 1969 season unfolded under clear, cold spring skies at Southern California's Willow Springs International Raceway on March 22-23. Unbeknownst to many in the sizable crowd of competitors, this Southern Pacific Division event would have special significance: On Sunday, California resident Jules Williams, driving a green Lotus 51B with a yellow stripe and a 1600cc crossflow Ford Cortina GT four-cylinder engine he'd tuned himself, would win the first official Formula Ford race in America.

Sadly, there were no prophets on the grounds and no one paid any special attention.

"My diary entry for the event described the Ford race in two paragraphs while devoting several pages to other classes; little did I know!" recalls journalist Ed Pitz who was then in the Navy and, coincidentally, had thumbed a ride from the motel to the track with Williams and his wife in their MGA.

According to the *Formula Ford Report* edited by Len Pounds, there were 11 Formula Fords in 27-car combined FF/FB field. Behind most of the more powerful Formula Bs but on the FF pole was Les Hill's Merlyn Mk. 11, with Gary Johnson's Lotus 51B next up. Jules' Lotus was third, ahead of Bruce Powers' Titan Mk. 4 and the rest.

"According to my diary, Hill broke away at the start, immediately showing his gearbox to all the FFs and several of the more powerful FBs," Pitz goes on. "But on the second lap, there was a mad scramble in Turn Nine, the last corner, a fast, right-hand sweeper. Hill's Merlyn slid off into the sandy infield while much of its fiberglass cartwheeled down the middle of the track, oncoming cars swerving madly in avoidance ..."

"I passed all the guys ahead of me, one at a time, between Turns Four and Five," Williams would recall at the FF 20th Anniversary gathering at Willow celebrating his triumph. "They were in Merlyn Mk11s and one Titan Mk4, I think, and my Lotus was not as good a car. I was also running Goodyear Blue Streaks and they weren't supposed to be as good as the Dunlops. But I had a real advantage in that one spot on the track."

Williams, who was a math and science teacher who later achieved great notoriety as builder of some of this country's very best FF engines—and as a partner in the ADF venture—took the lead for good with three laps remaining. His crew, consisting of "my wife—or was she still my fiancee?—and two guys from Edwards Air Force Base we found at the gate looking for a way into the races" was delighted.

"Titan driver Bruce Powers was initially given credit for the FF victory," adds Pitz. "However, while he was taking his 'victory' lap, Williams was presenting the officials with a lap chart that set the matter straight."

The *FF Register* recorded that the FF winner was eighth overall. Twenty years later, Jules could not recall the flap over the lap chart nor *not* getting to take a victory lap. He did remember that a few other drivers came over to congratulate him after the dust had settled.

The balance of Williams' '69 season was somewhat mixed: "I stuffed the car into a wall at Sears Point two weeks later. Fixed it and picked up a few seconds and thirds that summer, including a second at the last-ever race at the Tucson Airport Circuit.

By finishing third in the Division point standings, I qualified for the end-of-season SCCA Runoffs. But they were in Daytona and I didn't go—3,000 miles away and too much to think about."

Too much, but on a cool, clear March day at Willow Springs in 1969, Jules Williams had made history.

"The official results show Jules as the winner of the first National Formula Ford race," Pitz observes. "But they don't foretell or even hint at the heights the new class would reach. Nor does my diary ..." □

A sad postscript: Jules Williams was diagnosed with cancer some time before the 20th Anniversary FF Festival event held March 25-26, 1989, and succumbed to the awful disease, after a tremendous battle, just a few months later at the age of 50.

In 1989, several hundred FF enthusiasts gathered at Willow Springs to celebrate the 20th anniversary of FF racing in America. Ford, SportsCar magazine and the SCCA's California Sports Car Club sponsored the grand event.

A whole new generation of American racing car drivers grew up collecting FF PR photos—and dreaming. This is David Lazenby's angular Hawke DL2A. (INSET) John Crossle's first FF, the sensuous 16F.

minor chassis revisions and the 1600cc crossflow engine; the Hewland gearbox came with the 51C variant). Williams collected his car, chassis number 95, from Bill Smith's Lotus Southwest, an importer based in Dallas, and raced it in Formula B from mid-'68 on.

"It made a whole lot of sense," Jules would say of his purchase. "A low cost, stock, engine in a good Formula Junior chassis.

"Of course, the Formula B guys had mixed feelings about Formula Fords," Williams remembered in an article written in celebration of FF's 20th Anniversary

in the U.S. in 1989, just a few months before his death, of cancer. "We were 'low technology interlopers.'

"In 1968, FB was a marginally subscribed class featuring everything from clapped-out 1500cc Formula Libres to more contemporary stuff," Jules continued. "Formula C was even more sparsely populated. But FF was essentially looked down upon."

As the FF fields grew, though, by ones and twos, the attitude of the FB drivers turned to one of 'benign indifference,' Williams would add. By the end of the year, many FB fields were more than half FF. And still

No one in the business in America was as good at selling Formula Fords as Carl Haas—even when the cars weren't particularly good. The short-wheelbase T-200 was not much loved, but Lola's day would come!

the SCCA was in no hurry to formally recognize them. Jules Williams again: "I remember the Cal Club Regional Executive telling me we'd get a standalone class when 10 FFs showed up. Then it was 15. Then 20..."

Ultimately, there was no arguing the numbers. Formula F was recognized by the SCCA over the winter of '68-'69 and thus Jules Williams found his way into the record books, for it was he who had the honor of winning the first American Formula Ford National, at Willow Springs International Raceway on March 23, 1969. He garnered no special acclaim for winning that race until 20 years later when he was a guest of honor at the 20th Anniversary Formula Ford Festival sponsored by the Ford Motor Co., *SportsCar* magazine and the SCCA's Cal Club Region.

By then, of course, the significance of the first American FF race was pretty well understood.

The $10,000 Catalyst

Williams couldn't afford the time off necessary to journey to Daytona Beach, Fla., 3,000 miles to the east of his Southern California home, and so could not use

Skip Barber (at left) gets a check from Len Pounds.

FF bible: The **Formula Ford Report** *newsletter.*

his invitation to the '69 SCCA ARRC, aka "Runoffs," where the first-ever Formula Ford National Championship would be awarded. This would be the event where the Ford Motor Company delivered on its early '69 promise which made FF's success in America a certainty: a $10,000 prize fund directed at the SCCA National race program. The $2,000 to be paid the FF National Champion was a real carrot in an arena where the top prize was a handshake and a nice trophy, and a considerable talking point over the summer of '69.

As it had been in England, the direct participation of Ford PR was instrumental in the new class' early success. After announcing its $10,000 program, Ford Special Vehicles Activity boss Jacque Passino acted swiftly, putting Len Pounds in charge of a new Ford-backed FF Register. The Register dispensed the contingency money (in addition to the National Championship postings, top divisional finishers also drew a share) and, in Nov. '69, produced the first *Formula Ford Report* newsletter.

Eventually integrated into Ford's *Motorsports World* publication, the regularly arriving *FF Report* tied the whole, growing community together. When Ford's corporate interest in FF waned during the various Energy Crises of the early '70s and Pounds was reassigned, communication within the FF fraternity was dealt a blow from which it never truly recovered

(*Formula* magazine ['73-'80, R.I.P.] notwithstanding).

As important as FoMoCo's support of FF in club racing was, the SCCA could have gone along merrily without it. Not the case at all with the International Motor Sports Association (IMSA) which got its start in '69 sanctioning professional FF, FV and small sedan events.

IMSA President John Bishop, the former SCCA Executive Director whose talents were appreciated by no less powerful an individual in the American motorsports scene than NASCAR's Bill France Sr., did a lot for FF. While it's not quite true to call IMSA stock car sanctioning body NASCAR's road-racing arm, the connection was clear and IMSA's first-ever racing event in the fall of '69 was taken very seriously by the media.

This was an absolutely incredible 150-mile-long Formula Ford race, held Oct. 19 on Pocono International Raceway's 3/4-mile banked oval, and eventually won by outstanding SCCA Central Division FF racer Jim Clarke. Clarke needed 1hr 47m 0.08s to complete the 200-lap affair, his Caldwell D-9 finishing just 15 seconds ahead of Jim Jenkins' Winkelmann (nee Palliser). There were seven different leaders and an amazing number of lead changes in an event which featured several incidents but only one driver injured (that was

Lotus 51s were numerous in the U.S. in '68, less so in '69.

Titan Mk6 was beloved on the '71 American FF scene.

future sedan racing star George Alderman who looped his Lotus 61 into the barriers).

IMSA, which rose to international prominence with its Camel GT series, was a prime mover of FF racing '69-'72 and some of its events stagger the imagination: No fewer than 49 FFs battled for top honors (and a share of a $10,000 purse) at the Alabama International Motor Speedway in Talladega, Nov. 9, 1969, a wild 100-mile race won by Nils Sanborn in a Merlyn Mk11 by a victory margin of inches. (He didn't get his $2,000 check for winning until two hours after the race when film of the photo-finish was processed! The runnerup was poor Jim Jenkins who'd been the bridesmaid at Pocono.)

Skip Barber, who led briefly in IMSA's Pocono inaugural, skipped Talladega in favor of preparing for the SCCA Runoffs, held in Daytona that year. His readiness greatly affected the outcome of that Sunday afternoon, Nov. 30, race: The 34-year-old Harvard University graduate was forced to start from the back of the grid in his back-up Caldwell D9 (the D9 prototype, chassis no. 0001, he'd raced all summer) after wsrecking the new D9 he'd qualified on the pole (chassis no. 0044) in warm-up.

Ironically, Barber crashed when he was tagged by fellow Caldwell driver Jim Clarke, whose machine broke a rod end in the rear suspension.

Barber's drive was truly sensational: Starting 21st and last, he moved up 12 positions on the first lap. Third on lap two, he nipped past Dan Fowler's fast-starting Beach on lap three and started working into Jim Clarke's lead.

Once he caught him, the two battled mightily until lap seven when Skip seized the lead and made it stick. Sadly, a cable having fallen off the battery in Clarke's D9, he coasted into retirement on lap 13.

Barber won (despite losing third gear in the closing laps!) and won the Runoffs again in 1970, driving an F3-based Tecno. He would eventually make a few appearances in Formula 1 before "coming home" to start what would soon become America's premier racing school.

The Caldwell chassis that Barber, Clarke and many others used to good effect was America's answer to the Mk11 Merlyn, built by the Marblehead, Mass.-based Autodynamics, Inc. Ray Caldwell, Autodynamics' founder, made his name in Formula Vee racing and in making kits for VW-powered dune buggies. His market timing was sensational: the D9's similarity to the all-conquering Merlyn was easy to spot, parts were plentiful, and Caldwell's 100-chassis-plus sales tally (55 D9s and 48 of the lightly modified D9Bs) over three seasons remained the record for an American FF builder for over 15 years.

Talladega FF GP

One of the most amazing Formula Ford races in history was the Nov. 9, 1969, IMSA-sanctioned Talladega Grand Prix for Formula Fords which featured 49 qualifiers and 46 starters. Winner Nils Sanborn had to wait two hours for his prize money while film of the finish was being developed; his Merlyn and Jim Jenkins' Winkelmann were that close after an hour of racing.

Surprisingly, there were no major incidents in the 25-lap race around Talladega's combination infield road course and 33° banked tri-oval. The Dec. '69 issue of the Len Pounds-edited *FF Report* newsletter noted that "the first 16 cars finished on the same lap with 14 of them changing places on the last lap."

Pennsylvanian Sanborn took home $1,100 (including Champion Spark Plug prize money) for the win while runnerup Jenkins got $840 and everyone who started was guaranteed $100—substantial sums for FF1600 racing even today!

TALLADEGA GRAND PRIX

RESULTS of the 100-mile Talladega Grand Prix for Formula Fords, sanctioned by International Motor Sports Assn. at Alabama Intl. Motor Speedway, Talladega, Ala., Nov. 9.

Race Length: 25 laps of 4.0-mile road course; 59 mins. 20 secs. Winner's Avg. Spd. 101.1.

POS.	CAR NO.	DRIVER	CAR	LAPS COMPL.	PURSE	PTS.
1	31	Nils Sanborn, Media, Pa.	Merlyn	25	$1000	9
2	66	Jim Jenkins, Blauvelt, N.Y.	Winkelmann	25	750	6
3	39	Bill Scott, McLean, Va.	Climax-Royale	25	500	4
4	73	Gary Magwood, Scarborough, Ont., Canada	Merlyn	25	375*	3
5	6	Skip Adrian, Fresno, Cal.	Winkelmann	25	250	2
6	0	Jim Clarke, Garden City, Mich.	Autodynamics	25	225	1
7	8	Robt. Smith, Dallas, Texas	Merlyn	25	220	
8	33	Jack Cowell, New York, N.Y.	Winkelmann	25	215	
9	24	Bob Gardner, Wilmington, Del.	Lotus 61	25	210	
10	74	Fred Opert, Paramus, N.J.	Titan	25	205	
11	37	Dave Yoder, Ft. Lauderdale, Fla.	Lotus 61	25	200	
12	77	Jim Grob, Pompano Beach, Fla.	Winkelmann	25	195	
13	99	Lee Wiese, Tenafly, N.J.	Macon	25	190	
14	41	John Emery, Rockford, Ill.	Merlyn	25	185	
15	92	Dave Shook, Detroit, Mich.	Autodynamics	25	180	
16	7	Fred Phillips, Boulder, Colo.	Titan	25	175	
17	1	Hugh Kleinpeter, Key Biscayne, Fla.	Lotus 61	24	170	
18	46	John King, Atlanta, Ga.	Autodynamics	24	165	
19	71	Chris Cook, Holland, Texas	Winkelmann	24	160	
20	4	John Barrow, Henderson, Ky.	Winkelmann	24	155	
21	40	Bill McFarlan, Toledo, Ohio	Lotus 61	24	150	
22	10	Gary Weber, Vandalia, Ohio	Lotus 61	24	145	
23	13	David Piper, Huntington, Pa.	Climax-Royale	24	140	
24	44	Herbert Ladd, Grosse Pt., Mich.	Lotus 61	24	135	
25	11	Jim Needham, Greenfield, Conn.	Winkelmann	23	130	
26	25	Den Sziarto, Atlanta, Ga.	Autodynamics	22	125	
27	18	Jose Alvarez, Hammond, La.	Autodynamics	22	120	
28	9	Mel Tretheway, Warwick, N.Y.	Alexis	22	115	
29	98	Eddie Miller, Oklahoma City, Okla.	Merlyn	22	110	
30	19	Bill Morrow, Troy, Ohio	Lotus 51	21	105	
31	47	Haughton Smith, Montgomery, Ala.	Autodynamics	21	100	
32	30	Bert Gafford, Montgomery, Ala.	Lotus 51	21	100	
33	79	Kevin Glynn, London, England	Climax-Royale	21	100	
34	52	Theodore Wright, Kenosha, Wisc.	Lotus 51	20	100	
35	12	John Greeven, Miami, Fla.	Lotus 61	20	100	
36	27	Oliver Treiback, Greenwich, Conn.	Autodynamics	18	100	
37	70	Craig Hill, Toronto, Ont., Canada	Lotus 61	17	100	
38	22	Michael Richards, Chattanooga, Tenn.	Merlyn	11	100	
39	57	Gene Shelton, Nashville, Tenn.	Lotus 51	11	100	
40	14	Peter Quenet, Dearborn, Mich.	Autodynamics	11	100	
41	2	Horace S. Davis, Shawnee Mission, Ks.	Autodynamics	11	100	
42	3	Folis Jones, Memphis, Tenn.	Climax-Royale	5	100	
43	65	Jim Stevens, Detroit, Mich.	Autodynamics	5	100	
44	56	Bob Floeck, Greenville, Ohio	Lotus 61	4	100	
45	59	Robert Stewart, Baton Rouge, La.	Merlyn	4	100	
46	36	Wil Painter, Washington, D.C.	Climax-Royale	3	100	

* Includes $75.00 for Pole Position

Two other successful American Vee builders tried their hand at FF at about that time—Gene Beach and Jerry Mong (Bobsy); neither stuck with it.

Needless to say, Merlyn was huge in the U.S. in '69 following Tim Schenken's '68 Guards Championship headline gathering. Lotus' revised 51Bs and Hewland-equipped 51Cs also sold well although the wedge-shaped 61 which followed was much better. Also quite successful were the early Royales, called Climax-Royales in the U.S. to trade upon builder Bob King's reputation as a Coventry Climax engine specialist. These were resoundingly quick in American Bill Scott's (and several others') hands.

The prettiest of the first-generation Fords, though, were Titan's Mk4s and Mk6s (designed by Roy Thomas and built by Charles Lucas Engineering, a top British F3/F2 entrant in the middle '60s) and Crossle's 16F (designed by John Crossle and assembled by C.T. Wooler in Northern Ireland). Both marques would achieve great success in America.

March and Lola, too, had Formula Fords for the '69 and '70 seasons respectively; Lola took the class quite seriously and its early T200-series cars gave way to the fabulously successful T-340/342s of 1973-'76. March, meanwhile, was *not* serious about FF but had cars in the beginning because they came out of the gate with one of everything else, up to and including customer (!) F1 machinery.

Intriguing and somewhat avant garde machines designed by ex-Lotus Indy Car engineer David Lazenby, the early Hawkes would prove successful. But they would arrive a little later, as would the first Eldens and Dulons. Much later came the Van Diemens and Reynards which would be the imports of choice in the '80s, and the home grown Zinks and Citations. Neither the ADF nor its awesome complexity was a remotely comprehensible notion in '68-'72—except, perhaps, to designer David Bruns.

As FF caught on in America, examples of just about everything seen in Europe eventually made its way across the Atlantic. There were seven different marques represented at the first FF Runoffs race, and four different marques in the top five. In '70, when Barber won the Runoffs in the unique Tecno, Royale probably had the best "production" FF car there: James King qualified his RP3 on the pole and Bill Scott finished second in a similar car. But it was hard to support any argument about "dominance" for there were five different marques in the top six.

In '71, Titan began to make real inroads. Builder Roy Thomas, who picked up the reins of the

Skip Barber's Caldwell D9 was a regular visitor to victory lane in SCCA racing. It won seven Nationals and the ARRC.

company from ex-boss Charles Lucas, Titan offered a good car (the long-wheelbase Mk6A was very stiff, exceptionally quick and comfortable in fast corners), a great engine (the Titan Gold Seal), and two aggressive importers (Fred Opert and Pierre Phillips, who combined to sell over 150 Titan Mk6s from '70 to '75).

Titan won the '71 Runoffs—Doug Shierson Racing's Jim Harrell triumphed over the late Gordon Smiley (Merlyn Mk20)—and almost repeated in '72: Californian Boyd Pearce took pole with his Mk6A but fell out of the lead when a misrouted fuel line chafed through, handing victory to Eddie Miller in a Hawke DL2B.

More variety: There were *six* different marques in the '72 FF Runoffs top six.

Ford's new "Uprated" or "Kent" engine introduced in 1971 quickly became the rage despite the 50 lb. weight penalty Kent-equipped FF's had to carry. The Uprateds had better main bearing caps and a different cylinder head featuring larger valve diameters, reshaped combustion chambers and lower compression ratios. Initially they did not offer much of a horsepower advantage, but that soon changed.

There was a wealth of choice right from the word go in Formula Ford, which has always remained one of its charms. Price tags just under $3,000 when the

first Lotus' arrived in the U.S. did not climb rapidly, and the basic "affordability" fueled staggering success.

When Ford's financial support dried up, IMSA abandoned Formula Ford racing but by then the class had a tremendous amount of momentum. A particularly important event in '72 was the FF World Finals qualifier event run at Mid-America Raceway. At this early fall event, race winner Jack Baldwin, Bruce MacInnes and Ron Dykes all earned trips to England where they joined Jas Patterson (who had been there all summer racing a Len Wimhurst-designed machine) in the FF World Finals at Brands Hatch. None of the four finished particularly well, but America's presence in the very international world of FF was keenly felt.

The Mid-America event (and Bert Hawthorne Trophy presented to the FF winner) joined the Runoffs and IMSA pro races in presenting the best drivers North America had to offer. There were a lot of them, too: The FF Register reported 1,200 members at the end of '69!

The years '69-'72 were among the best of times in American FF racing. Happily, all the old battles are being brought to life again on the vintage racing scene. These races lack the desperate, frenzied, "cut and thrust" which FF racing in that era always featured. But they rekindle some wonderful memories.

(ABOVE) Daytona International Speedway, Nov. 30, 1969, the first American National Championship event for FFs. (BELOW, LEFT) Winner Skip Barber charged back to front! (BELOW, RIGHT) John Hancock's new Winkelmann.

More Daytona action: Above, Barber has sights set on Jim Clarke, both in Caldwells. Barber snuk past on lap seven (of 15); Clarke retired five laps later. (BELOW) Lotuses were well represented: Roger Chastain's 61 finished fourth.

4

Glory Road (1973-1983)

Looking back on it, the success of the first Formula Ford Festival in the fall of 1972 was another important turning point in Formula Ford's evolution. The next year, 1973, would prove to be a milestone year—the start of FF's best decade.

Never before (and never again!) was such a superb balance achieved in the class between engineering and evolution of chassis design (kept in check by a good set of rules); parity of engine development; and the lure of the intangible "star appeal" that attracted the world's best up-and-coming drivers.

A lot of really good new FFs debuted between the fall of '73 and spring of '74—indeed, the sheer number of competent chassis available all at one time was probably never surpassed. Consider what FF customers in England had to choose from in that 18-month span:

• The stunning Eric Broadley/Bob Marston-designed Lola T-340, the first FF with genuine lust appeal.

• The first Van Diemen—Lotus inspired and overly sturdy, perhaps, as Ralph Firman had racing schools in mind, but nonetheless the first car from a firm which would give shape to the class for the next 20 years.

• The Crossle 25F, which really stamped Crossle's name on the international arena (Gerry Birrell's '69 European Championship notwithstanding).

• The wonderful Roy Thomas-designed Titan Mk6C, one of the most beloved-by-its-owners chassis ever sold in the U.S.

Golden Era: (LEFT, ABOVE) David Kennedy's Crossle leads a pack of Royales and Hawkes in '76; (LEFT) Marty Loft's Lola vs. Crossles and Tiga at Sears Point Raceway that same glorious summer.

• The controversial Falconer-bodied Elden, Johnny Gerber's World Cup-winning Mk10A, which was a PR distraction taking away from the really good 'boat-tail' Elden 10B and even better 10C.

• The attractive Merlyn Mk24, which extended the Colchester firm's proud FF lineage (the Colchester marque's best years were by then behind it, but no one knew).

• The Royale RP16 which propelled FF away from the mid-'60s F1 look most of the designers clung to for the first five years.

• The Hawke DL11, a high-water mark for David Lazenby's company and a double championship winner.

• Dulon's Mp15, kind of chunky but a good example of productive (as opposed to destructive!) design evolution.

• Bert Ray's sensational 73F pedaled so quickly by up-and-comers Stephen South and Richard Morgan.

• And in America, from opposite coasts: The frighteningly advanced ADF MkII and the delightful Zink Z-10.

As they would be in America (a specific discussion of which follows later in this chapter), these were glorious years for FF as drivers danced to the music echoed by Schenken's and Fittipaldi's and Scheckter's success in Grand Prix racing. While the path narrowed sharply as the F1 pinnacle approached, the starting-off point was terribly confusing. Where to begin?

By '73, all doubts were erased: The way was Formula Ford.

(Two decades later, of course, all the doubt has returned. A determined teenager of the '90s stumbling onto this page will not believe it possible—he or she hears the siren call from at least half-a-dozen useful formulae in Europe and three or more in the U.S., and has a real problem of choice. But in '73, FF was the only way to fly.)

The career path was quite simple on paper: a racing school, and maybe its "in-house' series"; a novice championship, like the wonderful Dunlop Star of Tomorrow Championship (later sponsored by *Autosport*) which first appeared in '77; one or two outings at big national meetings just for experience; and then a go-for-broke year that was one's ticket to Formula 3 ... F2 ... *F1*.

A few drivers replaced the "racing school" part of the formula with something else, like karts or Formula Vee. But all the rest was carved in stone.

Which was great! "The thing about Formula Ford in the '70s," explains Paul Pfanner, publisher of the American *Racer* magazine, "was that you believed *anything* was possible."

Milestone chassis (CLOCKWISE FROM TOP LEFT): ADF Mk II, Lola T-340, Crossle 25F, Titan Mk6C.

In the middle of FF's '73-'83 glory years, stars of tomorrow engaged in sterling battles using a variety of chassis: Here soon-to-be-Dr. Jonathan Palmer leads a Van Diemen-Royale-Van Diemen-Royale chain at Donington Park in

Thousands of drivers did believe, all peril their education, real jobs, and, in many cases, families.

The flaw in the fabric, of course, was that the number of opportunities in Formula 3 was smaller than the number of successful emerging FF drivers, the ratio something like 10:1, which in a very short time meant a significant backlog of talent—we're not talking pikers here; we're talking championship-winners.

As with many motor racing problems, Motor Circuit Development's John Webb was quick to see opportunity in this, and so in quick succession the racing world got Formula 5000, F100, Formula Atlantic, Formula Ford 2000 and Sports 2000 ... and eventually the cleared path to F1 was muddied once again!

But in the '70s and early '80s, at least, anything—*anything*—that came at Formula Ford from the entry-level direction, failed.

Since FF success was the only way onto the career ladder (short of buying the whole hardware store), the intensity of each and every FF race rivaled the late, lamented, 1-liter Formula 3 (replaced in 1971 with a 1.6-liter, restricted intake, stock-block formula; bulked up to 2 liters in '74).

Actually, FF had everything but the great noise.

Because the FF races were invariably terrific, everyone on the grounds watched them and had to pay attention. And so a kind of unofficial star system emerged: Behind every filthy driver's suit was the next J. Scheckter; at the wheel of every homebuilt, tomorrow's Fittipaldi.

Race fans began to hang on some of the names—in the mid '70s, guys like Geoff Lees were *famous*, and what other entry-level racing series in history can say that about its participants?

Heady times.

Fancy threads

Back to chassis: In 1973, the English manufacturers began to pick up the tempo just a little bit. The front radiator "cigar" look was dead in F1 (killed by the Lotus 72), dying in F2 and 3, and looking its advanced age in FF.

There were various portents of change in items like the rocker-arm front suspension on the '69 Elden PH6 and the sports car nose on the original Hawke DL9. But nobody had done a Lotus 72 in FF yet.

Merlyn Mk24 and Titan Mk6 were typical of early '70s FF design: front radiator, outboard suspension, outboard rear brakes, carburetor ram air device, and bodywork one step removed from the "tube."

The Bob King-designed Royale RP16 didn't miss the mark by much. This one was raced by Englishman Geoff Lees, a triple champion and FF Festival winner with a Royale RP21 in '75.

If not for the Lola T-340, Royale boss Bob King might've gotten the credit his '73 FF probably deserved: The Super Vee bodywork-bedecked RP16 that rolled out of Royale's Huntington factory shortly before the much ballyhooed inaugural FF World Final event in Oct. '72 had a very nice "high-tech" look.

Unfortunately, it was basically an old RP3 underneath, with roots in moonlight work Bob Marston had done for Royale in the late '60s. In '73, King was distracted by bigger projects and by health concerns, and when Royale finally got around to the FF, developing the mediocre RP16 into the improved RP16A, it was too late: The Lola T-340 had landed.

Actually, the T-340 didn't have the impact on the English scene that it had in America, but it was certainly visible: Belgian Patrick Neve used one to win the '74 STP FF Championship as the T-340 stole the styling thunder from all the other FF manufacturers.

With so many parts interchangeable with other models in Lola's diverse range, the car was priced right too. This was a very well-conceived effort.

Suddenly, side radiators were the rage (except at Crosslé). But past that, the combination of T-340 and "ADF shock" in the U.S. somehow combined to lift the curtains in the minds of the best and brightest FF designers. Milestone cars appeared one after another throughout this golden era, all very inspired, all ultra-competitive: Lola T-340/2, Royale RP21, Hawke DL15, Royale RP24, Crosslé 30F, Van Diemen RF77 ...

There were a few turkeys, too, like Van Diemen's unloved RF75/76 and Titan's dreadful Mk8 follow-up to its wonderful Mk6C. Under the heading of "turkey" would have to be the Lola T-440 and Hawke DL17 even though there were a handful of drivers who could really make them go. The 440 and 17 respectively were the first generation of volume-produced FFs featuring long engine/gearbox spacers aimed at getting some of the weight off the back tires. Ultra-long bellhousings are now *de rigeur*, but in the '70s, the problems which resulted from torsionally stressing the Ford engine blocks and Hewland Mk9 gearbox casing were new.

In '77, Chico Serra opened the floodgates on a sea of young Brazilian superstars. Here his factory-entered Van Diemen RF77 leads David Leslie's Royale RP24 at Brands Hatch.

The Great Race I : The Formula Ford Festival

by Jeremy Shaw

The first Formula Ford Festival I attended was in 1975, at the bleak airfield circuit Snetterton in Norfolk, England. By then, the event was well established on the British motor racing calendar, providing a welcome end-of-season match up of the best protagonists from the various British series and an influx of challengers, many from abroad.

That year I well remember that drivers from the United States, Canada, Rhodesia, South Africa and Australia, not to mention a smattering of other European nations, arrived to take on our best. It was a wonderful event.

There was, of course, no shortage of wheel-to-wheel racing, nor of the category's regular drama and controversy. Royale driver Geoff Lees emerged as top dog—as usual that year—although only after Canadian Rod Bremner was penalized for jumping the standing start.

Lees subsequently drove a few Formula 1 races and these days is based in Japan where he remains a consistent front runner in both single-seaters and sports cars.

There were three Festival winners prior to Lees, none of whom went on to really establish himself in international racing, but several of the more recent winners are well known to race fans the world over. The '76 winner, for example, was Derek Daly who became a GP regular with Tyrrell and Williams before heading across the pond to the CART/PPG Indy Car series and then a new career in broadcasting.

Brazilian Chico Serra, the '77 winner for Van Diemen, went on to drive in F1 for Fittipaldi and Arrows, while Roberto Moreno ('80), Tommy Byrne ('81) and Johnny Herbert ('85) followed the same FF Festival-win path in climbing the F1 pinnacle.

The format of the event back in '75 was to hold four heat races in the morning, with the first 15 (I think it was) finishers in each progressing to the semi-finals. Once again, the top runners were whittled down before the eventual 30 finalists (from an entry of 114 that year) were determined.

Daly, relishing the '76 event's wet conditions in his Hawke DL17, was the first to score at the Festival's new-found home, Brands Hatch. The move to the Kent circuit's more hospitable surroundings enhanced the Festival's reputation immediately. Entries increased to a peak of about 250 in 1981 and the event was expanded to two days, with no fewer than eight heats taking place the first day. An extra "quarter-finals" round of competition was introduced, too.

In the mid-'80s, the rules were changed to require an International license. This cut into quantity but certainly not the quality.

For the acknowledged front runners, the system of heat races only serves to heighten the pressure of the entire event. No one wants to be eliminated in an early round, and yet no driver wants to wear out himself, his car or his engine before the all-important Grand Finale.

Reputations have been won and lost at the Festival, and not only by the drivers: Van Diemen's dominance—the firm won 10 of the first 20 FF Festivals—has been reflected in sales of its chassis over the last two decades, but also on the roster of winners are Dulon, Crossle, Elden, Royale, Hawke, Sark, Lola, Reynard and Quest.

Throughout its history, the British FF Festival has provided some of the most exhilarating competition of each racing season. And it may be improving with age.

FF Festival Winners 1972-1992

Year	Driver	Car
1972	Ian Taylor	Dulon LD9
1973	Donald MacLeod	Van Diemen FA73
1974	Richard Morgan	Crossle 25F
1975	Geoff Lees	Royale RP21
1976	Derek Daly	Hawke DL17
1977	Chico Serra	Van Diemen RF77
1978	Michael Roe	Van Diemen RF78
1979	Donald MacLeod	Sark 2
1980	Roberto Moreno	Van Diemen RF80
1981	Tommy Byrne	Van Diemen RF81
1982	Julian Bailey	Lola T-640E
1983	Andrew Gilbert-Scott	Reynard 83FF
1984	Gerrit van Kouwen	Lola T-644E
1985	Johnny Herbert	Quest FF85
1986	Roland Ratzenberger	Van Diemen RF86
1987	Eddie Irvine	Van Diemen RF87
1988	Vincenzo Sospiri	Van Diemen RF88
1989	Niko Palhares	Van Diemen RF89
1990	Dave Coyne	Swift FB90/1
1991	Marc Goossens	Van Diemen RF91
1992	Jan Magnussen	Van Diemen RF92

Geoff Lees: '75 FF Festival champion

Roberto Moreno: '80 FF Festival champion

Brazilian Raul Boesel took advantage of the opportunity presented him in '79 as a member of Van Diemen's factory FF team.

Works teams

The mid to late '70s in Britain featured some particularly turbulent battles among manufacturers, primarily featuring Crossle, Hawke, Royale and Van Diemen. Costs soared as Formula Ford's original £1,000 price ceiling was not only forgotten but obliterated by suddenly increased design and development costs. But even so, the international FF market continued to expand geometrically and the stakes for a manufacturer continued to climb.

This was a wonderful time for FF, though seeds of bitterness were planted that would flower ugly in the '80s. One of the problems was the phenomena known as a factory entry or "works team."

FF works teams were a fact of life from the very beginning in England, as evidenced by the success of MRS student Ray Allen and Jim Russell School leading light Claude Bourgoignie in 1967. The works teams always had the best equipment but that didn't matter a whole heckuva lot through FF's formative years: The very best cars, engines and tires (or very near copies of these cars, engines and tires) were for sale, available to all.

Almost all the way through the '70s, a working stiff with a modicum of talent could not only race Formula Ford but could win races and thereby cling to his dream.

Sadly, all that changed. By the end of the decade, the "best of everything" needed to win championships cost more than the average Joe (even one willing to make incredible sacrifices) could come up with. You couldn't lease a race car from anyone any more (the way James Hunt acquired his first Russell-Alexis) and sponsorship was harder to come by than ever because the sums were significantly larger.

For many years, the mere existence of works teams delayed the inevitable. Here was a place for the talented if penniless driver who could no longer afford to win on wages alone. His racing was subsidized by the manufacturer who capitalized on his success with sales. Geoff Lees (Royale), David Kennedy (Crossle),

Spectacular young Irishman Derek Daly proved worthy of the assistance lent him by Hawke Racing Cars, engine tuner David Minister and others in the mid '70s.

Derek Daly (Hawke) and Donald MacLeod (Van Diemen) were just a few of the deserving drivers in the middle '70s who probably would not have been able to sustain their early careers without factory assistance.

During this era, works teams abounded because so did the number of works! It wasn't just the manufacturers; engine tuners and prep shops were in on that act, too.

England being the mecca for anyone wishing to be a racing car driver, the very best racing was to be found in the major English championships. (Which is why Geoff Lees' extraordinary success in 1975 came as such a shock: The young Englishman won all three major titles plus the FF Festival in one season. Simply unbelievable!)

And every spring, the world's best young drivers flocked to England, including a regular number from South America.

The chassis war was wide open '74-'76, but the number of competitive works rides began to dry up once Van Diemen boss Ralph Firman figured out a way to cement his South American connection. Coincident with the arrival of the Dave Baldwin-designed Van Diemen RF77, Firman was at last able to draw on his friendship with Brazilian Emerson Fittipaldi, whom he ran in Formula 3. Starting with Chico Serra in 1977 and progressing through Raul Boesel ('79), Roberto Moreno ('80), Ayrton Senna da Silva ('81), Mauricio Gugelmin ('82), Maurizio Sandro Sala ('83) and a few others, Firman's Van Diemen factory-entered team featured a steady stream of South American superstars who were privileged indeed.

This parade antagonized a lot of people, especially English drivers left by the wayside, but the works team's success certainly brought sales to full boil: Van Diemen regularly sold over 100 FF chassis a year.

More and more often, though, the true privateer was shut completely out of the results as the once-non-existent gap between the FF haves and have-nots grew. In 1983, the end of the glory years in the view of this book's author, one still "had to" get started in Formula Ford. But by then, most could not.

An electrifying duel at Oulton Park in '78 featured Irishmen Kenny Acheson (Royale RP24) and Michael Roe (Van Diemen RF78).

Over 30 FFs charge into the esses at the now-defunct Riverside Raceway. And this was an '80 Regional, not a National!

The Promised Land

By 1973, Formula Ford's reach was truly global. An ocean away from England, enthusiasm for FF racing in America rivalled—even surpassed—the fun in the home market. American drivers were snapping up just about everything the English manufacturers sent over, but there was also some interesting home-brewed machinery. Two chassis in particular stepped into the the void left by the suddenly bankrupt Autodynamics, Inc., manufacturer of the Caldwell: The robust Zink Z-10, designed by noted FV man Ed Zink; and the frighteningly complex ADF Mk II, designed by aerospace engineer David Bruns.

Americans began buying FFs at a terrific rate as early as '68, and to an English manufacturer who felt tapped out in the home market, the U.S. became a land of plenty—a sales Promised Land. Early Royale, Winkelmann (Palliser) and Titan models sold better in the U.S. than in their own home market while Merlyn did well in both.

In about '72-'73, America and England really got out of sync on the chassis front—that is, marques doing well in one arena seemed to be doing poorly in the other. This was easily explained away by the big differences in tires (tall, treaded Firestones [later Dun-lops] in the U.K. vs. low-profile Goodyear racing slicks in the U.S.) and climate (cooling systems adequate for Brands Hatch in March sometimes melted at Riverside in July).

But these obvious explanations miss the mark: By 1973, there was more to the increasing separation between FF's two hungriest markets than skinny tires and water temperature. The separation wasn't strictly technical as was proven in '76 when the paths did converge again around Crossle's 30F, a wonderful car which was victorious in both arenas.

Similar equipment, maybe, but the game was played differently in America than in England.

Formula Ford racing in the U.K. was short, sharp, and physical—8-lap heat races, 10-lap finals, gears, gas, *go*, getthe*bloodyhell*outoftheway, *got it*, that's it, trophy, trailer-up, thank you very much indeed, on to the next.

The FF racing in the U.S. wasn't like that at all. A few of the English manufacturers, though they knew the facts, just couldn't *understand*—victims of the land of plenty.

One who did understand was Royale boss Alan Cornock (though because he couldn't seem to hook up with a well-funded, FF-focused, Carl Haas-quality importer, Royale faded from prominence in the mid-

50

'70s anyway): "In England, if a guy thinks for an instant he'll let the field 'settle down' before making his move, the leaders will have finished and gone to the bar before he gets to the first turn!" Cornock observed during one across-the-pond foray.

The dichotomy started with the time on the road getting to the races. The roads weren't so good in England then, but in the U.S. 1,000-mile tows were not unheard of and 500-mile journeys were routine in at least three of the seven SCCA geographically determined divisions.

Then there were the preliminaries: A few minutes to do or die in England; two and sometimes three lengthy practice and qualifying sessions at a U.S. National event.

Finally, the races themselves: 10-15 minutes tops in Britain vs. 30-40 minutes plotting and planning for the last lap in America.

In America, there was so much *time* that a car's little quirks were greatly magnified. High-speed oversteer is little hindrance to a fast-starting English driver with quick reflexes in a 10-minute race. But it's hard to live with for half an hour at Lime Rock (which may explain, come to think of it, why Elden's Mk10-series cars fell from grace so quickly on the East Coast).

While the U.K.'s best drivers were banging heads with one another all summer long, America's best met only once a year, at the National Championship Runoffs held at Road Atlanta (where everyone had a full *week* to engineer his car to the back of the grid).

Because of the vast distances, FF racing in America became regionally provincial almost as soon as the class was recognized by the SCCA in 1969. Communication among the SCCA regions was poor—the updated point standings that came once a month in the SCCA's *SportsCar* were two or three months behind due to the slick magazine's lead time.

So rumors appeared and flourished because there was no way to stop them—and these frequently hurt sales of many a manufacturer's fine machine. Great myths about cars and drivers emerged during the '70s summers which spoiled many a brilliantly hatched marketing plan: The Californians had all the trick stuff, the Northeast and Central Division guys played dirty, the Southeast FF guys had the unfair, home-court advantage, and the guys from the Pacific Northwest and Colorado had to be cheaters because none of their tracks were anything like Road Atlanta so how could they be so fast?

Oh yes, Road Atlanta. The week-long, one-race, winner-take-all SCCA Runoffs that was supposed to sort it all out was such an anomaly to begin with that the results we FF enthusiasts lived and breathed for meant nothing and everything *at the same time!*

Hard as hell for an English company to sell cars Stateside. The problem wasn't tires or climate or race tracks, it was this: There was no such thing as a Formula Ford for the American market because there wasn't a single American market.

In the '70s and early '80s, Titan, Lola, Crossle, Van Diemen and Reynard each had it figured for a little while. But for the rest, the promised land was a nightmare vision.

American FF great Bob Earl rests between sessions in '73.

The American perspective

As in England, the years '73-'83 were FF's glory years in America. At the start of it, Titan's purposeful new Mk6 dominated the American racing scene, ultimately finishing second, fourth and seventh at the '73 Runoffs. But strong Titan sales or no—and certainly the Roy Thomas-designed cars were sold by two of the best importers going in the U.S., Fred Opert and Pierre Phillips—the American-built ADF won the '73 Runoffs event and created a ripple of market disturbance.

Ultimately, fears about marketing head to head against the ADF proved groundless. At the '74 Runoffs, Marty Loft—a fine young talent from the Northwest—qualified his Crossle 25F on the pole and broke the ADF's magic spell. Loft finished third as Coloradoan Eddie Miller's aggressively driven Lola T-340 snatched victory from ADF-mounted Tom Wiechmann.

Every FF racer (not to mention retailer!) in America worried about the ADF over the winter of '74-'75 but, since it cost twice as much as any of its competitors, few drivers could afford one. Cigar-chomping Lola importer Carl Haas emerged the winner from all the doubt, selling a bountiful number of T-340s and the even sleeker T-342s between '73 and '76 on the strength of his solid marketing formula: Gorgeous cars which drivers of all skill levels liked sold for a fair price with awesome spare parts availability via a web of regional distributors.

But Lola came out with a less successful 340-series variant, the T-440, in 1977 and no amount of Carl Haas sales genius nor

(ABOVE) ADF train at the Canadian circuit West-wood. (BELOW) Wonderful Lime Rock battle in '78 featuring Tom Davey, Peter Kuhn (Van Diemens) John Herne (Hawke), and Mike Strawbridge (Lola).

number of Bertil Roos race wins could overcome the fact that, 1) it was hard to drive; and 2) its far-forward seating position left the driver's feet extraordinarily vulnerable. The long spacers between engine and gearbox that set the T-440 apart were 15 years ahead of their time.

(An aside: The small-tube-and-tear-off-tab-flexi-frame 340s/342s were a bitch to work on, and the author has often wondered if it wasn't a mechanics' backlash as much as the disappointing T-440 which led to Crossle's plucking away Lola's U.S. sales-winner crown ...)

Wiechmann laid on another ADF scare by winning the Runoffs in '75 (a sensational race featuring a classic Zink vs. ADF set-to), but by then everyone knew these were strictly low-volume machines, good on long courses but flawed on some of the shorter tracks found in so many regions. They were beatable if not *easily* beatable.

Dennis Firestone gave Crossle importer Ken Deeter a richly deserved '76 Runoffs victory, kicking off America's commitment to the Irish marque—a commitment which endured long after Ralph Firman's Van Diemens took over the European FF scene. Interestingly, one racing school (Motor Racing Stables) launched the FF class in '67; another (Jim Russell) contributed to the Van Diemen's successful launch in '73; and still another made a significant difference in Crossle's blossoming: After putting a toe into the driver training waters with a partner, Tony Scotti, ex-FF National Champion, ex-F1 driver, and recently retired F5000 regular Skip Barber plunged right in: In 1976, Skip opened a racing school bearing his name which featured Crossles for many years.

America came late to the Van Diemen party, but did so finally when the English FF marketing king found an importer up to the job: As sales manager for the New York-based Grand Prix Race Cars, Inc., transplanted Englishman Mike Gue got some good cars to sell (RF78s, touched-up versions of designer Dave Baldwin's first Van Diemen, the RF77) and put some excellent Ted Wenz-tuned engines in the back. Then he stirred two terrific Northeast Division drivers—Tom Davey and young Peter Kuhn—into the blend, a recipe for 1) selling cars by 2) winning races.

Out on his own as Essex Racing shortly thereafter, Gue sold Van Diemens in great numbers in the early '80s as Ralph Firman finally got the acclaim in America his cars attracted in Europe.

Van Diemen arch-rival Reynard, meanwhile, attacked a few years later with its lovely '82 machines, while PRS, Tiga, Royale and to a lesser extent Hawke and Merlyn all achieved some regional success during the golden era '73-'83 as well.

Competing against the English marques' price advantage, achieved through volume manufacture as well as currency conversion, was tough. Zink was the only American manufacturer to hang in all the way through that period; ADF came and went, Eagle came and went, and LeGrand came in small numbers. A few others, like the hideous, California-built Carom and Corsa, were gone before they came ...

The fit and finish of the American cars was not up to English standard, but the Eagle DGF, Zink Z-10 and Citation-Zink Z-16 were plenty fast and extremely safe—and they won a lot of races.

In the years '73-'83, a great FF time was had by all.

A classic confrontation between two American FF greats: Bruce MacInnes (Zink Z-10) vs. William "The Fox" Henderson (Crossle 30F).

Developmental differences

One of the benefits of having so much 'time' in the U.S. was that the American drivers could do more tinkering than their U.K. counterparts. At Snetterton, a Van Diemen was a Van Diemen was a Van Diemen, but at Laguna Seca a Van Diemen could be a long-tail Van Diemen or a high-tail Van Diemen or an old Lotus with a Van Diemen body. These differences led to an interesting array of machinery—truly something for everyone in the FF paddock.

Tom Davey, advertising genius and one of the Northeast's best FF drivers, summed up one of the most exciting things about FF racing quite completely in *SportsCar* magazine in 1978: "As the seasons have gone by," Davey wrote, "enterprising competitors have worked long into the night trying virtually every trick known to modern science in order to make their racers go faster. The list is endless: snorkles, ram-air boxes, brake scoops, front radiators, rear radiators, wide noses, narrow noses, sports car noses, needle noses, wedge-shape designs, fat and bulbous designs, thinly disguised wings, not-so thinly designed wings, short tails, long tails, high tails, low tails, no tails at all, front spoilers, rear spoilers, gearbox spacers, inboard brakes, inboard suspensions, outboard suspensions, faired-in mirrors, big sway bars, little sway bars, hydraulic sway bars, no sway bars, torsion bars, stiff chassis, flexible chassis—even radial tires pumped up to 50 lbs."

"Development" has always been a buzzword in FF racing, but in the '70s, FF drivers were drivers first and engineers last, and surprisingly few of them knew what they were talking about! (Which made for some .... er, *unique* newspaper and magazine articles: There was at least one American journalist writing about Formula Ford racing in the mid '70s who knew a whole lot less!)

"Development? I'm sure if you were quick and painted your hat green, everyone would have to have a green hat!" explained Royale proprietor Alan Cornock.

Another decade would pass before guys like ex-David Loring/Brian Goodwin wrench Chris Wallach started bringing affordable multi-channel computerized instrumentation devices to bear on FF, and for a long time "development" in FF racing was mental rather than practical and very heavily related to inspired use of right foot.

But, when genuinely advanced technology (as opposed to green hats) began taking advantage of race-savvy right feet routinely in the early '80s, FF's promise died quickly. And promise gone, FF became just another racing class—easy prey for the entrepreneurs with new entry-level classes up their sleeves.

In the '80s, FF technology exploded in England and the U.S., and the FF world came to an end.

The Great Race II: The SCCA Runoffs

There is no weirder, wilder, more wonderful event in the Formula Ford universe than the Runoffs, the fall flagship event of the Sports Car Club of America's club racing program.

Until 1973, the enduring event was called the American Road Racing Championships (ARRC), and for the next decade-and-a-half, it was the Champion Spark Plug Road Racing Classic (CSPRRC). But it has never been called anything but 'The Runoffs' by the participants. (In the old days, a few promoters and PR people tried to call it the "Olympics of Motor Racing." But despite the fact that it's a true amateur event—i.e. everyone involved makes money except the volunteers who make it work—they got lawsuit-threatening letters from the IOC.)

To understand the Runoffs, one has to understand that the SCCA club racing program, which has always featured dozens of classes, is more a lifestyle than a hobby. In many of those classes, "winning the Runoffs" is an end unto itself, something one tries to do *every year* rather than do once and then move on from.

The Runoffs are a full week long! Practice and qualifying take four days, racing another three. And as an invitation-only affair, they are strictly provincial: do *not* send us your tired or your poor, longing to compete.

Formula Ford never fit particularly well into this environment. Half the field were young guys on their way to Formula 1 or Indy Car racing who cared nothing about the "club racing family"; the other half were full-time club racers kicked out of the family for their association with Formula Ford!

Drivers had to be aggressive just to survive in FF's cut and thrust, and because of the closeness of competition, there were always a lot of accidents—which meant an awful lot of extra work for the volunteer corner workers and safety crews who came to despise FF.

Runoffs glimpses: (TOP) Skip Barber's Caldwell charges to victory in '69. (BELOW) Bob Lobenberg scored ADF's third Road Atlanta triumph in '80. (BOTTOM) America's greatest FF champion Dave Weitzenhof.

No question, though: Since Pro Formula Ford racing never amounted to much in the U.S., since the popular June Sprints at Road America never attracted drivers from west of the Rockies, and since the various divisional champions got no publicity away from home whatsoever, the Runoffs was far and away the most important FF event in what was, for almost 20 years, the biggest FF marketplace in the world.

This, plus the fact that it was such a weird event, set an awful lot of English constructors to teeth-gnashing.

The Runoffs settled permanently at Road Atlanta in 1970—previously, the huge event alternated between tracks on the east and west coasts—and that forever altered the course of FF history. The northwestern Georgia circuit has some unique features, and it is nowhere near as easy to get around quickly as the preponderance of long straights and sweeping corners on the track map would imply.

Brute horsepower, clean aerodynamics, and bravery count most at Road Atlanta, but subtleties are important, too, in ways they are not on the tight, twisty courses of the Northeast, Central and Midwest Divisions. Or of England.

Years passed before the English chassis manufacturers truly came to grips with Road Atlanta, a point not lost on an eclectic group of Southern Californians who stood the FF community on its ear by winning the '73 Runoffs with a hideously complex, previously unraced, California-built machine. The ADF Mk II was a heretical machine which featured inboard front shocks/springs, inboard front brakes and ponderous if functional bodywork. It also featured a ponderous price: a cool $10,000 in a year when other FFs could be acquired for just slightly more than half that.

Bob Earl won the Runoffs in '73 with the ADF prototype, ADF customer Tom Wiechmann won in '75, and the brilliant Bob

Lobenberg gave the ADF marque (by then long gone from the race car construction business) still another Road Atlanta victory in 1980.

The ADF's '80 triumph came in the middle of a streak of Runoffs success by American chassis: Dennis Firestone's Crossle won in '76, the last time an English chassis won the Runoffs until 1984. This was particularly bizarre because during those years, the English constructors dominated the sales charts and won most of the SCCA Regionals and Nationals. But in '84, the picture changed: American-built Swift took off in the sales arena. So what won the next Runoffs? An English-built Reynard.

History can be perverse.

It wasn't all ADF down there in Georgia, although the marque might have claimed a few more trophies if Dave Weitzenhof had driven one of their cars: The intense, mustachioed Ohio resident and Firestone tire engineer appeared on the FF scene in '73 after winning the '72 Formula Vee National Championship. His first Ford was a Royale RP16, but his next was a Zink Z-10, and Dave has been faithful to the marque and its Citation successors ever since.

Weitzenhof won a barn-burner of a '77 National Championship race, and backed it up by winning with the new Citation Z-16 in '79. He won again in '81 (Z-16) and again in '87 driving a Citation (the Indiana Citation-Zink and original North Carolina Zink firms having gone their separate ways), although he was helped to the '87 title by the disqualification of the on-track winner, Brian Ongais.

Also in on the American marque Runoffs win-streak was Eagle: David Loring, America's FF boy wonder in '71-'72, utterly dominated the '78 event. Sadly, Dan Gurney's FF project went nowhere.

And then there was the Viking: Ace engine tuner Arnie Loyning produced a small number of FF slipstreamers, one of them used by Bob Lobenberg to strike Runoffs gold in '82.

More about Swift, which won the Runoffs for the first time in '83, elsewhere in this book. Suffice it to conclude this essay

by noting that a 10-year-long Swift winning streak at Road Atlanta has been broken only three times: in '84 by the brilliant Jackson Yonge driving a Reynard; in '87 when, as mentioned, the winning Swift was disqualified for a carburetor infraction; and in '90 courtesy Tony Kester's much-modified Reynard.

The numbers are: 24 FF Runoffs races '69-'92; 17 victories by American chassis; just seven victories for the Europeans.

Nothing at all like the FF sales numbers in North America. But, then, the SCCA Runoffs are like nothing else in the world.

SCCA Runoffs Winners 1969-1992

Year	Driver	Chassis
1969	Skip Barber	Caldwell D9
1970	Skip Barber	Tecno
1971	Jim Harrell	Titan Mk6A
1972	Eddie Miller	Hawke DL2B
1973	Bob Earl	ADF Mk II
1974	Eddie Miller	Lola T-340
1975	Tom Wiechmann	ADF Mk II
1976	Dennis Firestone	Crossle 30F
1977	Dave Weitzenhof	Zink Z10
1978	David Loring	Eagle DGF
1979	Dave Weitzenhof	Zink Z10
1980	Bob Lobenberg	ADF Mk II
1981	Dave Weitzenhof	Citation Z16
1982	Bob Lobenberg	Viking 82
1983	R.K. Smith	Swift DB-1
1984	Jackson Yonge	Reynard FF84
1985	Scott Atchison	Swift DB-1
1986	Jim Vasser Jr.	Swift DB-1
1987	Dave Weitzenhof	Citation 87F
1988	Kenny Hendrick	Swift DB-1
1989	Richard Bahmer	Swift DB-1
1990	Tony Kester	Reynard FF88-X
1991	Richard Schroebel	Swift DB-1
1992	C. T. Hancock	Swift DB-1

No expense spared: After graduating from the Skip Barber and Bertil Roos racing schools, Mario Andretti's oldest son Michael hit the N.E. Div. FF world like no one before or since: Few drivers (even including veteran Englishman Syd Fox!) have had four different chassis at their disposal in one season: Young Michael raced a Lola T-440 (TOP LEFT) in early February (that's John Paul Jr.'s damaged Crossle alongside); a Scandia (TOP RIGHT) in late Feb., and again in the summer; a Van Diemen RF81 (LEFT) in fall; and a PRS RH02 (FAR LEFT) in between!

5
Trials (1984-1992)

After several years of domination by Brazilians and Irishmen, the British journalists were understandably relieved in 1982 to get their own back in Formula Ford racing, Englishmen Julian Bailey (Lola) and Rick Morris (Royale) claiming two of Britain's most prestigious FF1600 championships.

Of course, Brazilian Mauricio Gugelmin *did* nab the third.

In summing up that trio's '82 success, journalist Jeremy Shaw, writing in *Autosport*, offered some extremely salient comments about what FF racing in the early '80s had become:

"Apart from the top three men, no one else managed to challenge for the lead on anything approaching a regular basis (in '82) and it must be said that a great deal of time, effort and money went into creating their success. It is a sign of the times, though, that a true privateer only once managed to break into the winner's circle from a total of 37 races that comprised the three major championships in 1982 ...

"There are probably two main reasons for the virtual monopoly that the works teams now enjoy. Firstly, of course, they possess the technological and financial resources to conduct proper test programs and really extract maximum potential from their cars. And secondly, they have the time and inclination to work out any deficiencies and correct them.

"An example of this can be seen in the way that the works teams 'solved' a potentially major problem last year: the supply of sub-standard tires ... It was said during the year that Mauricio Gugelmin went out testing with his Van Diemen RF82 at least twice per week, and that on numerous occasions he would spend

Mauricio Gugelmin worked hard at testing in 1982.

a whole day pounding round Snetterton just trying to find four matching tires to use for the following weekend's racing!"

For all its popularity and intensity, the bill for Formula Ford racing finally came due, just as cost had finally swept away the equally entertaining 1-liter Formula 3 (giving way to FF's birth) in the mid '60s. FF chassis and spare parts were extremely expensive as manufacturers had to absorb horrendous development costs (see "Mauricio Gugelmin testing his Van Diemen twice a week" above). Engines and engine components were extremely expensive as tuners had to absorb tremendous development costs (i.e., had to buy roomfulls of expensive new computerized test equipment). Tires were extremely expensive as the tire makers had to absorb tremendous development costs in other arenas and tried to recoup some of it by selling FF rubber.

By the early '80s, chassis, engines and tires were priced well beyond the available resources of the average racing newcomer and FF had traveled light years away from Geoffrey Clarke's original concept of a class which tested drivers' mettle, not the depths of their pocketbooks.

With full fields of cars at key events on circuits like Brands Hatch (LEFT, ABOVE) and Road Atlanta (LEFT), Formula Ford looked healthy enough. But in truth, through the '80s, it was clinging to life.

Sports Renault was an instant success in the U.S., on the strength of low-cost entry, technical simplicity, and a pro series. (ABOVE) SRs at the '84 Detroit GP. (BELOW) FF star Dave Weitzenhof—traitor!—tests the SR prototype.

Winning had never been easy, of course, especially in a class as hard-fought as Formula Ford. As early as 1968, Tim Schenken faced a formidable summer-long management task tying together all the loose ends of his successful Merlyn program.

Winning took nothing less than complete commitment but suddenly, one day, that commitment could be bought.

"Today, people (beginners) are not focused on the steps they need to take. Today, they go and buy engines and tires, they don't practice!" said Swede Bertil Roos, a Vee and Super Vee star who graduated briefly to

Formula 1 in the mid-'70s. Roos knows of what he speaks: These days, he runs a successful racing school in Pennsylvania that preaches finding and then learning how to drive at the limit.

The beauty of FF for many years, as explained in the last chapter, was that wins could *not* be bought. Money helped, of course, as it allowed more practice time and more component choices; but it was only part of the blend. In the '70s, desire could and often did win out; by the early '80s, that was no longer true.

Formula Ford's original promise came with one guarantee: that the winners were the real thing, had what author Tom Wolfe would define as The Right Stuff. When that guarantee could be broached by a new generation of drivers who led with their Visa cards instead of their right foot, FF was finished.

Villains of the piece

Interestingly enough, the seeds of FF's destruction were sown not in England, where the story began, but in America. Enter, stage right in '83, the two most visible villains of the FF whodunnit: David Bruns and Nicholas Craw.

In 1983, Craw, the coolly calculating and newly hired Executive Director of the Sports Car Club of

America, unveiled a new club racing master plan that, incredibly, would put the sanctioning body in the manufacturing business! The SCCA would be producer and director both of a new one-design sports racing class dubbed "Sports Renault."

When the prototype was unveiled at the '83 Runoffs, Sports Renault put the SCCA in direct competition not only with the world's production race car manufacturers but also with the hundreds of race shops in the U.S. that depended upon SCCA club racing for their livelihood. Most of these were FF shops as, despite the creeping costs, FF was far and away the SCCA's most popular class.

Craw's plan was brilliant and well timed, kicking FF where it was most vulnerable—Fords were expensive cars with no resale value; tires were expensive and short-lived—knowing the manufacturers and prep shops were far too competitive with each other to pull together and fight the thing.

The four-cylinder, Renault-powered sports racers were very much like modern-day Lotus 51 FFs in that they were cheap, reliable and available. Unlike the world's first purpose-built FF, Sports Renaults were also dog slow and butt ugly. But fueled by low price, the promise of non-obsolescence (the chassis design would be locked in for several years) and the immediate announcement of a Pro series, Sports Renault exploded: The SCCA took 111 deposits at the Runoffs and sold another 100 over the next six months, more new cars than all the English FF manufacturers combined had sold in the U.S. in several years.

Clearly, there was a need for an entry-level racing class that wasn't being met (in the U.S. at least) as hundreds of drivers young and old clamored—*tripping* over each other!—to buy one of these graceless and ungainly sports racers.

Where had FF gone wrong?

Suddenly, in 1984, all the young up and comers were gone. For the first time in 15 years, there was no "next generation" in Formula Ford to pick up the baton from the veterans.

But Sports Renault wasn't the worst of it ...

Even as Craw and his SCCA cronies were fiddling with their spec-sports racer scheme, Southern California-based designer David Bruns and *his* friends were preparing for the Oct. '83 debut of a no-compromise Formula Ford to be called the Swift DB-1, the first in what was expected to be a line of cars from the newly created Swift Cars Inc.

Incredibly enough, history repeated itself when, 10 years to the day later, the new Swift won the prestigious SCCA Runoffs in its debut. In '73, the Bruns-designed ADF Mk II had done likewise—an amazing feat then, made all the more unlikely for being done again!

Bruns' Swift was a wonderful race car and a simply awesome Formula Ford with many strengths including traction, a very reassuring balance and refined aerodynamics. It had very few vices.

It *was* more expensive than the English chassis then available but not frighteningly so like the ADF. Between Oct. '83 and Feb. '87, Swift sold 120 cars,

Swift comments (L to R): "A super car (that) jumped two full generations," said Van Diemen's Ralph Firman. "The Swift phenomenon was a failure of the other people in the business," said Citation's Steve Lathrop. "Fun!" said Swift's Paul White.

and every one of them was a nail in the coffin of the English FF constructors who took far too long to respond.

"The Swift immediately captured the imagination of the American public," Van Diemen proprietor Ralph Firman acknowledged in an interview taped several years later. "It was a super car, but it jumped two full generations (of FF development).

"Like Ralt, you see, we preferred to move along a little bit at a time, walk gently, keep it cost effective and reasonable. We looked after our own business and with that attitude, FF maintained fairly steady growth—we believed in FF very much.

"The daft part about the Swift was that it brought FF down in the U.S. The whole scene went crazy! In '84, the dollar was strong against the pound, but the importers all whacked the prices up to meet the Swift.

"And there you go. That was it. Whether it (FF) will ever come back, I don't know."

"The Swift phenomenon was a failure of the people in the business," said Citation Engineering's Steve Lathrop, builder of the Centurion FF raced by Dave Weitzenhof and others, in an interview with *On Track*'s Bill Mitchell. "The English car builders and I didn't build the best car possible. We had designs on the shelf but we chose to keep improving our old models."

The one-two punch—Bruns' Swift, Craw's Sports Renault—all but KO'ed FF. The class' National racing numbers tumbled as newcomers flocked to Sports Renault and, by 1988, top-line FF racing in America was just about finished off.

Back across the pond

FF racing in England had its own problems. For one, taking advantage of Ford's decade of disinterest in Formula Ford, its biggest competitor General Motors decided to jump into the single-seater fray at the

Road Atlanta, Oct. '83: R.K. Smith at the wheel, the Swift DB-1 wins the Runoffs in its first compeitive appearance.

World class confusion

Geoffrey Clarke offers an apocryphal tale that seems to be an appropriate lead-in to a discussion of Formula Ford's modern-day competitors. It also fills in some historical gaps as there's no mistaking the ex-Motor Racing Stables proprietor's bitterness towards MCD boss John Webb in this one!

"John tried desperately for years to create a class as successful as Formula Ford—there was F100, F5000, FF2000, S2000, all the rest of it. He was jealous of FF's success—it wasn't his, wasn't his baby," Clarke remembers.

"I recall the day I was asked to tag along as he took several VIPs to a lunch near the circuit (Brands Hatch)—we went to a pub called 'The Rising Sun' or 'The Piddling Horse' or some-such—to announce Formula 5000. Afterwards, he'd arranged an exhibition: Tony Lanfranchi, one of my instructors for a time at MRS, was going to drive one of these big V8-powered machines around, show it off for us.

"Well, we're all in John's car, driving under the pit tunnel onto the club circuit, when Tony whizzes by for the first time. Webb reaches over, pats me on the knee and says, 'Geoff: Formula Ford was yours. This is mine.'

"And just then, accelerating out of Clearways, Tony spins and crashes! How telling."

Clarke's dislike of Webb aside, **Formula 5000** was ultimately successful for a time, while **Formula Atlantic**, **Formula Ford 2000** and **Sports 2000** are thriving even today.

Webb's **Formula 100**, introduced in '69, featured Ford's 1300cc four in a small, spaceframe, two-seat chassis. Named for its use of Firestone F100 radial tires, it tried to compete with Clubmans and failed.

Then there was **Formula Turbo Ford**, which threatened in '84, but a series planned for '85 featuring Garrett turbo-equipped, 2-liter Ford-powered cars did not materialize.

Still, though F100 lasted only two seasons and Turbo Ford was stillborn, former MCD boss Webb can claim a significant legacy in the form of healthy racing classes.

More classes have emerged in England since Webb quit the game and retired to Spain. Indeed, the preponderance of classes now inhabiting the range between racer drivers school and Formula 3 is quite staggering—a very confusing array.

As mentioned, there is Formula Ford 2000 (called F2000 in Canada and **Formula Continental** in the U.S.). It was introduced in Jan. '75, featuring Ford's new SOHC 2-liter four, revised FF1600 chassis and wings. It is now all but dead in the U.K., but was extremely popular for 10 years or so.

In '88, FF2000 was split into A and B categories, the latter for pre-'87 machines.

Sports 2000, introduced in Jan. '77, a sports racing class which also featured the 2-liter Ford four, also attracted a large worldwide following.

Then there was **Formula Talbot**, launched in 1980 after years of hearing about the Big Energy Crisis to come (which would be bigger than the last Big Energy Crisis). Talbot's gimmick was that the cars used methanol. It got a lot of media attention as P.M. Margaret Thatcher's son Mark raced in it, but was gone by 1984.

In May '86, John Foulston led a takeover of the Brands Hatch group of companies, and one of the first things Brands Hatch Leisure (BHL) did was reorganize its racing schools and announce a new school and school race series-aimed **Formula First**. The class featured a new 1600cc Ford engine mounted transversely. Van Diemen won the contract to build all the cars, the number quickly running to over 100.

In 1989, BHL introduced **Formula Forward** and soon thereafter, the sports racing one-marque **Multisports** as BHL stretched successfully to include more and more of the motor sports ladder under the shelter of its own program.

Launched in April '88, **Formula Vauxhall Lotus** (called Opel Lotus on the European continent) took off on the strength of a terrific 16-valve, 2-liter engine and GM's aggressive PR. By 1992, there were no fewer than six regional championships supporting the premier EFDA-run Vauxhall Lotus Euroseries. Reynard-built monocoque chassis were extremely handsome for a one-marque class, the cars were quick, and the series immediately yielded world-class drivers, starting with Mika Hakkinen.

Van Diemen builds cars for the no-less-notable **Formula Vauxhall Junior**, an entry-level class introduced in 1991 that has already produced some good racing. The Juniors are powered by Vauxhall's 1.6-liter Nova GSi four generating about 112hp and they use Avon slick racing tires. The class was, says GM, "designed for competitors embarking on their motor racing careers and kartists wishing to graduate upwards." The parallels to FF1600 are extraordinary.

Another success story is the new **Formula Renault** which came to England in '89 after a rules revolution: Out were the old semi-monocoque Formula Renault chassis; in were spaceframes. Out were the old turbocharged engines; in was a new normally aspirated SOHC 1721cc four. As all the English manufacturers had FF2000 designs they could adapt, interest was intense and immediate.

If all of the above is not enough to fog one's brain, consider what's happened in England to Formula Ford 1600: In '79, the BRSCC introduced a new **Pre-'74** class for FF chassis built prior to Jan. 1, 1974. That was so popular so quickly that in '82, the rival BARC introduced a **'74-'78** FF class for cars built after Jan. 1, 1974 but before Jan. 1, 1979.

Later, the newly formed Formula E Register announced ... Formula E. The "E" stands for "Economy" and the rules admit any FF with outboard suspension. Next, in '88, came **Pre-'85**.

Wonder what's next?

A brand new purpose-built "vintage FF" from Elden.

The race to the Swift: At the SCCA Runoffs in '88, there were only a very few non-Swift interlopers.

bottom end with the one-design Formula Vauxhall-Lotus (called Opel-Lotus on the Continent) featuring GM's tidy 2-liter four. Reynard produced some very handsome machinery for this new class, and once GM's PR machinery got the bit between its teeth, interest in Formula Ford 2000—already flagging—dipped considerably.

Although there were many stirring battles over the years, there was something not quite right about FF1600's big brother FF2000 which had been conceived by MCD's John Webb and introduced in time for the '75 racing season. Designer Adrian Reynard won his spurs here and for a time the racing was good, but FF2000 lacked *panache*—it simply wasn't a big enough jump up from 1600.

Ayrton Senna at speed in an FF2000 Van Diemen.

Interestingly, after years of sanctioning body disinterest in America, 2-liter FF racing got a toehold in the mid-'80s and today Formula Continental, as it's called in the U.S., is quite popular.

A third Ford-based formula—Sports 2000, introduced in '78 for the '79 season—has been far more succesful over the long run. But, while entertaining, it was really nothing more than a diversion for a young driver intent on a professional motorsports career.

Then Brands Hatch Racing announced the very cheap, entry-level Formula First. Then Formula Renault came to England, a formal rebuke, perhaps, for Ford introducing FF to France in '84? Whatever, new FR rules introduced in '89 dispensed with semi-monocoques in favor of spaceframes. Featuring Renault's normally aspirated SOHC 1721cc, there was immediate interest in England as all the manufacturers could adapt existing FF2000 designs.

By the end of the '80s, Formula Ford 1600 racing in England was getting pounded on all sides.

Ralph Firman again: "Even though we won contracts to build some of these cars, we continue to believe in open competition among manufacturers—that's why Formula Ford was so good for so long. We could sell a new car every year, not only because it looked different, but because it was developed a little more.

"With these one-design formulas (like Formula First), we *don't* sell a new car every year and we don't make what we should on spares: As the years go by, the pirates get more brave."

Firman is far too pragmatic an individual to waste time getting misty-eyed about FF. Still, there is emotion not far below the surface of a man who was involved with the class almost without interruption for over 25 years.

"FF1600 had its day in the late '70s and early '80s. In England, every young, budding, racing driver who wanted to prove himself saw the main FF championship as the place to start his career. It's very unfortunate that Ford and the RAC did not accept that fact or promote that fact—that would have ensured that someone look after it as a way of training racing drivers.

"Regardless of the PR, they (Ford) had some responsibilities. These were ignored; Ford simply re-

(TOP, LEFT) Ford's presence in FF racing all but vanished in the '80s. (ABOVE, LEFT) SCCA Northeast Div. FF star Bill Shearer practices touch and go's with his DB-1. (ABOVE, RIGHT) FF racing had lost its spark by '85.

fused to see the logic. In '85, the decline started and (the class) may not be bottomed out yet."

It least it started down with a bang. That year, 1985, Van Diemen sold 124 RF85 FFs.

End of an era

Happily, Van Diemen has many other projects to sustain it in the face of a fading Formula Ford: In 1985, after 12 years in business, it delivered its 1,000th car, a FF1600 RF85 that was part of a 25-car order from Ford for Portugal. In 1993, just eight years later, it will deliver its *2,000th* car.

Other companies which specialized in FF were not so fortunate. The upward component cost spiral claimed Merlyn and Hawke in the late '70s. Royale, PRS, Tiga, Sparton and FF Festival winner Quest were all gone by the mid- to late-'80s. Newcomers to the class in '85, both Anson and Talon faded quickly from the FF scene.

Survivors? Atop the list, besides Van Diemen, there was Reynard. Though the brilliant Adrian Reynard's personal ambition to do F1 may have hampered his FF efforts in the early '80s, there were signs of a resurgence of interest when Reynard contracted with

ex-Royale boss Alan Cornock and Mike 'Fulmar' Taylor to distribute Reynard's small-bore production cars. Cornock immediately contracted with an American firm he had admired for decades—Carl Haas Automobile Imports—to distribute Reynards in the U.S. A sound move.

Crossle thrives, doing a whopping parts business, as does, in the U.S., Citation and of course Swift (though its DB-1 FF design was 10 years old and still counting).

Two traditionally small English FF manufacturers, Jamun and Ray, blossomed in the late '80s as a handful of newcomers specializing in FF seemed to have made it over the hump: ex-Crossle designer Leslie Drysdale's Mondiale and Frank Bradley's Swift U.K. were both doing well into the '90s, while two intriguing new American machines, the Piper and the Stohr, were beginning to attract considerable attention.

But once costs escalated beyond the entry level and FF came under real pressure from several quarters, the class lost its most important feature: By 1990, FF1600 was no longer the obvious choice, the only way to get started. And already, new stars of F1 and Indy Car racing were beginning to emerge from someplace else.

Would Formula Ford every return to the peaks it once scaled? In 1992, a better question, perhaps, was "Could Formula Ford be saved?" The prospects appeared bleak. (ABOVE) Scott Rubenzer's Citation leads at Blackhawk.

RF85 was a Van Diemen FF best-seller.

The Stohr is a promising new American-built machine.

Ten years after, it's still Swifts as far as the eye can see.

Formula Ford racing arrived in France in '84.

That man Bruns and his marvelous machines

A pivotal machine, the Swift DB-1 which was designed in '83 not to revolutionize (like its '73 ADF FF predecessor) but to rapidly evolutionize a popular but increasingly complex and expensive racing class.

"The English FF constructors have found that the secret to sales success lies in the old Detroit adage of change for change's sake and regular fall facelifts," wrote John Rorquist in a *SportsCar* magazine series entitled 'Race to the Swift.' "Sometimes the changes are cosmetic; more often these days they are major. The top drivers buy or are loaned new cars every year and because they are the top drivers they, of course, win. Potential winners must therefore have the latest too, or so the thinking goes."

Despite the modern-day belief that he could proceed entirely unrestrained, Swift designer David Bruns admits there was a heavy hand on his DB-1: the need to provide quality at a price close to what the British manufacturers were then getting in the U.S. Exotic materials (chrome-moly steel, carbon fiber and the like) and advanced construction techniques were out.

"The Swift's focus is on straight-line speed. The design treads no new technological ground," Bruns told journalist Rorquist in the summer of '83, months before the car's winning debut at the Runoffs. "The design's evolution followed a logical path: conceptualize, eliminate all unnecessary parts, relocate components to more efficient locations."

An aerospace engineering graduate of Arizona State University, Bruns used an extremely wide track and narrow body to eliminate aerodynamic suspension clutter and spent weeks on the computer working on suspension geometry. He agonized over some of the parts that would be cast, especially the complex bellhousing adapter.

His partners in the Swift Cars venture, meanwhile, invested heavily in molds and tooling required for "mass production" and reduced component costs. Their faith in Bruns' design ability was rewarded quickly, driver R.K. Smith breezing to victory in the car's debut and Swift principal Paul White accepting more than 30 deposit checks that weekend. And that was really just the start of the Swift FF story.

Comparisons to the ADF were inevitable—and unfair.

(ABOVE) DB-1 design brief: straight line speed. (BELOW) A Bruns gallery: Lightning Indy Car, Autoresearch Super Vee, and "The Homebuilt," a Formula Ford which emerged from the aerospace engineer's basement in '71.

6

And Again (1993-?)

In 1992, Formula Ford 1600 race entries were down once again, but in England there was something to cheer about: A superb battle between Jamie Spence and Andrew McAuley for the Rapid Fit British Open Formula Ford Championship, and the late-season arrival of Jan Magnusson whose winning streak carried right over to the FF Festival.

Spence—suspended for three months for a driving infraction—was hardly missed at the '92 FF Festival at Brands Hatch which featured top drivers from seven countries. There was great chassis variety in the final won by Magnusson's Van Diemen: Ray, Swift, Jamun, Mondiale, Reynard and, of course, Van Diemen, all had car (or cars) in the top 10.

There were good engines aplenty at the Festival, too: Auriga, Gatmo, Quicksilver, Zagk, Loyning, Greenwood, Auto Cooper and Scholar were in the top 10; Nelson, Minister, Ivey, Reid, Searle and Bastos were in the hunt.

Autosport reporters Andrew Benson and Nick Phillips concluded their FF Festival story by observing of 19-year-old Magnusson: "This is the start of something very special indeed."

A lot of this rings like old times. But is it all a promise only to deceive?

Formula Ford is not what it used to be, though in '93 it could be more: This year, FF in England gets the new 1800cc Ford Zeta engine, a fairly impressive little mill that the engine tuners seem to like.

But what's sorely needed is interest from the top: Formula Ford's 25th anniversary in 1992 and the '93 adoption of the Zeta engine may rekindle fires of interest at Ford ... or may not. Other manufacturers like Opel/Vauxhall and Renault have really taken advantage of the PR vacuum left by Ford at the entry level. That alone has seriously dimmed FF's future, exciting new engine or no.

"Now, Ford has taken an interest again," says Van Diemen's Ralph Firman. "They appear to want to do it. Why the hell they didn't do it 10 years ago, I can't imagine, but the good news is, they're not letting it drop."

Well, maybe not in England. But in America, it looks almost certain that Ford will step in to replace Renault supplying engines for the SCCA Spec Racer (nee Sports Renault) class. That will use up any budget or energy that Ford might have applied FF.

This Zeta four may be a hit—in winter '92-'93 testing, it looks good. But for a glimpse at Formula Ford's future, we may have to look to its past. The one area where interest in FF racing is really bursting is the historic racing scene.

The BRSCC's John Nicol wrote in the '87 *Formula Ford: A 20-Year World Success Story*: "So long as the requisite engines are produced and there can be stability with such components as gearboxes and tires, Formula Ford 1600 should continue without hiccup beyond the year 2000 (Pre-'74s may have wilted a little by then!), and championship Formula Ford racing will remain the mainstay of innumerable race programmes. As each year passes, organizing clubs will inevitably look to categorize or sub-divide the increasing resources: Pre-'74, '74-'78 and Formula E could find themselves just part of the backdrop to contemporary FF1600, with Pre-'89 and Pre-'95 assuming equal status."

FF enthusiasts hope Nicol is right. But frankly, a starring role in vintage racing is not something FF was ever meant to have. Through its first 15 years, Formula Ford was a celebration of the "new": hot new cars, promising new drivers. Minus that ever-renewing freshness, what is FF's appeal?

Well, the memories are wonderful. Thanks, FF.

(LEFT, ABOVE) Wiet Huidekoper's sexy Vector— will it be the Swift of the '90s? (LEFT) Van Diemen RF93 prototype featured the new Ford Zeta 1800cc engine around which promise swirls.

Is there a future in FF for firms like Ray (ABOVE) and Piper (BELOW)? How will Swift UK (RIGHT) fare?

(BELOW) With few exceptions, Reynard's Formula Ford's have been among the most graceful and well-engineered.

(ABOVE) Two views of Wiet Huidekoper's stunning new Zeta 1800-equipped Vector FF.
(BELOW) Will we see Formula Ford grids like this one of 20 years ago again? No, probably not.

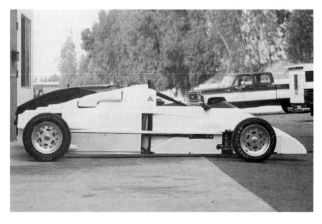

7

Chassis Builders

With help from Jeremy Shaw and Marcus Pye, the author set out in '91 to produce a very narrow supplement to some of the existing motorsports encyclopedias, this one noting every manufacturer of FF1600 chassis since the class' inception in 1967. Shaw, one of Indy Car racing's most reliable correspondents, remains hopelessly addicted to FF1600. *Autosport* National Editor Pye, meanwhile, is the first and last bastion of enthusiasm for this class—a walking encyclopedia of FF people, places and things.

As for the author, he has always been almost as intrigued by the people who built race cars as the people who drive them, producing a "Guide to FF Chassis" chart for the now-defunct *Formula* magazine as long ago as 1977.

We three had a lot of fun coming up with a list, but ... well, come to find out, the project is quite hopeless—at least "hopeless" insofar as the three of us wanted to make this historical supplement complete and authoritative.

Our original, single criterion was straightforward: This was to be an encyclopedia of legitimate manufacturers, not one-offs. So we decided to include only those companies/people which produced more than one FF.

But this left out a dozen homebuilts more intriguing or technically advanced than some production cars (like Harvey Templeton's HR2760). And it left out a few interesting if erstwhile manufacturers who never got past the first FF but did other things (like Supernova). And it left out a few nameplates that we think were nothing more than dreams or drawings, but we aren't sure (like Vista).

(LEFT, TOP) Dreams: David Bruns' Swift DB-1 prototype. (QUARTET AT LEFT, CLOCKWISE) Nightmares: Titan Mk8, Lola T-440, Van Diemen RF84, Hawke DL1.

Which is what brought us on the day this book goes to print to the final tally of over 190 names.

Unfortunately, "final" is probably not the right word. For instance, after a February '92 week in England which included a wonderful day spent in *Motoring News'* amazing downtown London library, the author added over two dozen names to his final-complete-we're-done-this-is-it list, winter '91-'92 edition.

When Pye printed this list (featuring a few revisions of his own) in the "25th Anniversary of FF" *Autosport* supplement, he got several phone calls, leading to several *more* additions and deletions.

Then, one fall '92 evening, Shaw rang up to say that on an airplane flight he'd thought of a couple more.

This encyclopedia will never be "final." But the publisher is frustrated with the delays, and so, off we go.

Needless to say, this chapter could have been a book all by itself, but we would have had to leave out the historical overview and the pictures of all those great drivers. So we had to make some compromises: Because there is a world of difference between McGregor, say (which built three FFs total), and Van Diemen (which built on the average *two FFs a week* in the peak period '77-'87), there are two different kinds of entries. Twenty marques get a whole page or more while all the rest get a few sentences only.

But space grew very tight at the end, so the author resorted to subjective opinion rather than production quantity in determining which marques got the space and the extra pictures, and which didn't.

If you are a Dulon, Mondiale or PRS enthusiast, yes, you were robbed. Sorry!

More regrets: In many cases, despite all our hard work, little more is known than the name. In a few other cases, the author had to resort to the dread "educated guess." Hopefully, that the principals who survive will contact him via the book's publisher and put things right for an update.

Otherwise: Enjoy!

Canadian super-homebuilt Aero 81.

Anson SA-7 was a striking machine.

Engine bay details of the Anson SA-7.

ADF (USA)

See expanded entry on page 74.

Aero (CDN)

The Aero 81 was designed and built by Dobroslav Hajek, a Toronto aeronautical engineer who raced an old Hawke through 1978. Short on funds with which to buy a new chassis, Hajek built one. The advanced Aero prototype featured inboard front suspension, a front radiator, and an enclosed engine compartment fed by NACA ducts. The engine was pushed forward and the space between engine and gearbox filled by oil and catch tanks. Hajek then announced that copies would be available both in kit form and complete.

In the late '80s, brothers Ian and Keith Willis purchased the project and started work on the Aero 2, which has proven to be extremely competitive. An Aero 3 was said to be on the way ...

Agent (GB)

Designed by Lucas Research Centre employee David Rendall, the Agent DR1 was an FF2000 car funded by David Winstanley's Lodge Corner Agencies (thus the name). Six cars were built in 1981 at Brian Martin's Yorkshire premises. Purpose-built for the 2-liter formula, one or two of the cars apparently raced in FF1600 trim that year type-numbered DR2.

Alexis (GB)

See expanded entry on page 76.

Alta (GB)

The Alta BT1F was a Formula Ford raced by Tony Rivers and Mike "Alta" Taylor in the early '80s. Mike was a descendant of Geoffrey Taylor who founded the Alta marque in the '20s and built its first GP car in the '40s.

Anson (GB)

Ex-Brabham and McLaren F1 mechanic Gary Anderson, his brother-in-law and Tyrrell F1 mechanic Bob Simpson, and Simpson school chum Jeff Hills founded the machining and fabrication company Anson Ltd. in Sept. '80. They became a full-blown chassis constructor with the '81 debut of their tidy SA-3 Formula 3 car.

Though there was success in F3 and especially Super Vee, it was slow in coming and Anson's principals eventually succumbed to financial concerns, selling out to Pacemaker Performance Cars of Bridgnorth in '84. The advanced Anderson-designed SA-7 Formula Ford stretched the Anson range when it appeared

Anson (cont.)

in Pacemaker's workshops late that year, clearly destined for the American market. The U.S. FF racing summer of '85, though, was virtually a Swift-only affair and the attractive SA-7 would be numbered among the casualties. Pacemaker's chassis construction aspirations soon followed.

Anderson, meanwhile, rebounded rather well: Chief mechanic at Brabham during some of Gordon Murray's best years, the Irishman is, of course, the designer of today's trend-setting F1 Benetton-Fords...

Argo (GB)

Anglia Cars Ltd. was founded in Nov. '76 by Jo Marquart, Nick Jordan and American John Peterson. Marquart was an ex-Lotus and -McLaren (with stop-overs at Huron, GRD and Modus) designer; Jordan an ex-Roger Williamson and Tony Brise mechanic.

Argo's tidy wares were destined primarily for F3 and FSV, but the firm unveiled a purpose-designed FF2000 car in Jan. '83—the JM14—and a replacement for it (the JM17) in '86. Away from the factory, one or two owners reportedly converted their JM14s to FF1600 trim.

Arian (GB)

John Markey was in charge of sales at the Cobham, Surrey-based Arian Auto Developments which acquired the assets of Huron in the early '70s. Arian's Michael Chambers handled design development work on the Jo Marquart-designed range of cars. Rob Wilson raced an RP3 in '75.

Arrow (GB)

The Arrow CH78 was a one-off machine built in Purley, Surrey. It was raced (and wrecked!) in 1978 by future Brands Hatch-series star Chris Hall at the start of his career, before he became a Jamun stalwart.

There must surely be a connection between this car and another Arrow campaigned by Eddie Johnson at Brands Hatch a few years before, but if so, the author was unable to make it.

The Anson SA-7 was a striking FF designed by future F1 pen-man Gary Anderson. Regrettably, its lifespan was short.

ADF (USA)

Paul White founded the Southern California-based firm Automotive Development (AD) in 1965, pretty much a "moonlight" outfit until he was laid off from his job in the computer industry in 1970. AD specialized in engines for drag racing until road racer Jules Williams, a math and science teacher who had a shop in the same small industrial complex, came aboard. Williams was a pioneer of sorts, winner of the first "proper" Formula Ford race in the United States driving a Lotus 51.

With a third partner—entrepreneur Dick Cooney, who soon left to open the FF retail firm Pacific Formula—Automotive Development turned its attention to the FF1600 scene in '71, and built engines which dominated the American west coast for years.

In '72, 26-year-old aerospace engineer David R. Bruns came to AD for an engine for his advanced, home-garage-built FF built in 1970. That first meeting would lead, ultimately, to the first ADF (called the "Mk II" in deference to Bruns' Mk I, literally built in his basement).

The ADF project grew out of White's belief—carried over from drag racing—that "you can't be big in a class where you don't do your own hardware. We just didn't want to race the bricks they (the English) kept sending us."

Bruns was assisted in the Mk II's design by Al Thomas—"Al was a general science guy, a great guy to bounce ideas off of," he explained. Funded by enthusiasts Hayla and Gary MacLeod, the first Mk II was more frighteningly complex than anything seen before in FF racing—except, perhaps, Bruns' Mk I homebuilt. With features like inboard front suspension and brakes—and a price tag more than double the ones on its English competition—the ADF Mk II was not a big seller. But, it did win the Runoffs in its very first attempt despite being crashed by test driver Bruns just three weeks before the event: He backed the prototype into an earth bank at Willow Springs when a front hub broke, destroying everything aft of the roll bar.

Repaired just a few days before the late-October event, the car was rushed to Road Atlanta where it was raced by Northern Pacific Division superstar Bob Earl. Earl was the fastest qualifier in each session and led the race from start to finish.

Not really designed to be built in quantity, orders flooded in. Customer cars won the Runoffs again in '75 (thanks to Northwest businessman Tom Wiechmann) and, incredibly, in '80 (courtesy the rapid Bob Lobenberg). The ADF was not the first American-

made chassis to win America's most prestigious FF event; that honor belonged to Caldwell. But unlike the Caldwell, which was patterned along European (specifically Merlyn) lines, the ADF was uniquely a product of American imaginations.

Though AD built fewer than a dozen ADFs, the car was a foretaste of an era to come: Bruns and White would conspire again in 1983 to build the Swift.

Years before, they had sold the whole ADF project to local racers Steve and Rick Anderson who added a few more cars to the production tally before realizing that despite their manufacturing experience, profitable "mass" production of an FF chassis or anything like it was out of the question.

In '81, the remaining ADF assets were sold again to Southern California-based chassis specialist Marc Bahner. Today, the jigs are still around, the Andersons have the drawings, and one can still find parts for these fabulous cars that were way ahead of their time.

ASD (GB)

Englishman Bob Egginton's ASD Engineering has been building racing cars since 1974. A Can-Am "dog's body" (the American phrase is "go-pher") for drivers Al Pease and Ludwig Heimrath in the late '60s USRRC days, Egginton wound up at Surtees as production foreman in '70-'72. When a U.S. racing team that subsequently lured him away folded, Egginton founded his own company, Advanced Systems Design, out of necessity. Initially a component supplier to Rostron and others, ASD produced five copies of its own car in '76-'77. Called the 003, it featured a radical rising-rate, pullrod front suspension. Its successor was the '78 007 or Type 7, a more conventional machine. The 008 or Type 8 was the '79 car with side radiators and a needle nose. Six 007s/008s were built before ASD, which now produces an exciting Maserati 250F replica, turned to other arenas.

Ash (CDN)

Regrettably, the author knows nothing about this FF but has been trying to track down information for years, ever since seeing a classified ad in *Autoweek*!

Avanti (USA)

Avanti, Inc., of North Hollywood, Calif., announced plans to build a tubeframe Formula Ford in Sept. '72. There was no other information forthcoming, though, on its development and the car never appeared.

Baker (USA)

The marketing name in America (the surname of the southeastern U.S.-based importer) given English-made Nikes imported in the very early '70s.

BarrCarr (USA)

Roger Barr was an talented SCCA NEDiv. FF racer in the late '60s, who raced Crossles and may have had something to do with this FF raced by Joe Freeman.

Barney (GB)

An ad in a Jan. '72 *Autosport* listed a Barney FF for sale from M.A. Barney Competition Developments of Epsom, Surrey, England.

Beach (USA)

Eugene Beach's Clearwater, Fla.-based Competition Components Inc., a successful Formula Vee constructor, built the Type 11 Formula B/C in 1967. In '68, while SCCA was still deliberating whether to accept the British FF rules, Beach created an 11-based FF.

By Jan. '69, the first Beach Formula Fords were being delivered to customers, and one finished second in the first-ever SCCA FF Runoffs race that November.

Beattie (GB)

After spending the '68 season assisting with the preparation of Tim Schenken's Merlyn, former Chequered Flag designer Chas Beattie, in partnership with New Zealander Bruce Smith, went back to designing and building his own cars. A number of Beattie FF cars and a prototype F100 model were turned out, as was a monocoque conversion of a Lola T-142 F5000 car called the Beattie P1100.

Bob Bailey's Beattie (in the foreground) at Mallory Park.

Bee Gee (GB)

Six Bee Gee Mk1 and Mk2 FFs were built by the Northern England-based engineering firm of Bamford, Pickering and Grey (BPG) in '69-'70 (the "Pickering" was Rod Pickering, a successful Libre racer). John Bright, who bought chassis #6 in a crashed state and rebuilt it, gave the marque its only victory at Mallory Park in '71.

BEF Priamos (GB)

A one-off BEF Priamos MkII built by BEF Engineering in Coventry was raced in '77 by Martin Ochiltree, promoter at Coventry Stadium, whose father Charles is one of the legendary promoters of U.K. stock car racing.

Begg (NZ)

Begg single-seaters—including several FFs—were built in Drummond, South Island, N.Z. by George Begg. (Among the drivers of the Begg FM2 FB in the '70 Tasman Championship was well-known American racing car importer Pierre Phillips.)

Alexis (GB)

Formula Ford came along fairly late in the game for Alexis Cars Ltd., a firm founded in 1959 by Alex Francis, a builder of trials cars in the '50s, and Australian engineer Bill Harris (ALEX + HarrIS = ALEXIS).

A noteworthy player of the Formula Junior game, Alexis would score several successes in FJr's Formula 3 successor, and moved up as far as F2.

Allen Taylor took over the reins of the Birmingham-based company in '65 when Harris returned home to Australia. It was he—Taylor—who did the deal with Jim Russell which led to the fall '67 debut of the Russell-Alexis Formula Ford (later type-numbered, in retrospect, the 14).

This attractive machine followed along the design lines of the one-off Mk9 F3 car Alexis had previewed in '66. Though extremely fragile, the Hewland-gearbox Russell-Alexis was straightaway better than its only FF rival in '67, the Lotus 51 which was saddled with a Renault 'box. Indeed, the upstart Russell-Alexis won more races in FF's first season than anyone else, largely thanks to Belgian Claude Bourgoignie, a Jim Russell School graduate who was surely the unofficial '67 FF champion.

Fully 57 production examples of the Russell-Alexis were sold over about 12 months before the Russell/Taylor arrangement ended in Oct. '68. The split occurred when Russell was enticed back into the Lotus camp by Colin Chapman himself. Alexis carried on in FF for a half dozen more years: The Russell-Alexis evolved into the Mk15, previewed in mid-October '68 and peddled in the U.S. in '69 by famed marketers Fred Opert Racing, Pierre's Motor Racing, and Grizzly Engineering & Machine. The 15 was followed by the sturdier 1970 Mk18 (celebrating the firm's move from Ward End to Coleshill); the '71 Mk18B; '72 Mk22; '73-'74 Mk23; '75 Mk24; and '76 Mk24B that, near as can be gleaned from the author's collection of old *Autosports*, was the final FF word from Alexis.

As well as launching Claude Bourgoignie's career, an Alexis helped Aussie Dave Walker gain some notoriety in his first year in England. Ian Ashley raced a Mk15, too. But surely the most famous Alexis driver of all time was one James Simon Wallis Hunt, a youngster who sunk every penny he could scrape together into the deposit on his first race car, a Russell-Alexis that he financed in '69.

Improving with age: (ABOVE) An immaculately restored Alexis Mk15 at Donington Park in '92. (BELOW) Formula Ford vs. Formula 500 Invitation Race at Longridge in '78 featured an Alexis Mk18.

Birrana (AUS)

The Australian Birrana firm was founded in 1971 by Malcolm Ramsay and Tony Alcock, and the first car from the fledgling Adelaide-based constructor was an FF. Later, they were successful in Australian F2 and Formula Atlantic, and produced an F2 chassis for Europe which became the Minos driven by Bob Muir.

Sadly, designer Alcock was one of the people killed in Graham Hill's 1975 airplane crash. Shortly thereafter, Birrana's doors were closed.

Blackjack (GB)

Sports car driver Alan Minshaw bought an out-of-date Brabham F3 chassis in '66 and, just for fun, made it into a Formula Ford for the still-new class in '68. He gave it a great name (you do remember three-time World Champion Brabham's nickname, don't you?) but gained nothing like the fame with it that he would in founding the Demon Tweeks concern in '72.

Bobsy (USA)

Bobsy Cars of Medina, Ohio, began building racing cars in '62, Jerry Mong the founder. Primarily known for an excellent Formula Vee, Mong took a stab at FF in '69. Four cars were built before he decided an American chassis just could not compete in price with those produced in Britain.

Bowin (AUS)

Bowins were designed and built by John Joyce who worked in England for both Team Lotus and Lotus Components for five years in the mid '60s as a project and design engineer. (Joyce, in fact, was on the team which produced the Lotus Europa.) Returning home to Sydney in '68, Joyce set up as a race car constructor. The '69-'71 P4/P4A Formula Ford was an extremely light spaceframe version of his '68 P3 F2 car, while the improved P6 debuted in '72. Malcolm Oastler, now chief designer at Reynard Racing Cars, was one of the more renowed Bowin FF owners.

BPG (GB)

See Bee Gee.

Brabham (GB)

In the late 1950s, GP driver Jack Brabham persuaded designer Ron Tauranac, who had worked on Jack's first real racing car, a Cooper MkIV, in Australia, to join him in Britain. Together they built a Formula Junior in 1961, initially called an 'MRD' which were the initials of their company Motor Racing Developments. This had unfortunate consequences in France, but that's another story.

By the time FJ ended in 1963, Brabham had built 32 cars for the formula, and they went straight to the top of the heap in F3, building 13 cars in '64, 59 cars in '65 and 79 cars in '66, the years leading up to the introduction of FF.

Unlike F3 competitors Lotus, Merlyn, and Titan, Brabham never built a purpose-designed Formula Ford. Tauranac was quoted once calling it "a fiddle formula," and Brabham personally turned down an opportunity to build 10 cars for Jim Russell in '67.

Nonetheless, Brabham played a significant role in early FF history. Many Tauranac-designed F3 Brabhams ('64 BT9s, '65-'66 BT15s, '66 BT18s and '67 BT21s) were converted by their owners to FF spec.— Frank Williams mechanic Tony Trimmer, for example, used a BT18 rescued from the dumpster to great effect in 1968. A few of these conversions got special names, including Brian Smith's 'Bardahl Special' and Alan Minshaw's 'Blackjack', both seen in '68.

And then there were the one or two constructors of questionable integrity who offered FF models which clearly 'borrowed' frame design, suspension geometry and more from Tauranac's F3 line ...

Bradley (GB)

Frank Bradley (who today owns the thriving Swift UK) bought Design Formula (Elden) from the Hampsheir brothers in 1973—temporarily; they bought it back a few years later, only to sell it again in '77 to someone else!—but raced a Formula Ford which bore his own 'Bradley' name in that mid-'70s period.

The Bradley, raced by future Swift UK principal Frank Bradley in '74.

Caldwell (USA)

See expanded entry on page 79.

Carom (USA)

The late '77-early '78 Carom FF project was financed in part by actor and racing enthusiast Gene Hackman, while the prototype was tested by Formula Vee driver Bob Campbell. The Carom was a fairly complex beast, expensive for the times: development costs reached a reported $75,000). Sales interest was slim, though, and after the car crashed in its first race at Riverside, the project was abandoned.

Centaur-Scholar (GB)

Centaur was a reasonably well-known producer of kit car Formula 1200 and Reliant Formula 750 cars for many years. Chassis were initially assembled in Richard Scott's workshop in Suffolk, but in the late '70s, were being built by the Penistone Hardmetals Co. in Sheffield. The Centaur Mk9 (or Mk9X) was a one-off, originally called a 'Centaur-Scholar' as it was a joint venture between Scott and Scholar's Doug and Alan Wardropper. First driven in '69 by Tony Youlden, it was sold in '70 to Chris Alford and again to Jim Cartwright in '71.

Centro-Scott (GB)

A driver G.P. Stewart raced this machine at Croft in the late '60s.

Cheetah (GB)

Chevron (GB)

It's possible that a few of designer Derek Bennett's '67 B7, '68 B9 or '69 B15 spaceframe Formula 3 cars were raced in FF, but in Bennett's lifetime, Chevron never participated in FF. Sadly, Chevron's founder was killed in '78 in a hang-gliding accident; less than two years later, the Bolton, Lancashire-based firm had gone into receivership.

The assets were taken over in Apr. '80 by Robin Smith, Laurence Jacobsen and Leslie Cuthbertson who moved Chevron to Scotland. In the middle '80s, Chevron was passed along again, to long-time racer Roger Andreason. Andreason later took over the assets of Quest Racing Cars, and the first "proper" Chevron FF1600—the B68—was designed by Quest's Mike Thompson in 1987.

The latest Chevron FF1600—the B70—is another Thompson design, given its first shakedown runs in Mar. '92.

Designer Mike Thompson picked up at Chevron where he left off with his Quests: The B68 was tidy, aerodynamically clean and very effective.

Caldwell (USA)

Swift Cars now holds the record for greatest number of Formula Ford chassis built in America. But the largest volume producer of racing cars of all time in America is a now-defunct firm located at the opposite end of the country: Autodynamics, Inc. (the first "AD").

In the decade between its founding by 29-year-old Ray Caldwell in '64 and the first American energy crisis of '73 when it folded, the Marblehead, Mass., manufacturer produced over 1,000 cars. Most were Formula Vees but over 100 were Formula Fords. Founder Caldwell was a first-class marketer, and as his company's "Rally 'Round the Flag, Boys" ad campaign trumpeted, AD produced the first really successful built-in-America Formula Ford. As both the ADF and Swift would do in subsequent decades, Caldwell won America's premier FF event—the SCCA Runoffs—in its first attempt, courtesy of future F1 driver and racing school proprietor Skip Barber.

AD, which built a DeDion rear axle/solid-beam front axle (about which its luckless test driver Sam Posey has many a tale to tell!) in '67, went conservative with the '69 D-9. The Bill Woodhead and Del Trott-designed machine, heavily influenced by the all-conquering Merlyn Mk 11A, was extremely sturdy, quite forgiving, and very competitive on American rubber.

As the reputation of Automotive Developments' engines would promote interest in the '73 ADF, so did the power developed by Doug Fraser's great DFRE Cortina engines propel Caldwell sales in '69-'70.

In D-9 and '70-'71 D-9B trim, 103 Caldwell chassis were sold over three seasons. Sadly, cash flow never quite kept up with the firm's ambitions. A Chrysler-backed Trans-Am effort in 1970 greatly distracted Caldwell himself even as the then-new D-13 Formula Vee created a firestorm of interest.

Besides Barber, several great American drivers started their careers in D-9s, notably including SCCA National and IMSA front runners Jim Clarke (who retired prematurely after suffering an eye injury), Bill Alsup and David Loring.

In '72, Autodynamics announced a new DL-15 FF. Sadly, "real ones" were never built as AD was soon forced to close its doors. After a teaching stint in nearby Salem, Mass., Harvard Business School-graduate Caldwell went to work for former AD customer Reeves' Callaway's Turbosystems firm in Connecticut.

As a postscript, the DL-15 moniker was eventually applied to a hideous "update kit" (sic) offered to DL-9 customers in '75 by ex-AD sales manager Bob Fletcher whose short-lived Fast Company operated for a time out of the abandoned Autodynamics factory in Marblehead.

(LEFT) Today, a used D-9 in good condition will fetch a pretty penny. (BELOW) Caldwell FF stars Jim Clarke (#0) and Skip Barber (#99) battle for the lead at Daytona in the '69 SCCA Runoffs.

Chinell (GB)

See Wiet.

Cirrus (GB)

The Cirrus 006 was a spaceframe chassis designed in 1980 by Alan Morgan who, with his father Bill, owned the Egham, Surrey-based Cirrus Race Engineering. Originally a kart manufacturer, Cirrus built its first proper racing car—the Formula 4 004—in '78. The 006 was adaptable to FF1600, FF2000 and Formula 4 specifications.

Citation (USA)

See expanded entry on page 81.

Condor (B)

A one-off designed and built by Belgian Peter Vennic, who would later be associated with March's F3000 works team.

Cooper (GB)

Brothers Alan and Martin Cooper opened the Caine, Wiltshire-based Cooper Racing Services in 1984 and built their first Formula Ford in '86. Primarily used at the Castle Combe Racing School, Cooper FFs were also seen in several junior series.

Cooper-Chinook (CDN)

Fejers Racing Cars Ltd. in Ontario, Canada, built a McLaren-style Group 7 car called the Chinook in 1967. Two years later, founder George Fejers bought the assets of the British Cooper concern. In the early '70s, he apparently constructed a FF, announced for sale in the U.S. through Speed Components in Inkster, Mich.

Corsa (USA)

The Paronelli brothers of Los Angeles' interesting and ill-fated Formula Ford project of 1973-'75. Designed by Hank, a builder of F1 racing aircraft and veteran USAC mechanic, the curious device had an 88" wheelbase, a 56" rear track, and a body shape that was said to have been worked out by the Jet Propulsion Laboratories (JPL).

Rick Paronelli debuted the car at Riverside Raceway in Feb. '75, but did not start.

The Peter Vennic-designed Condor: sleek and simple.

(ABOVE/BELOW) The '74 Corsa was a curiosity.

Introducing The CORSA CORSA (The Racer's Racer)
For 1974

1974 CORSA-Lubri-Metal Special Formula Ford Specifications and Features:

FRONT TRACK.. 62"	STUART RADIATORS
REAR TRACK..... 64"	MAGNESIUM WHEELS
WHEELBASE...... 88"	SUN INSTRUMENTS
CHROME MOLY FRAME	DOUBLE ADJUSTABLE KONI SHOCKS
FLAME RETARDANT FIBERGLASS	ON-BOARD FIRE SYSTEM
SIDE-MOUNTED RADIATORS	LEFT & RIGHT FOOT BRAKE PEDALS
INBOARD REAR BRAKES	FUEL TANKS SEALED FROM COCKPIT
GORDEN SCHRODER RACK & PINION	DEFORMABLE CHASSIS STRUCTURE

THE SAFEST FORMULA FORD BUILT TO DATE

For Price & Delivery Information contact:
CORSA WORKS, LIMITED
6600 N. Figueroa St.
Los Angeles, Ca. 90042
(213) 255-0168

Citation (USA)

Citation's Steve Lathrop is one of the true geniuses of FF design and engineering—don't let his "aw, shucks" good ol' boy demeanor fool you. But sometimes there are so many good ideas bouncing around in there that things get a little complicated: marketing and model designations have sometimes become complex. In 1992, for instance, one could buy the advanced 92FF; the same car with less expensive outboard rear suspension, called the 92CF; and/or a "major component only" kit (at an absurdly low price).

Lathrop started racing Formula Vees in '68 and opened the Indiana-based Citation Engineering in '74. Originally a distributor of the North Carolina-produced Zink Vees and FFs, Citation officially became a constructor in the '78 when Zink Manufacturing was sold and moved to Florida.

Lathrop began calling the cars his firm produced "Citation-Zinks" and ultimately just Citations and/or Citation Centurions. Lathrop's great relationship with many-time American FF champion Dave Weitzenhof and other Zink customers like Bruce MacInnes, Tim Evans, Rollin Butler and R.B. Haynes, was largely responsible for the improvements which made the original Ed Zink-designed Zink Z-10 and subsequent Citation-Zink Z-16 a world-beater in the Northeast and Central SCCA divisions.

The Citurion 85FF-92FF range of cars, penned with the help of Race Ahead Consulting Engineering's Randy Wittane and Max Schenkel, have been extremely quick and thus extremely popular as Lathrop has worked hard on aerodynamics and suspension developement. Citations have been particularly successful in a very difficult era for any manufacturer which was not called "Swift."

(TOP) Citation-Zink Z-16. (ABOVE) Lathrop oversees work on Weitzenhof's machine; (BELOW) Citation 85FF was a revelation. (LEFT) Citation Centurion. (LEFT, BELOW) Centurion frame carries on the Zink heritage for strength.

Cougar (GB)

Many FF fans remember the Cougar, type-numbered the 73F, which ran particularly well at Croft in the hands of driver Peter Harrington, the '73 Tate Trophy/Northern Clubs FF champion.

Crossle (GB)

See expanded entry on page 84.

CTG (GB)

The wildly diverse product mix of Cyril Maylem's CTG Racing Ltd. included the '76 Viking F3 and the last P207 and unraced '79 P230 BRM F1 cars, as well as suspension components for others including Ralt. In partnership with Design Auto's Len Terry, CTG-built SF77-SF81 FF2000 cars were quite competitive in the late '70s-early '80s. A few may have been run in FF1600.

(RIGHT) Cougar on the prowl in the early '70s. (BELOW) Dastle founder Geoff Rumble selling "Raceboxes."

Dastle (GB)

Geoffrey Rumble, a heating and air conditioning engineer, built his first racing car—a 500cc motorcycle-powered special—in 1959 and acquired much notoriety for his success in the midget racer class. The name Dastle was an anagram of his middle and surnames (Geoffrey DAvid STanley rumbLE). Between Dastle Types 2 and 3, Rumble did his national service, then went to worked for the Chequered Flag concern as second to Les Redmond, designer of Gemini FJr.'s. The Dastle Mk6 was a prototype FF of late '60s, never built; the Mk11 another prototype of '73 which, when finally produced in '74, was renumbered Mk16. Six were built and, with Paul Jackson driving, were reasonably competitive. (The Dastle Mk9, incidentally, was the '72 Hesketh F3 car raced by recent FF graduate James Hunt.)

Rumble was also involved as designer and chassis builder of the Sparton FFs. Racing ex-Barrie Maskell cars in historic classes in the '70s and '80s, Rumble needed a good trailer; today, that's what Dastle—calling them "Raceboxes"—builds.

Davron (GB)

Davron Racing Components of Buckingham produced a very tidy Super Vee in the late '70s designed by ex-Javelin designer John Lipman. At least one, apparently, appeared in FF1600 trim.

Delta (GB)

Formula 4 enthusiast Glen Hyatt's Low Cost Racing Ltd. was acquired in 1976 by one-time F3 driver Nick Crossley. The mustachioed Crossley renamed it the Horseless Carriage Co. and commissioned ex-Lola and -Scott designer Patrick Head, who had penned a similar car two years before for Starfire, to design an FF2000 chassis. The Delta T77 emerged very much along the lines of the of the '73 F2 Scott and subsequent evolutionary versions of it would achieve significant success in the 2-liter class even as Delta tackled the new for 1980 Formula Talbot.

Delta formally ignored the FF1600 market until '83 when Northern and Midlands Delta agent Ray Joyce pushed through the 2-liter derivative T83.

Delta (I)

Italian Lorenzo Sassi entered an apparently Italian-made Delta 69F in the first-ever Formula Ford World Final in '72, crashing it in practice, then borrowing his teammate's car ... and spinning off in the same place, hitting his own safely parked Delta later on!

De Sanctis (I)

Founded in Italy in '58 by Gino and Luciano De Sanctis, father and son, the firm folded soon after Formula Ford was launched and never produced a purpose-built car for the class. However, at least one of its late '60s spaceframe F3 chassis found its way onto an FF grid.

Design Auto (GB)

See CTG.

DRW (GB)

David Warwick's Highgate, London-based DRW Developments produced a small number of very interesting clubmans and hillclimb machines starting with 1172cc Ford-powered specials in '59 and including the Len Terry-designed, Renault gearbox-equipped, Mk4.

The DRW Mk8F was an FF1600 produced in 1970, and perhaps the most interesting thing about it was that virtually unique to the times, the fiberglass, spaceframe and most of the suspension bits were all designed and fabricated in-house.

Shovel-nose DRW Mk8F in 1971.

The Mp15 triggered a Dulon resurgence in America.

Crossle (IRL)

The author apologizes for the bias leaking through, but John Crossle's FF1600 machines have played a pivotal role in my life: my first FF (co-owned with my best friend John Herne) was a 16F; most of my friends and SCCA racing heroes (Brian Goodwin, Tom Davey, Dennis Firestone, R.K. Smith and Fox Henderson to name just a few) drove Crossles at one time or another; and even a few of my current heroes (Nigel Mansell and David Kennedy to name just two) raced one of these Irish-built machines in the past.

John Crossle was a college of agriculture graduate and very succesful motorcycle racer, born in Scotland but raised in Ireland, whose first racing car was a homebuilt 1172cc Ford-powered special. Successful in a move from two to four wheels with this car, he built another example in '59, another in '60, and then two replicas which would become the first production Crossles.

Initially, cars were assembled in the laundry room of a house in Rory's Wood, Holywood—just a few miles from Belfast—that John bought in '60 after his marriage to Rosemary. Today, the laundry room has become a fairly expansive racing car factory.

Crossle's first single-seater was the '60 3F special; his first rear-engined single-seater the '61 4F Formula Junior. Mid-'60s Crossle machines included an F3, FLibre, and both FB and FA cars for the U.S. market. His first FF was the beautifully constructed late-'68 16F which evolved into the striking '71-'72 20F.

The '73-'74 25F was a squarish new FF which did not depart at all from the Crossle ideal: His cars cars have rarely been revolutionary but have always been safe, sturdy, and (unlike the very popular Lola T-340-series) easy to work on.

Skip Barber acquired Crossle U.S. importation rights in '75, coincident with the introduction of his racing school, and with a flood of 30Fs landing in the U.S., Crossle parts availability was soon second only to Lola (which had Carl Haas). This made an enormous difference in the expansive U.S. market.

With a solid toehold in America, Crossle battled tooth and nail with Van Diemen through the late '70s and early '80s for the mantle of largest volume FF producer. Crossle's '77-'78 32F and '79 35F models, though, were without question the significant cars of the U.S. scene in the latter part of that decade.

The narrow-track 40F (introduced in '80) was very difficult to drive and hurt the marque's reputation in the U.S. But with the 45F ('81), side-radiatored 50F ('82) and excellent 55F ('83-'84), the firm appeared to be rebounding nicely. Unfortunately, Crossle was one of several marques whose U.S. sales were devastated in the mid '80s by the arrival of the Swift. In late '83, Crossle also lost long-time designer Leslie Drysdale, who started the new Mondiale firm right down the road.

Crossle's 60F ('85-'86), 65F ('87) and 67F ('88) were excellent FFs which never really got the credit they deserved. Then, in Apr. '89, heretofore conservative John shocked the world with the introduction of the 70F, a wildly styled FF he had designed in collaberation with aerodynamicist Frank Costin—the ex-De Havilland aircraft engineer responsible for the revolutionary late '50s Vanwall GP cars.

As well as continuing to crank out beautifully finished new machines, Crossle today is doing a booming business in spares as its 30-series cars are overwhelmingly popular in the various vintage FF and Club Ford series.

Hey, whatever John Crossle decides to do is alright with this book's author. Long may his FFs reign!

(BELOW) John Crossle poses with a 16F.

(LEFT TO RIGHT) John Herne in a 16F; Eddie Jordan's 30F (right) battles a 25F; Marty Loft's 30F.

(LEFT TO RIGHT) William Henderson's 32F; R.K. Smith in a 35F; Chip Ganassi wins at Lime Rock with a 40F.

(LEFT TO RIGHT) U.S. Crosslé star Dennis Firestone tries a 45F; Russell Long, a winner in a 50F; Firestone again, aboard a 55F in '83.

Striking 70F featured Frank Costin-designed bodywork.

The lovely and underrated 60F.

Ian Taylor's Dulon LD9 leads at Oulton Park in '72.

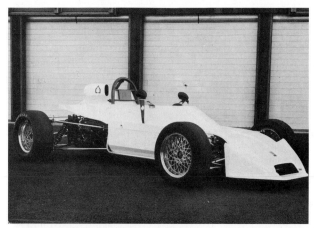

Dulon's regal and shapely '75 Mp17.

Dulon Mp21: final FF fling for Maxperenco Products.

Dulon (GB)

Several pioneering FF marques started off by converting existing Formula 3 chassis into FF machines but, as near as the author can tell, engineers Andrew Duncan and Bill Longley (DUncan + LONgley = DULON) were the first to produce a *Formula 1*-based FF. Incredibly, their '67 Dulon LD3 FF prototype was an ex-Tim Parnell Lotus 24! A subsequent one-off—the LD4—was their own design, though, and 24 LD9B and LD9C production examples were built and sold by their firm, Maxperenco (for MAXimum PERformance ENgineering COmpany—were these guys into anagrams or what?) in '68-'69.

The late Ian Taylor skyrocketed to prominence as Dulon's works driver during this time, winning the inaugural FF Festival in '72 with an LD9 shortly before Longley sold his interest in the firm. Teenage Eddie Cheever drove a '73 Mp15 in half a dozen races while Derek Lawrence won the '73 FF Festival in a similar machine, Dulon then a mainstay of the British FF scene.

The '75 Mp17 was a particularly good-looking car but, sadly, Dulon's FF Festival success failed to translate into huge sales numbers. The 17 evolved into Mp19 and Mp21 models, but by the late '70s, following something of a revival in rock star Ken Hensley's hands, Dulon faded into obscurity.

Eagle (USA)

Taking a page from sports car wizard John Wyer's book, brilliant ex-F1 driver and race car constructor Dan Gurney hit upon the concept of keeping his All American Racers fabricators occupied during the occasional slow times by moving in at the bottom end of the production race car business. And so rookie Indy Car designer John Ward was turned loose on a Formula Ford project in 1977, from which emerged the potent if unattractive Eagle DGF.

An excellent car, as FF veteran David Loring proved in dominating the '78 SCCA Runoffs, the Eagle was not a sales success and, when production began to dilute the focus on AAR's primary projects, the fixtures and inventory were sold to local Southern California club racers Dick George and Sandy Dells.

Egan (GB)

Eifelland (D)

Albert Hamper's German racing team used Reynard-based chassis in the late '80s (and won the '88 German championship), but announced plans to produce its own FF1600 in mid-'92.

Elden (GB)

See expanded entry on page 88.

Elfin (AUS)

Cliff Cooper and his son Garrie founded Elfin in Adelaide, S. Australia, in '58, and built first a sports racer then a Lotus 18-based Formula Junior. Formula Junior was introduced to Australia in '61 and, as most components were locally produced, Elfins enjoyed a significant cost advantage over imported British cars.

The first monocoque Elfin appeared in '67 and the first FF shortly thereafter. The sturdy spaceframe '68 Elfin 600 would be used in formulae as far-flung as FF, F2 and even F5000 (!), the 600B FF winning the '70 and '71 Australian FF championships. Larry Perkins finished third at the '72 British FF Festival in an Elfin 600.

The side-radiator-equipped 620 was produced between '73-'75, and many were exported.

Elwyn (AUS)

Another Australian constructor about which very little information filtered over to the U.S. The principal is Elwyn Bickley.

Eutectic (NZ)

Several different cars raced in the Southern Hemisphere have apparently been given sponsor Eutectic's name.

Faster (CH)

The Swiss-built Faster AF91 was a fairly advanced machine raced in the British FF Festival in 1991 by Andreas Jenzer.

Ferret (CDN)

The '75 Bulova Championship and Canadian Road Race of Champions-winning Ferret Mk4 was designed by Alec Purdy, a UBC Engineering School graduate. The Hanover, Ontario-based Ferret Industries (founded by Purdy and engine tuner/partner Fred Wilken) was primarily a service business, but the success of the prototype, which debuted in 1974, meant five cars were produced.

Incredibly strong, the Ferrets had one feature admired by every FF mechanic in the paddock: Purpose-designed depressions in the fiberglass cowl on which to set your beer ... er, *soft drink* can.

Focus (GB)

An early-'70s FF which was raced in England by Terry Horrocks.

AAR's John Ward, David Loring and Dan Gurney in '77.

Loring's Eagle DGF romps at the '78 Runoffs.

U.S.-spec Elfin 620 in '74.

Elden (GB)

The twists and turns of the Elden story could fill a book, but it starts with the Hampsheir brothers—Brian, who retired from club racing at age 23 after a major accident in '63, and Peter, an industrial engineer who designed (but never completed) his first sports racing car at age 16.

In 1967, the brothers produced a Formula 4 prototype powered by a 650cc Triumph engine. Called the Briham and numbered PH2, it triggered enough interest in the new-to-Britain class that five replicas were subsequently sold. The '69 PH6 was a tidy FF1600 prototype which bore the Elden name ("It doesn't stand for anything," explains Brian, "but our backer and friend John Thompson just came up with it and we kind of liked it!"). It had rocker arm front suspension, like the Lotus 21, and it led to the production PH8. This car was a huge success, particulary in the hands of 18-year-old Tony Brise who claimed 33 victories in '71!

Orders for the PH8 (48 built '70-'72) and the even better PH10 (121 built '72-'74!) led to a 1972 move from New Ash Green to Wrotham Hill. A PH10A with bodywork by Dennis Falconer won the inaugural World Cup race at Brands Hatch in the hands of Johnny Gerber, its fiberglass raising the eyebrows if not the ire of RAC scrutineers.

The worldwide energy crisis hit small constructors hard in the early '70s, though, and Elden was one of the victims. In '73, they sold out to future Swift U.K. boss Frank Bradley—who sold the company back to the Hampsheirs three years later!

In 1979, the name and inventory were sold again, this time to Howard Drake of Dartford. But Drake couldn't make Elden go either and Brian Hampsheir, after a brief fling at Saracen, got the project back for the third time in 1980.

Elden was one of the few supporters of Formula Talbot and, while the firm has not returned to its early '70s glory, financial backing from Techpro has enabled it to remain in the news. An early '90s Formula Renault was not particularly successful but the new FR-based PH34 FF announced in Jan. '92 looks quite attractive.

Elden Gallery (CLOCKWISE FROM ABOVE): The original '69 PH6 Formula Ford; Elden PH10 squadron in '72; Johnny Gerber's Falconer-bodied PH10A wins the FF World Finals; "New Era" '89 PH27; Howard Drake-built Elden 79F.

Forsgrini (USA)

Coming off a Runoffs victory in 1968 in the American Formula C class, Seattle, Wash.-based Forsgren Engineering built a few Mk12 FFs in late '68-early '69. The firm probably has the distinction of being the first American FF builder, narrowly beating Beach.

Galloway (AUS)

Gemini (USA)

See Jen.

GES (GB)

Getem (GB)

Initially produced in Lancashire, England, by a firm founded in 1973 by Martin Down and designer Alan Brunning, a Ford engineer, limited production Getems were driven by Andy Best and others including John Hayes-Harlow who used a Getem GBB77/78 in '78 to good effect.

That particular model featured a tiny frame cross-section (just 18" wide by 9" deep), inboard front suspension and very attractive *plywood* bodywork!

Subsequently, production moved to Down's workshop in Ash Green, Kent, and Ken Baker came on board as a partner in the venture. Rick Shortle gave the '83 GD113 and '84 GD114 several good outings, first in novice races and then the Champion of Brands series. The GD115 and GD116 were later variants.

By 1986, the company was being run from Ash Green by Down and Ken Baker. The GD117 was the '87 model raced well by Mark Salter and in June '89, Getem announced a new Martin Down-designed GD119 for Shortle that would have pull-rod suspension.

Ginetta (GB)

The '69-'70 G18 and '71 G18B Formula Ford chassis were something of a departure for Ginetta. The firm run by the famed Walklett brothers had carved out a reputation primarily as sports car builders beginning in the late '50s.

Shortly after debuting the stunning G4 front-engined coupe in the mid '60s, though, Ginetta surprised by introducing a n FF. Several were built over a three-year period. Among the more notable Ginetta drivers was young Adrian Reynard who made his four-wheel racing debut with a G18B in '72.

(CLOCKWISE FROM FAR LEFT) John Scratch in one of the fabulous Ferrets; Andy Brunning-designed '77 "Tyrrell-Getem 007½"; Getem through the spray in '78; '82 Getem GD113 draws a crowd.

Ginetta G18 charges into the lead at Rufforth in '69.

Don Halliday's '78 FF built for friend Dave Ryan.

This particular Hamlen is sidelined for the time being.

GNF (GB)

Geoff Bedding, a Saracen employee until the firm was liquidated in '80, founded the Brands Hatch-based GN Fabrications in '81 and debuted a modified Peter Hampsheir-designed Saracen FF1600 chassis that year as a GNF, planning to produce the car in quantity.

Griffon (CH)

A Swiss-built chassis, one of which was raced by Laurent Ferriar in the inaugural FF World Finals at Brands Hatch in '72.

Halliday (GB)

The Halliday FF was built by Kiwi McLaren mechanic Don Halliday for his friend Dave Ryan, another McLaren employee, in '78, shortly after his arrival in England. The JF-1 was a Vee built before Halliday left home in New Zealand, which makes the Ford (sometimes called a 'Ryan') the JF-2. Halliday subsequently worked at Lyncar and de Cadenet, and designed the TDC S2000 chassis which, in '80, became the first non-Lola or Tiga to win a British S2000 event.

Hamlen (GB)

A Formula Ford produced by David Martin in the late '60s. The engineer (who would later produce the Martlet) rented space in the back of the Lenham-Hurst Racing workshop, thus the name "Hamlen" ("Lenham" backwards). The car, designed by Peter Coleman and featuring Julian Booty bodywork, would become the basis for Lenham-Hurst's own '69 T80 FF.

Hampe (F)

A spectacular FF1600 introduced at the '86 Paris Motor Show by the famed Formula Renault builders. Seemingly out-of-date suspension (with outboard shock/springs no less!) was actually a "mask" for fully variable geometry that was paddock adjustable.

Hawke (GB)

See expanded entry on page 91.

Hayashi (J)

Hayashi was a successful Osaka, Japan-based constructor of quality automotive components as well as single-seat race cars, first lured to America by the Jim Russell School's Jacques Couture who contracted with them to build all of his Russell-Mazda pro series machines. Hayashi followed through by setting up a separate American sales agency, which imported the Masao Ono-designed 412 Formula Ford in '83. The

Hawke (GB)

The mercurial David Lazenby, Jim Clark's mechanic at Indy and a principal at Lotus Components during those frenetic first few months of Formula Ford's existence in 1967, founded his own business in 1968 with a grand plan to capitalize on a significant failing of the first Lotus Formula Ford: The fragile quill shafts in the Renault gearboxes and the lack of changeable ratios for same. In '69, having stayed in close touch with the market for chassis, Lazenby decided that anyone could do a better job and why not him? After all, he had built his own car—an 1100cc Ford-powered special—while in the Air Force working on twin-boom Vampires.

The answer to the rhetorical question was the long-nosed Hawke DL-1, which bowed in '69 and became the production DL-2—a great car as Tom Walkinshaw (yes, the same T.W.) would prove in winning the '69 Scottish Championship. Lazenby built 35 DL-2s, 2As and 2Bs over the next two seasons.

The DL-2A was an evolutionary model and strong sales gave Hawke the cash necessary to get involved in other areas, including Super Vee and Atlantic—even F5000 courtesy of Lazenby's taking over the failed Leda LT22 project.

But Hawke stretched too far, and was just about to go under following an expensive move from a barn in Waltham Cross to a modern factory at Hoddesdon when Lazenby was rescued by Mac McKinstry. McKinstry settled Hawke in less ambitious premises, and also entered Syd Fox (who had done a lot of test driving for Lazenby in the DL-2 era) in a factory DL-9 in '72-'73. "The 9 was a good car, though a little bit overweight," Lazenby remembers. Originally fitted with a sports car nose, this was discarded when it proved to have too much downforce.

The '73 DL-10 was a DL-9 equipped with an ungainly John Bicht-designed body–very slow in a straight line. The '74 DL-11 (of which 30 were eventually produced) was much better.

Young Rupert Keegan was a Hawke DL-11 customer in '74 and his repair bills, says Lazenby only partly in jest, kept Hawke afloat! Shortly after the late '74 debut of the DL-12—"a super slipstreamer, but sales crashed in the face of the oil crisis," Lazenby remembers—Rupert's father Mike (head of British Air Ferries) stepped in to buy a controlling interest in the firm.

Keegan hired Adrian Reynard to design a Hawke F3 car (there was also a Hawke F1 machine, which got to the clay model stage) and to assist Lazenby in designing the wonderful, rocker-arm front suspension DL-15 (Adrian's big contribution to the 15 its engine bay triangulation). The DL-15 was probably the most successful Hawke of all time; 65 were built!

(PHOTOS TOP TO BOTTOM) Hawke DL-1 prototype; DL-9 with its original sports car nose; John Bicht-bodied DL-10; Derek Warwick in a DL-15.

The design objective for the late-'76 DL-17 which followed was to get weight off the rear tires. The objectives were met by long engine/hearbox spacers, but the car was not particularly good in the dry. Lazenby then designed the more conventional DL-19, but had wearied of the politics in the Keegan-controlled company and sold out completely in '78.

George Burda was left in charge of Hawke's expansive Essex factory while Vic Hollman (who would soon depart to found PRS) took care of sales, but the Frank O'Connor-designed Mk20 was simply not market competitive. Keegan, growing tired of the whole thing, finally closed Hawke Racing Car's doors for good in Aug. '79.

'79 Hermes 16/79 featured a Nike frame.

Great man, great car: Harvey Templeton's HR2760.

Jo Marquart-designed Huron FF, circa 1971.

Hayashi (cont.)

cars never achieved much of a following outside Southern California and, after a couple of abortive seasons, importation of the FFs ceased.

Hermes (GB)

TC Racing Ltd. of Thetford, Norfolk, England was a "race car refurbishing" company owned by Tony Clarke who was impressed enough with the sturdy frame in a customer's Nike 10B to do a deal with Nike's Ken Nicholls when he decided to become a constructor. A Nike chassis was used with a Clarke-designed body in the first Hermes 16/79 completed in March '79; a few production examples followed. The '80 prototype was the 16/80, with a new Nike chassis built to Clarke's specifications. The cars never caught on, though, and the marque was gone by '81.

(An interesting selection of names, here—these guys must've been well-read: Nike is the winged Greek goddess of victory and Hermes the Greek messenger of the gods.)

HR2760 (USA)

Sometimes mistakenly called the Ringwraith (in deference to his Formula Vees, named after Tolkien steeds Shadowfax and Ringwraith), the HR2760 was built by American Vee racing Lord of the Wins Harvey Templeton in '78. The Tennessean, then aged 69, gave the car features some chuckled at: hydraulically controlled camber adjustment, door-spring rear suspension, tube bodywork and a 60" front track. But on the big Southeast Div. tracks like Charlotte and Daytona, Harvey had the last laugh.

The FF, named after the U.S. House Bill introducing the Social Security laws which provided his racing budget, was raced competitively by its builder through '86 when Harvey, born in 1909, was age 77 ...

HTR (GB)

Huron (GB)

Canadian Jack Smith, Englishman Ray Ireland and Swiss ex-Lotus and -McLaren designer Jo Marquart founded Huron Auto Race Developments in 1970. Their plan to build a full range of single-seaters and sports racers included a '71 FF1600, but the firm folded later that year. Its assets were sold to Arian.

Hustler (NZ)

Image (GB)

Founded by Alan Langridge and Dominic Filmer-Sankey in '74, FSL Cars debuted its first Image FF at the '74 Showboat exhibition. The hideous but affordable FF1 was followed by '75 FF2, '76 FF2B and '77-'78 FF3 models which were all reasonably successful, evolutionary examples of the first Tangmere-built car. Many were sold at a very attractive price, fully assembled and in kit form.

Filmer-Sankey was long gone when Image moved to new premises in '77—the Super Shell building at Goodwood. Shortly thereafter, works driver Frank Bayes was seriously injured in a racing accident and proprietor Alan Langridge suffered a nervous breakdown, which left new employee Robert Synge in charge. Synge stepped in as general manager, and in '79 Image returned to manufacturing with the advanced, new, Langridge-designed FF4 model previewed in '78. The FF5 appeared in '80 while the FF5-based 681 was unveiled shortly before financial difficulties overtook the firm in 1981.

Synge, of course, went on to great success as the founder of Madgwick Motorsport.

Jamun (GB)

J. Anthony Mundy, an aeronautical engineer specialising in engines, and original partner Mike Sirett, started work on an FF/F4 prototype—the Jamun T1, which was never completed—in 1968. But only in the last half-dozen years has Mundy been able to make the greater time commitment the firm needed to blossom beyond the part-time "hobby" stage.

Though American Fred Sigafoos had several good outings with a Jamun T3 in the '70s, the "professionalism of Jamun" really began with the introduction of the T12C (later renumbered M87) in '87.

As the firm is based at Brands Hatch, it is not surprising that Jamun (largely courtesy loyal Jamun driver Chris Hall) dominates the Champion of Brands and Brands Hatch Winter Series' FF championships. Volume is up from about one car a year to six cars built in '90.

Javelin (GB)

Skilled FF racer Richard Eyre raced a John Lipman-designed Javelin JL2 in '75, but a far more famous Javelin driver was Nigel Mansell who drove an Alan McKechnie-sponsored JL5 model in '77. Mansell raced it only part of the year. The car was fast but proved to be brittle, and the future World Champion switched to a Crossle at mid-season.

Image FF1: A low-bucks alternative ...

Image FF4 prototype tests in '78.

(ABOVE) '80 Image FF5. (BELOW) '75 Javelin JL2..

'87 Jen 001 was a homebuilt Swift!

1975: One of three Jomics built charges into the lead.

Jen (USA)

Jeff Rieffle liked his Swift DB-1, but thought he might be able to improve it. So he built his own version of the Swift in '86-'87—*at his house!* Rieffle, who built the Gemini FF in the early '80s, used measurements and a body mold taken from his Swift as a basis for the project. But other than purchasing a Swift bellhousing, he fabricated the entire car himself—even having his own uprights cast.

The car was named after his daughter, Jennifer.

Johnston (NZ)

A Van Diemen RF80 replica, built and raced in the Southern Hemisphere.

Jomic (GB)

John Peters and club racer Mike Wallaker used up nearly two years' worth of weekends building the first Jomic which debuted at Snetterton in Oct. '73.

Eventually, two more copies would be completed, the trio of nicely built cars serving the pair well for several years.

Jamun collection: (ABOVE) Conventional for the day '70 T3. (ABOVE, LEFT) '85 Jamun driven by Brands Hatch-specialist Chris Hall. (BELOW) Gorgeous T12C, aka M87, debuted in '87. (LEFT) '92 M91/92 in the U.S.

Jomo (GB)

Keith Vickery's Birmingham, England-based Jomo Motor Racing was founded in 1967, and first built an F750 car. A Jomo FF was announced later that year, and a pencil sketch appeared in *Autosport* in Jan. '68, the car apparently set to debut at Brands Hatch in April driven by John Skinner.

A Jomo JMR7 was raced in '77, but the author has no details on the intervening years.

King (GB)

Mike King Racing announced the King FF in Nov. '67, but nothing else was heard until late '68 when a pair of bizarre letters appeared in *Autosport* from King and Roy Adlam Racing. The latter claimed to have King Mk3 FFs (with torsion-bar front suspension, rear-mounted radiator and wedge body) for sale. In an ad, King "denied legal contracts on premises other than Mike King, Liss., Hants." Oh.

Kittyhawk (USA)

Syracuse, N.Y.-based designer/driver Brad Wright started work on an FF project in 1981 which emerged as the low-profile Kittyhawk BW-1 first raced at Nelson Ledges in '84.

Konig Heath (GB)

See Palliser and Nomad.

Ladybird (GB)

Ladybirds were a series of one-off cars built by English club racer Derek Walker starting in about 1961. The first seven were 1172cc specials and clubman's cars. The Mk8, though, was a front-engined Formula Ford built in '68 and followed up by a more conventional, rear-engined Mk9 in '69.

Lago (GB)

A prototype Formula Ford built in 1980 by Automotive Designs, the Northampton, England-based company better remembered for producing the prototype Magnum 813 F3 machine. The Lago FF prototype was built by Dave Fullerton, based on the Andy Brunning/Andy Best-designed Getem design—quite a complicated device that apparently never went into production.

Lanan (GB)

Founded in Leicester in 1973 by schoolmates Robin Webb and Bill Bray, Lanan Racing entered Clive Braughton in a Ray, then John Bright in a Royale, before starting work on the Bray-designed 1601.

Brad Wright's Kittyhawk BW-1 was introduced in '84.

Early Lanan, Crossle-nose equipped, Jeremy Shaw driver.

Lanan's latest, the 1604, at the FF Festival in '89.

Show crowds gathered around the striking Laser HD87.

LCR P12s running 1-2, Heini Jeker in the lead machine.

LeGrand Mk10 was introduced in 1968.

Lanan (cont.)

Named after a small village in France (where an unrepeatable chapter in Lanan history transpired), Lanan subsequently produced the 1602 and 1604 FFs. "1603 was some sort of farm equipment thing," remembers journalist Jeremy Shaw, one of Lanan's original inner circle.

Webb now handles the sales side of Swift UK. At Lanan, meanwhile, a good time was had by all.

Laser (GB)

Howard Drake bounced back from the disappointment he experienced trying to rebuild Elden in the late '70s to found a new company, Laser, in 1985. Works driver Peter Rogers put the first Laser HD85 chassis, designed by Drake himself in '84, on the pole at its first race and starred at the FF Festivals in '85 and '86 (finishing third in the latter).

New footbox regs demanded almost a clean sheet of paper design—the HD87 was a sensational slimline version of the HD86 which debuted at the Alexandra Palace Racing Car Show in Jan. '87. There were plans to build a dozen, with four previously sold. But following Rogers' fatal racing accident at Donington in '87, the project was wound down and eventually sold to Ben and Tom Osmaston, proprietors of Lowfold Racing Developments, in '88.

LCR (CH)

The Swiss Louis Christen Racing, notable for building racing sidecars and Vees, produced a series of excellent Formula Fords in the early '80s. One—the type P12—won the '82 Swiss FF championship driven by Benoit Morand.

LeGrand (USA)

Ex-U.S. Marine Alden 'Red' LeGrand set up shop in N. Hollywood, Calif., in the early '60s and started building modifieds and single seat Formula Juniors which became Sports Racers and FBs/FCs when the SCCA introduced its new class-naming system.

His first FF was the conventional-appearing Mk10, designed in '68 and available in every conceivable form, from a set of drawings to complete cars (as were all LeGrand models).

The Mk10 received a significant overhaul in '72, and was re-numbered the Mk13; the Mk13B appeared in '74. The Mk21 which came along in '77 featured all-new bodywork.

After a few years' absence from the formula, LeGrand 'cut loose' in 1980 with the revolutionary

LeGrand (cont.)

Mk27. This car, with its 77" wheelbase, was one of the stubbiest machines of all time, not particularly reassuring in fast corners but thrilling to watch in the hands of an ace like works driver Phil Krueger.

LeGrand passed away Nov. 12, 1988—"in his shop with his son, doing what he liked best," wrote Joe Puckett in *Victory Lane* magazine—but the firm still operates from workshops located at Willow Springs Raceway.

Lenham-Hurst (GB)

Lenham-Hurst Racing was founded in 1968 to combine Roger Hurst's racing efforts with those of the Lenham Motor Co., successfully exporting sports cars to France (Lenham is the name of a small French town). Hurst, then involved in F3, thought the new FF was great: "It's a wonderful thing to be able to get rid of all your old F3 cars!"

The firm produced FFs from '69-'73, and probably a dozen were built altogether, Hurst recalls today. Designed by consultant Peter Coleman with bodywork (shared with the firm's F3 car) by Julian Booty, the most successful example was driven by Chris Alford, a quasi-works driver. The last few cars were a complete redesign.

The Lenham Motor Co. withdrew in '72; Hurst then moved to Folkestone, Kent, where it thrives today as a component supplier.

Lola (GB)

See expanded entry on page 98.

Lomas (GB)

A Lomas Formula Ford was announced by Lomas Racing Cars of Mere, Cheshire, England in a Jan. '68 *Autosport* ad which trumpeted three versions of the Lomas Type V, for FF, F4 and FV. Only the Vee was pictured. Firm founder Geoff Lomas was an Oulton Park specialist who raced a Lomas K 1172cc Special in '66.

Lotus (GB)

See expanded entry on page 101.

Lynx (NZ)

The Australian Lynxes (Lynxii?) were Formula Junior cars designed by Ron Tauranac before he moved to Britain to join Jack Brabham. Of the Lynx Formula Fords which are probably unrelated but otherwise listed in N.Z. race results, there is no info.

Californian Alan Holly tries on a LeGrand Mk10.

(ABOVE/BELOW) '77 LeGrand Mk21 got a new body.

Phil Krueger at speed in the tiny '81 LeGrand Mk27

Lola (GB)

What Lola wanted, Lola eventually got, in *West Side Story* and in motor racing. Certainly over the last three-and-a-half decades, Lola Cars has become one of the most widely respected names in the history of the sport.

A manufacturer of everything from exotic Formula 1 single-seaters to sensuous Group C sports cars, Lola's importance was nowhere greater than in the Formula Ford arena, its seven distinctly separate series of FF chassis contributing greatly to the development of the class.

Founded in 1958 by Eric Broadley and R.E. "Rob" Rushbrook, M.B.E., Lola Cars has produced a vast range of enormously successful cars. Moving from Slough to an ultra-modern factory in Huntington in 1970—about the time its first T-200 FF model appeared—Lola was a giant in the FF realm. In the U.S., suburban Chicago-based Carl Haas had served as Lola importer since 1960. Today, Lola is perhaps best known for its successes in Indy Car racing, but well into the '80s, Eric Broadley's company retained a strong presence in the grassroots level of the sport. American importer Haas (not forgetting the dealer body he created) had a lot to do with the firm's impressive reputation.

Lola's short wheelbase T-200 (introduced in Jan. '70 and followed by evolutionary '71 T-202 and '72 T-204 models) made a splash on both the European and North American continents, but it was nothing compared to the reaction to the late-'73 T-340, designed by Broadley and ex-Marcos, -Cooper and -Surtees man Bob Marston (who arrived at Lola in Oct. '69). The T-340 (and tidied up '75-'76 T-342) featured a flexible "fifth-spring" chassis that was forever cracking, but when it was whole, gave the car a fantastic balance and feel that made every customer a hero.

Draped in the sexiest fiberglass Specialised Mouldings ever produced for FF, with F1-style seat and flawless quality of fit and finish, the 340-series cars were just about irresistible—and superbly competitive (as long as one *didn't* stiffen the frame).

Not so good was the '76-'77 T-440 which was 340 series-based but featured long engine/gearbox spacers, a far-forward center of gravity and put the driver's feet in a precarious position. It was built in response to America's request for "something more technically advanced," explained Lola Sales Manager Mike Blanchet, but customers stayed away in droves.

Happily, they flocked to the T-540 (called the 540E in Europe) which Blanchet himself debuted in Oct. '77. A wonderful, stiff and sturdy FF, the 540 was one of the few narrow-track Fords that ever worked on American slick tires

The 540 was followed in '82, after a long and successful four-season sales run, by the attractive, Andrew Thorby-designed T-640 which, like its predecessors, was successful in both Europe and the U.S. The 640 was followed by the lightly modified '83 T-642 and revised '84 T-644.

Regrettably, Lola did not have a small-scale slipstreamer in the production pipeline with which to battle the Swift. Though a T-740 FF was discussed, it never materialized and Lola has so far not returned to the FF scene.

Sexy Lola T-340 (ABOVE) and T-342 (BELOW) sold in huge quantities on several continents.

LOLA T-342 FORMULA FORD

To fill the vacuum left by Lola's departure from the entry end of the market, Carl Haas began importing Reynard FFs and FF2000s in '87—a successful marketing arrangement, but to an American enthusiast of the '70s, it somehow seemed heretical: Lola was Haas was FF was Lola. Period.

Lola's short-wheelbase T-200 FF debuted in Jan. '70.

Two views of the '71 Lola T-202 on a PR photo distributed by the Huntington, Cambs., manufacturer.

Brian Goodwin's winning MRG-prepared T-342.

Before his employ by Swift, John Gianelli raced a T-540.

Mike Andretti excelled in a Lola T-640.

Jerrill Rice at speed in the long-tailed '84 T-644.

At the end, Lola was distracted by bigger game (F1 and GpC), and had no answer for the Swift slipstreamer which ushered in a new era of FF racing.

Macon MR8B was previewed in 1971.

Mallock U2s were front-engined and fast.

The March 708 FF won no beauty contests.

Macon (GB)

The first MR6 Macon Formula Ford was introduced in Oct. '67 by monoposto racer Tony Macon, and the marque made headlines when ex-soldier Ray Allen, winner of the first-ever standalone FF race at Brands Hatch in July '67, debuted the MR7 at Brands in Sept. '68 with a victory.

The MR7B ('69), MR8 ('69-'70) and MR8B (1971) followed, the Harrow, Middlesex-based firm in business through the early '70s. Several were exported to the U.S.

Mallock U2 (GB)

Sir Arthur Mallock started building racing specials as a teenager in the '40s, and produced the first front-engined U2 in 1958 for the 750 Motor Club's 1172cc Ford formula. In '60, two copies of the lightweight spaceframe machine were adapted for Formula Junior. The clubman's formula introduced in 1965, though, is what finally turned Mallock Racing into a volume constructor.

The road-going U2 Mk6R became the prototype for the new Formula Ford class in '67, son Richard entering the car in the first-ever standalone FF race at Brands Hatch in July '67. The '69-'70 Mk9 was the 'productionized' front-engined FF, the 9B following in '71. The '69-'71 works Mk9DD featured a deDion rear axle and was the last purpose-built Mallock FF.

Mantis (GB)

Jim Lee Racing produced the first FF2000 chassis designed by its owner at the end of '87, and ran a very attractive FF1600 derivative at the '88 FF Festival. The subsequent JL89 was similar but featured pushrod front suspension.

March (GB)

The March Engineering master plan was to have a chassis for every single-seater formula, and so they had a Formula Ford 1600 for the '70 season. The Robin Herd/John Clark-designed March 708 (called the 709 in North America) borrowed as much as possible from the firm's existing F2/F3 spaceframe and so was fairly heavy for FF. The 708 claimed only one truly notable victory, Ian Taylor's European Championship race win at Hockenheim in 1970.

The same 'too heavy' complaint was voiced about the poor-selling '71 718/719 which at least had a purpose-built frame. By 1972, all the interest in March's FF wares was coming from the U.S. where Southern Calif.-based Wayne Mitchell Engineering

Lotus (GB)

In the beginning was Lotus, the archetypal production race car manufacturer founded by the late, great Colin Chapman in the '50s. Buried in the flood of customer cars rolling out the door of subsidiary Lotus Components between 1967 and 1971 were several hundred Formula Fords.

In fact, the first car to have the words "Formula Ford" painted on its flanks was a Lotus 31 owned by the Motor Racing Stables school. The first purpose-built Formula Ford was also a Lotus, called a 51 but essentially a 31 spaceframe Formula 3 car equipped with a Renault gearbox. The 31 was one of the most ignored cars in the Lotus inventory, although Jim Russell, who owned a lot of them, thought highly of them as school cars.

The 31 was, in turn, a revised 22 Formula Junior which had roots in the 20, so the 51 was venerable the day it was new!

Anything but sophisticated, the '67-'68 Lotus 51's biggest handicap was that Renault 'box: This featured a quill shaft that was not splined but epoxied, and standing starts did horrendous

Lotus 51 Formula Fords live again in historic racing.

Lotus 61 was a revised 51 with a wedge-shaped body.

Historic 51 with a proper roll bar and a Hewland.

things to the glue. Still, a 25-car supply served the Motor Racing Stables school well in '67-'68 as did an even number sold on the open market (Mark Litchfield took delivery of the first customer [i.e. non-school] 51 on July 20, 1967).

The '68 Lotus 51B featured a rear suspension geometry change and accommodation for the new 1600cc FF engine, while the mid-year 51C got proper rod ends and (at last!) a Hewland gearbox as the RAC began to relent on its £1,000 price ceiling on Formula Ford costs.

Beaten in all the important early races by first Russell-Alexis ('67) and then Merlyn ('68), Lotus struck back toward the end of the '68 season: First, Colin Chapman personally wooed Jim Russell back into the family; then Lotus Components stuck a radical wedge-shaped body on the 51. In '69, the Lotus 61 made a strong run at every British and European Formula Ford championship. Russell-entered pseudo-works Lotus 61s proved to be particularly effective, and Dave Walker rewarded the marque with the prestigious '69 Les Leston FF Championship.

Lotus ran the 61 again in '70 (as a 61M, with a lower nose profile) and it was a mistake: The aging design was humbled by more advanced new cars from Merlyn, Palliser, Titan and Dulon LD4. Lotus' '71 FF, though, rectified the mistake: The 69 was a

Wilson Fittipaldi in one of the great Lotus 69 FFs.

development of the spaceframe 59 F3 car, and the Dave Baldwin-designed machine was a good one. (There was also a semi-mono-coque version for F2, also called a 69 just to confuse historians.) It sold extremely well, and was still winning races—and even a few championships —well into the '70s. It was also the general layout of this car that Ralph Firman and Ross Ambrose followed in producing the first Van Diemen FA73 FF in 1973.

Sadly, Lotus shut down its production race car arm, Lotus Components, at the end of the '71 season and so production of the first great FF marque halted. The hallowed Lotus badge was immediately missed, but the popularity of historic racing has given all these old cars a new lease on life. At the heart of FF, there is still Lotus.

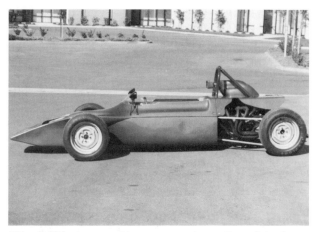

March 729 was a vast improvement over the original.

A Martlet loses a wheel—not typical of a very sturdy car.

March (cont.)

gineering (Mitchell was a friend of Herd's) planned to take over production of the March FF and did assemble a few cars. There were no March 728s, just 729s for North America only. The '73 739 was announced but never built; March simply had bigger things on its corporate mind.

Martini (F)

Naturalized Frenchman Tico Martini, a very good hillclimber in the '60s, built many great chassis bearing his name starting in that decade. He was a close friend of Richard Knight, founder of Winfield School, and one of his early jobs was looking after the technical side of the school at Magnys Cours. This was founded in '65, and used used Lotus, Merlyn and Cooper F3s.

A few F3-based Martini MK3s, 4s, 5s, or 7s may have appeared '69-'71 in FF guise. (Incidentally, the "MK" is for "Martini-Knight," not "Mark.")

Martlet (GB)

Martlet is the county bird of Sussex. The Hon. Jeremy Plunkett drove the first Formula Ford chassis designed by ex-Ian Raby F1 mechanic and historic car preparation expert David Martin, who was then chief mechanic at the Goodwood-based Winfield Racing School. The DM1 was followed by DM2 ('80), DM3A ('80), DM3B ('81) and DM4 ('81) models, Martin announcing but apparently never realizing plans to produce FF2000 and Formula Talbot derivatives.

Matek (GB)

McGregor (GB)

The name sounds Scottish but the '79 McGregor FF1 was designed by Dutchman Kees van der Grint and built by Englishman Len Wimhurst. It got its name from an American sponsor. One of the two FF1s built was driven by Dutchman Glenn Bosch.

A one-off FF2 built in '80 was sold to an American before the company decided to take aim on F3.

Design engineer Kees van der Grint tries the Len Wimhurst-built McGregor ZFF1 in '79.

McNamara (D)

Francis McNamara was an American serviceman who raced Vees and then started building them while stationed in Germany. Eventually McNamara set up a factory in Lengreis, Germany, which produced an F3 car in '69 and Andy Granatelli's bizarre-looking STP Indy Car in '71, the latter designed by Austrian ex-Lola designer Jo Karasek. In between came the fairly conventional FCA Formula Ford, also designed by Karasek but based on the McNamara F3 car designed by Dan Hawkes.

The FF was marketed in '69-'70 in both Europe and the U.S. McNamara's firm also modified the STP March F1 car driven by Andretti that was written off in Austria. It was out of business by the end of the '71 season.

Melton (GB)

The Melton firm was founded by Stephen and David Young, who unveiled the MMS1 Formula Ford at the 1988 British FF Festival.

Merlyn (GB)

See expanded entry on page 104.

Micron (GB)

Mirage (GB)

JW Automotive Engineering was founded in late 1966 by famed entrant John Wyer and Ford dealer John Willment who took over Ford's factory sports car project and Advanced Vehicles operation. Looking for a way to keep good mechanics employed over the winter, the firm decided to take a stab at production race cars: In March '70, JWA introduced the Mk5 Formula Ford designed by Pat Rochefort who had previously designed the Pringett-Mistrale. It was an attractive car, but really nothing special and its name alone (as Dan Gurney would discover eight years later after introducing the Eagle FF) was not enough to stimulate many sales.

Mistrale (GB)

See Pringett-Mistrale.

McNamara FF seen at the '71 FordSport Day at Brands.

McNamara's FF was simpler than its bizarre Indy Car.

The Mirage name did nothing to stimulate sales ...

Merlyn (GB)

Emerson Fittipaldi and Ray Allen streak away at Snetterton in '69 driving Merlyn Mk11As.

Johnny Kastner's Merlyn Mk24—a new path for CRD.

(ABOVE) Denny Moothart's Mk29. (BELOW) Mk31.

Colchester Racing Developments Ltd. (CRD) arrived on the Formula Ford scene a few months behind rivals Lotus and Alexis, but succeeded in stealing the sales thunder from both in 1968, the first full year of FF racing.

The Merlyn Mk11 FF produced by CRD was a conventional, F3-based machine that utterly dominated the first important British FF title race: Aussie Tim Schenken's incredible 33 wins from 38 starts (many of them in the 27-round Guards Championship) set Merlyn on an incredible sales roll.

The first Merlyn, designed and built by brothers Selwyn and Clive Hayward and Chris Maskery who founded CRD, was a front-engined Formula Junior built in 1960. The first car's name and its unusual spelling came from Welshman Maskery, a merlin ("merlyn" in Wales) being a hawk-like bird of pray.

Through the '60s, Merlyn specialized in production single seaters, though some of its best cars were sports racers. Its first FF, the Mk11, was essentially one of its '67 Mk10 F3 cars with some lightening of components; the 11A, introduced late in '68, featured a purpose-designed body (produced as were many others by Specialised Mouldings) with a less expensive windscreen.

Like the 11 had been in Schenken's hands, the 11A proved to be the car to beat in '69 and was a foundation for Merlyn offerings well into the '70s.

The 11A was succeeded by the 17 (which got a detachable nose and attracted a large order from the Jim Russell School at Mallory Park) and mildly revised 17A. The Mk20, introduced very late in '71, featured greatly increased chassis stiffness (thanks to larger diameter frame tubes) and a significantly revised front suspension. The '72 Mk20A, largely designed by Clive Hayward, was a wonderful car—a little on the heavy side but very well balanced and exceptionally strong.

Subsequent Merlyn FF models failed to reach their predecessors levels of success: The '73-'77 Mks 24, 25, 025, 29 and 029 were distinguished by their modern, shovel-nosed bodywork, lightweight fabricated uprights, and the rearward migration of their radiators. The '77 029 was a wide-track car produced largely at the request of Chet Kastner who ran the Jim Russell School on the American West Coast and whose son Johnny scored many triumphs in Merlyns.

By the middle '70s, though, Merlyn's race car construction business was in decline even as its mainstream engineering business flourished. Following a '77 move from the old dirt floor Church Rd., Little Bentley, premises to a modern new factory in Manningtree, the Hayward brothers' interest in FF racing declined still further. There was a brief flurry of international interest in Merlyn's '78 Mk31 machine but, having lost its remaining Jim Russell School business to Van Diemen, Merlyn production was formally halted in '79 sometime after the 400th FF model emerged from the factory. Over 250 Merlyn FFs were sold in the U.S. alone.

Selwyn Hayward retired to the south of France in '84; today, younger brother Clive minds the engineering and fabrication store. In addition to its many industrial accounts, Colchester Racing Developments does a booming business producing spares for all the wonderful old Merlyns which are still out there active in vintage FF racing.

Mondiale (GB)

The Northern Ireland-based Mondiale was founded in 1984 by long-time Crossle designer Leslie Drysdale and partners Dennis McGall and Colin Lees. Its first M84S FF was immediately successful on the home front, and was very effectively developed over subsequent seasons.

The fledgling company was aided by a significant order from the American Skip Barber Racing School starting in '86: As well as providing the school with specially designed FF chassis, Mondiale builds all the SAAB-powered machines used in the popular IMSA single-seater pro series.

MRE (GB)

Jim Gleave's Bourne End, Bucks., England-based company employed ex-Nemo F3 designer Max Boxtrom to design a straightforward, front radiator-equipped FF which appeared as the MRE 73F in 1973. Subsequent 74F and 75F models were successful in several markets, and were also the basis for the first Tiga FF: Gleave sold MRE's assets to Tim Schenken and Howden Ganley over the winter of '75-'76.

One of the most successful MRE drivers in the U.S. was Bob Earl, '73 U.S. National Champion driving an ADF, who raced an MRE entered by West Coast importer ProFormula.

Mygale (F)

Mystere (GB)

Apparently a Formula 3 Cooper "improved" by Mike Greenwood and raced in FF's first year, 1967. A Mk2 example, offered for sale in a Sept. '68 issue of *Autosport*, boasted a Brabham body and Jack Knight Imp gearbox.

Nike (GB)

Like many who came early to the FF manufacturing business, engineer Ken Nicholls' first car (named for the winged Greek goddess of victory) was a front-engined Formula Junior. The Bideford (later Holsworthy), Devon-based firm also built a few sports racers and Formula Vees before completing its first FF (co-designed by Nicholls and Mark Erwood), the Mk4, in '68. Subsequent models were the Mk6 ('70), the Mk10 ('71-'74), Mk10B ('75-'76) and Mk10C ('77-sometime in the early '80s).

Early Nike models exported to the U.S. were called Bakers while Nike frames were used in the first Tony Clarke-designed Hermes.

Mondiale M84S was an immediate hit worldwide.

Leslie Drysdale has trouble hiding his Crossle background!

The author celebrity-races a Barber School Mondiale.

Even more attractive: Mondiale's '88 M88S.

Max Boxtrom-designed MRE 74F.

MRE 75F was the starting-off point for the '76 Tiga.

Nike's first Mk4 Formula Ford appeared in '67.

North Devon-built '75 Nike Mk10B.

Nomad (GB)

The Nomad name went with noted sports car driver Mark Konig and first appeared on a BRM-powered Group 6 sports racer in 1967. In '73, Konig and Ian Heath bought the remains of the Palliser Formula Ford project and Nomad was the "rightful" name of the dozen or so subsequently produced Len Wimhurst-designed '73 KHF/1 (aka WDF4) and '74-'76 KHF/2 machines which were correctly called Nomads when imported by Ed Cunningham; Konig Heaths when one or two slipped in directly; and Winkelmanns WDF5s and WDF6s when sold with American-produced bodywork by Ron Hunter. (Are you confused yet?)

The Palliser project and Nomad badge changed hands again sometime between '76-'78 when chassis specialist Frank Coltman acquired all the fixtures and spares. Coltman would later partner Geoff Creber in Coltman Creber Racing Services which unveiled a new Nomad FF prototype, the FWC81/16, in 1981. *See also Palliser.*

Oscar (GB)

A hastily scribbled note in the files reminds the author that the Oscar Mk1 was designed by Frank Bayles, formerly with Cooper, and built by the Oscar Car Co. in Lynchwood, England. When he wrote that note and what became of the Oscar Car Co., he does not know ...

OX (GB)

John Oxborrow, former Ray driver and champion of Lydden, designed and produced his own FF chassis—the OX-1—in a very short time over the winter of '84-'85. It was a superlative effort, and the rapid Oxborrow has since extended the series of one-offs up to type number OX-6 which raced in '92—and in which Oxborrow suffered a very serious accident, emerging with a broken neck.

Pacer (GB)

Hawke found David Lazenby, proprietor of Pace Products Ltd., was dragged out of retirement to design the Pacer Formula Ford by wealthy Max Groos and sons Trevor and Kevin. The prototype BMG 79 was first raced by Howard Groos at Silverstone in March '79, and the chassis was further developed by Trevor as cars were produced through at least '81 in the family's Manchester, England-based workshops.

Palliser (GB)

Ex-Brabham and Lola designer Len Wimhurst was commissioned by driver and BOAC airline pilot Hugh P.K. Dibley to design and build a twin-cam Ford-engined Formula B car in 1967. This was completed, it is reported, in Wimhurst's "back garden" at his home in Catford, southwest of London. Three copies were built in '68 and at the end of the year, Palliser (the "P" in backer Dibley's initials) Racing Design Ltd. was formed and premises acquired in nearby Clapham.

Palliser FBs were raced and sold successfully in the U.S. by Northern California-based Bob Winkelmann who gave all the cars—including the FFs which first started appearing in '69—his own name. The WDF1 was Wimhurst's first FF design and it was a good one, competitive well into the '70s, its trademark a big cockpit which was comfortable even for the tallest driver.

The lightly modified WDF2 arrived in '70, the WDF3 (not to be confused with the '70 WDF3 F3 car) in '71 and the WDF3A was new in July of that year.

Dibley sold his interest in early '72 to Winkelmann and engineer John Plumridge. They in turn sold the rights to the FF in '73 to Mark Konig and Ian Heath, who resumed production, giving the cars their "Nomad" name. A few Palliser/Nomads exported to America were re-bodied and called Winkelmann WDF6s by veteran Colorado campaigner Ron Hunter; others were badged as Konig Heath WDF5s and still others as Nomads.

Whatever, the Palliser name was resurrected one more time in late 1974 when Wimhurst and Les Oakley built the Palliser 742 F2000 car for Damien Magee. Dubbed the 'Old Nail,' it was still winning years later with Syd Fox driving.
See also Nomad.

(ABOVE) '86 OX. (BELOW) '82 OX-6.

Max Groos, sons Trevor, Kevin, Howard, and the Pacer.

Early Pallisers were loved for their speed and comfort.

Graham Tomlinson's '67 Piper at Brands Hatch.

(LEFT TO RIGHT) Alexis, Titan and Pringett-Mistrale.

The startling—or is it frightening?—Prowess.

Pro Racing Services' RH01 was a terrific late-'70s FF.

Phantom (USA)

Not to be confused with the British Clubman's cars built in Essex in the early '70s, the Phantom FF was all-American, a project headed by driver Dick Ferguson at the RV assembly facilities of Power Performance Products. The TF-3 was quite advanced for 1974, featuring rising-rate suspension at all four corners, but the prototype never finished a race. Production was planned and all the jigs and fixtures were made, but to date only one example was ever completed.

Photon (GB)

Piper (GB)

The name Piper was from the trademark of Campbell's Garages, Hayes, Kent, England, managed by George Henrotte. A new company organized by Brian Sherwood settled in Wokingham, Surrey, in the mid '60s. Piper's first FF win came at a Brands Hatch 10-lapper on Aug. 20, 1967, one of its cars entered that summer by the Lydden Racing School. In 1968, a new Piper F3 car and FF derivative were announced; none were subsequently produced and Sherwood was killed in '69.

Piper (USA)

Donald Sievenpiper, director of engineering at an Illinois, U.S.A.-based hydraulics company, set about building a slipstreamer Formula Ford that "a big guy like myself could fit into" in 1990, racing the prototype quite successfully in the U.S. Central Div. By Jan. '92, the first production batch of three DF-2s was under way at Piper Race Cars, St. Charles, Ill., two of which qualified for the '92 Runoffs.

Pirola (I)

An early '70s Italian-built chassis, one of which was raced by the soon-to-be-world-famous Giorgia Francia in the '72 FF World Final at Brands Hatch.

Pringett-Mistrale (GB)

A lovely car designed by Pat Rochefort and first produced by Gerry Corbett in 1969; by mid-1970, 12 copies had been sold. The shop was in Eastbourne, Sussex, and the name is an anagram of PRINGle and CorbETT who were partners and brothers-in-law.

Syd Fox was one of the marque's more well-known drivers. The sturdy machines were eventually used by Motor Racing Stables and coincidentally or not Gerry Corbett was manager of the Silverstone Racing School in the early '80s.

Prowess (GB)

Among the most startling FF designs of all time, the Prowess was designed by Hugo Spowers ('Prowess' is an anagram of his surname) and unveiled in Oct. '86. Extremely low, the car featured a far-forward, lay-down driving position and an all-but-fully enclosed cockpit. Side radiators were located up front, alongside the inboard shocks/springs operated by pushrods. Regrettably, the car didn't go very well and volume production was never commenced.

PRS (GB)

Pro Racing Services (PRS) was founded in Dec. '77 by ex-Hawke man Vic Hollman, engineer Ray Hughes and driver Derek Daly. Based in Welwyn Garden City, the first Hughes-designed RH01, which debuted in March '78, was very "Crossle-like" and very good: The original and the RH02 which succeeded it in '79 won several important races over the next few years, both in Europe and abroad.

Though Hughes retired from racing, PRS remained a key FF player in the very early '80s. But the attractive Sergio Rinland-designed 82F was not particularly successful, and PRS, then being run by Vic Hollman and his younger brother Steve, quietly folded in '83.

Quest (GB)

The Oct. '79 FF Exhibition at Goodwood was highlighted by the debut of the startling Quest, the name borrowed from designer and full-time market researcher Mike Thompson's computer software firm. The Quest prototype was a very advanced machine featuring inboard front suspension and very small frontal area. Many of its components were made by ASD which had also produced bits for Thompson's previous venture, Rostron.

In '85, Quest won the FF Festival, courtesy young Johnny Herbert who made an unbelievable comeback after crashing in practice. Sadly, sales volume was never high, the firm was never particularly profitable, and it was finally liquidated in '87.

Happily, Thompson took his design creativity to the "new" Roger Andreason-run Chevron.

Quick One (USA)

RACE (USA)

A press release in Nov. '70 touted the three R.A.C.E. Mk21 FFs that had been built by Royal American Competition Enterprises of Chicago, Ill. But apparently the press release had a wider circulation than the cars.

RH02 PRS showed well in the U.S.

If looks could kill: The Sergio Rinland-designed PRS.

The prototype Quest caused a stir in '79.

Sensational Johnny Herbert in a Quest 85FF.

Clay model of the stillborn RAM.

American-edition Ray 74FF.

Into the '80s with Bert Ray: (ABOVE) 84F; (BELOW) 87F.

RAM (USA)

A clay model and an FF rolling chassis designed and produced by Robert Metcalf were shown to the SCCA club racing community in '85. But apparently, the Dallas, Tex.-based RAM Race Cars didn't get much further with its high-tech RM22J.

Raven (GB)

ASD Engineering's Bob Egginton recalls that the Raven was the brainchild of Paul Smith, a customer in the early '70s of the Carl Rostron/Mike Thompson-owned Rostron for which ASD produced several components.

Ray (GB)

Former Brabham mechanic Bert Ray, a skilled Clapham, London-based fabricator who made parts for his neighbors (including Palliser) for several years, began producing complete FFs for select drivers in 1972. A prototype Len Wimhurst-designed Ray FF72 was qualified by American Jas Patterson at the first World Cup in Oct. '72, but the most successful early

The most famous Ray of all? Stephen South's 73F.

model was the FF73 driven by brilliant ex-karter Stephen South who took Ray with him up to F3.

Ray FFs were built in small numbers each year right up to '77 when Bert Ray took a short "break." He returned in '79 with a new FF design (which carried the firm through the '83 season) as well as the London sales franchise for Crossle Cars. A new range appeared in '84 and closed out the decade while new '90s examples are ultra high tech and state of the art. Rays have also been produced under license in South Africa.

RCS (GB)

Reynard (GB)

See expanded entry on page 111.

Reynard (GB)

Having designed and built his own 250cc sprint motorcycle—with which he gained five World Land Speed Records—and while attending Oxford College, teenager Adrian Reynard turned his attentions to four-wheelers in 1970. He'd been hooked on auto racing at places like Lime Rock and Watkins Glen as a teenager living for two years in Connecticut, and he bought a Ginetta G18B FF. Results, in the few races he ran on a student's budget were, he remembers, "strictly forgettable."

A few years later, near the end of a four-year apprenticeship with British Leyland, he decided to build a new FF himself because he didn't have the funds to buy one.

That very first Reynard FF, called the 73F, was wrecked at Brands Hatch in '74, rebuilt, then traded outright to Jeremy Rossiter (the Spax shock absorber man was a close friend of Adrian's) for a Dulon. The latter was subsequently sold to finance a Reynard prototype for the new 2-liter FF formula introduced in '75. Thus, the Bicester-based Reynard Racing Cars was born, with most of the important components for its immediately successful FF2000 cars manufactured by Sabre Automotive, a firm founded by ex-March man Bill Stone and Reynard himself.

In the middle '70s, as sales of the 2-liter Reynards took off, the mercurial Adrian took on a consulting job with Hawke, assisting David Lazenby with the DL15 FF as well as heading up separate Hawke F3 and F1 projects. Also, between '76 and '78, he somehow managed to build 12 tidy Reynard-badged FF1600 cars as well—eight 76Fs built at the Hawke factory, two 77Fs, and a pair of 78Fs.

Reynard's company really wasn't on the map in FF1600 circles, though, until 1982 when it brought out the scintillating FF82—a state-of-the-art machine brimming over with good ideas and sex appeal. Derivative FF83 and FF84 cars were also good, and sold in extremely large numbers.

Adrian himself was by then distracted by higher formulae and so left the design development of a new range of FF1600/2000 cars to promising young Dutchman Wiet Huidekoper. Unfortunately, those '85 cars took some developing. The '86 car featured the old '84 rear suspension and in mid-year got a front radiator; it all looked cobbled together and despite the best efforts of super sales manager Rick Gorne—an ex-FF2000 ace himself—Reynard lost a lot of momentum in FF.

Given the pressures of F3000 plus the laborious search for funding with which to launch a F1 team of his own, Reynard thought about quitting the FF business altogether. He might have had not successful businessman and club racer Mike "Fulmar" Taylor and ex-Royale boss Alan Cornock made him an offer to market those cars. Fulmar Competition Services opened in April '87 and has been responsible for distributing Reynard's "small formula" offerings (including both Ford- and Vauxhall-powered machinery) ever since.

Given the experienced Cornock's daily attentions, Reynard has bounced back in the FF marketplace: Its latest generation chassis are as aerodymically slippery, well-balanced and appealing as the '82-'84 range was in its day.

The eclectic Adrian Reynard himself, meanwhile, remains a central player in modern day motor racing. His company's products—like his own interests—cover a very wide range.

The first Reynard FF.

First of a beloved series: The FF1600 FF82.

Summer-'86 FF86 looked decidely cobbled-together.

Typical of the terrific new generation, the FF89.

Rondeau (F)

LeMans winner Jean Rondeau staved off the bankruptcy of his company with an involvement in Formula Ford, new to France in 1984. The first M584 FF, a Reynard FF83 with Robert Choulet bodywork and several detail changes to the frame and suspension, won the inaugural

The first Rondeaus were re-bodied Reynard 83FFs.

Rostrons are terrors in Britain's Pre-'74 formulae ...

Sideways in the Roni at Croft in '78.

French FF championship. The subsequent M585 was a similarly fine car.

Sadly, Rondeau's untimely death meant the promising FF project was parted off with his estate.

Roni (GB)

Apparently a very quick one-off, produced and raced by Croft regular Ronnie Whittaker.

Rostron (GB)

A Kent, England, firm owned by Carl Rostron and Mike Thompson. Rostron's first '69 CT-1 was a "Brabham-ish" compilation of designs; ASD Engineering built the chassis and other components for this prototype and for approximately 10 subsequent CT-2, CT-3 and CT-4 production models.

Thompson, a market researcher by profession, won the MCD championship in a CT-3 and ultimately acquired the firm wholly in '77, only to sell it again in '78 as he prepared to launch Quest. One car raced in '77 was numbered RT77 while a '78 machine was labeled the CT78 in a few race programs.

Rotor (GB)

The Rotor JT1 was designed by Graham Millar and built in Scotland in '83. It was raced on a few occasions by multi-time Scottish champion Tom Brown whose primary weapons were Van Diemens.

Royale (GB)

See expanded entry on page 113.

Royale USA (USA)

See Royale (GB) entry on page 113.

Russell-Alexis (GB)

See Alexis.

Ryan (GB)

See Halliday.

Saracen (GB)

Brian Hampsheir had sold Elden for the second time when, as legend has it, he met ex-telecommunications industry executive Alan Weller at a Manpower Service Commission business management course. The two formed a partnership in '76 and began producing small formula cars designed by Brian's brother, Peter.

Saracen survived despite low volume into the early '80s. Soon after its demise, the Hampsheirs were given the opportunity to buy Elden back.

Royale (GB)

Bob King was first a mechanic for two Kiwi speedway stars—Ronnie Moore and Ray Thackwell (father of Mike Thackwell)—and later a London-based car salesman who one day took in an Elva in trade and decided to race it.

Competitive juices rekindled, King quit the sales business and started a race prep firm at his home garage called Racing Preparations Ltd. In the middle '60s, with his reputation as a Coventry Climax engine specialist blossoming, King moved RP Ltd. from home to shop under a railway Arch in London, joined there by a new assistant, Alan Cornock.

In the late '60s, faced with declining interest in the Coventry Climax engine, King started casting around for new things to do: The new Formula Ford class suggested an answer and, in '68, he contracted with Surtees man Bob Marston to design an FF chassis for him. The one-off RP1, called a "Royale" because of the firm's Park Royal address and King's surname, led to the RP2 production version which was instantly successful in the new class.

Another new racing car manufacturer was born.

In the three seasons '69-'71, Royale built an amazing 61 RP2s, 3s (identifiable by the twin ducts on the top of the nose), and 3As, most going to the U.S. where ex-Formula Vee champion Bill Scott and others were usually dominant.

Flush with his FF success, King pushed on into faster formulae including Formula B and Super Vee and moved the company to a new factory in Huntington, near Lola. But the rapid diversification took a tremendous toll on King's health: After an exhausting '73 season, King chose to retire in November.

Former assistant Alan Cornock took over the company, moved it to an abandoned WWII quonset hut at Little Staughton Airfield, near Bedford, in '74, and set about reorganizing.

The most important task was FF: All-new for the FF World Festival race in Oct. '72, the FSV bodywork-bedecked RP16 was a good but not great car that at least sold in good numbers; it got Royale through. In '74, Cornock hired young South African designer Rory Byrne who came up with the RP21. This delightful car was a big hit, Englishman Geoff Lees using one to win all three major British championships and the Festival in '75!

Byrne's follow-up RP24 was also good, but he left suddenly for Toleman in '77. His successor was ex-Ford engineer Pat Symonds whose boxy '79-'80 RP26 proved to be the best-selling Royale FF of all time—104 produced! But in that time period, Van Diemen's "Brazil Connection" really took hold and in the tally of championships, Royale was left behind.

Though Symonds' graceful RP29 was a solid machine, Royale sales crashed to earth: fewer than three dozen examples were sold. Original Royale designer Bob Marston was brought back to try and salvage the marque's FF fortunes, and he made some headway: Forty RP31Ms were produced in '82 and 26 RP33Ms in '83. But the numbers were a far cry from what Royale needed to stay afloat. The Wiet Huidekoper-updated '84-'85 RP36 would be the historic firm's final fling in FF racing.

A portion of the company had by then been acquired by American vintage racer and Argo importer Hugh Kleinpeter, a Georgia resident, who bought the remaining assets and put them under the Royale U.S.A. umbrella. Cornock, meanwhile, resurfaced in '87 as co-proprietor of Fulmar Competition Services.

The first production Royale FF was the '69 RP2.

Geoff Lees' all-conquering Rory Byrne-designed RP21.

Best-selling Royale ever: Pat Symonds-penned RP26.

Designer Marston, Hugh Kleinpeter, driver Rollin Butler, and the RP33M.

Saracen was another chapter in the Hampsheirs' FF book.

'78 Sark 1 would finish fourth in its FF Festival debut.

Michael Andretti splashes off to play in the '81 Scandia.

Sark (GB)

Real estate developer Gavin Hooper and former Lola and Scott designer Patrick Head introduced the proto-type Starfire FF2000 car in Dec. '74. Failing to stimulate much interest, they sold the car a year later to Richard Piper and Christopher Parsons who renamed it the Sark and built four production examples.

Interest waned again—but once again, Head's tidy design was revived, this time in '78 when John Mortimer, ex-works Van Diemen FF1600 driver Donald MacLeod, and MacLeod's brother Hamish took over Sark Racing Ltd.

While Donald raced a 2-liter Sark, Hamish began refettling the design as an FF1600, finishing the first car in November. This Donald used to finish fourth in the FF Festival just three days after the new car's first test!

In '79, Donald won the Festival for the second time in his career, driving a new Sark 2. His great talent, though, likely cursed sales of what was probably a very decent car. The assets were sold in 1981 to Wandsworth-based James Howe who produced the Sark 2B and 2C through at least '83.

Scandia (USA)

A sturdy and extremely narrow FF, the Scandia was designed by veteran racing driver Bertil Roos for young Michael Andretti in '81. The 1600 car was a one-off, but 2-liter derivatives have been built in fair number for Roos' wonderful Pennsylvania, U.S.A.-based racing school.

Silverstone (GB)

See Zeus.

Sparton (GB)

Founded by constructor Paul Jackson and Postal Service employee Norman Pierce in Feb. '78, Sparton flickered briefly in FF, FF2000 and especially Formula Talbot, then flamed-out and was gone by '84. Based initially in Warlingham, Surrey, Sparton's first FF78 FFs featured chassis designed by Geoffrey Rumble (of Dastle fame) who also did much of the fabrication, while Sparton's principals did their own bodywork.

The '83 SE316 was much more advanced, but it was Sparton's final fling in FF.

Spectrum (AUS)

The advanced '92 Spectrum 05 was designed by Australian engineer Michael Borland who founded the company in '86 and whose '88 car had been very successful in the home market.

Star (GB)

Radio Victory, the Portsmouth-based independent radio station which produced the beloved "Track Torque" program starting in Oct. '77, co-sponsored an FF team which ran its own car, designed by Ian Skinner and built in Worthing for Ian Cross and Alan Kimber. The team manager was on-air personality Rob Widdows and apparently only two cars were produced.

Stohr (USA)

Lee Stohr, a Hillsboro, Ore.-based mechanical engineer, started racing FF with an Elden in 1981 but decided to built his own car in '87. Discovering that his FF1 was "too radical," Stohr "hooked up with a few of the guys who used to do the Vikings for Arnie Loyning in Portland" and set about building the FF2. This followed slightly more conventional lines and first appeared in '89, turning heads.

In '91 and '92, the sleek machine showed extremely well—one of the cars qualified on the front row of the '91 Runoffs—and Stohr, a great FF1600 enthusiast, steams ahead.

Supernova (GB)

The small Supernova concern in Sussex, England, built a one-off FF in 1975. Designed by Ian Williams and ex-BRM mechanic Stan Collier, the prototype was imported into the U.S. by Fred Opert Racing and prepared by Jack Clark's C & S Racing for rapid Jamaican Peter Moodie. Sadly, the car was written off by another driver late in '75. While rumors circulated that Supernova was building more FFs for America in '76, the company folded.

Swift (GB)

See expanded entry on page 118.

Swift (NZ)

The Kiwi Swift is apparently a homebuilt being raced by its constructor, Bruce Smythe, in New Zealand FF events, with no connection to either the original Swift U.S.A. or Frank Bradley's Swift G.B.

Swift (USA)

See expanded entry on page 116.

Talon (GB)

Ex-U.S. Reynard importers Mick Penfold and Richard Martin, plus Ken Taylor, who built the Delta FF2000 chassis, founded Advanced Racing Concepts in 1985. Originally intending to produce an ultra-modern

Early Spartons were sturdy cars; this is a '79.

Barry Pigot was quick in an '82 U.S.-spec Sparton

'83 Sparton SE316 was a head-turner

Stohr prototype was ... er, interesting.

Swift (USA)

Sept. '83: The shape of things to come.

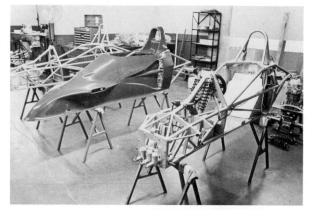

By March '84, business was booming at Swift Cars.

(ABOVE) By Sept. '86, Swifts completely dominated SCCA National starting grids. (RIGHT) An '85 long-tail.

The Swift DB-1 was the car that completely, inexorably, changed the future of Formula Ford racing starting in 1983. A sensational chrome-moly frame, inboard suspension, midships radiator-equipped machine designed by the brilliant David Bruns, the Swift virtually destroyed the FF1600 class in America by virtue of Swift Cars Inc.'s meeting all of its objectives: The DB-1 was a vastly superior machine made available at an insignificant premium in cost, to the ruin of a FF class which had thrived on marque vs. marque rivalry and interest for 15 years.

True, by '83 FF racing had already begun to price itself out of existence. The Swift, however, accelerated everyone's frustration by showing what the phrase "high-tech" really meant.

Though a very accurate line drawing of the DB-1 appeared in the American *SportsCar* magazine as early as May '83, rival manufacturers lost little sleep: Bruns' previous FF, the '73 ADF Mk II, had been extremely fast but the wildly advanced machine was also hard to build and exorbitantly priced, and it sold in very small numbers. The new Swift Cars, Inc. partnered ADF principals Paul White and David Bruns with attorney Alex Cross and businessman R.K. Smith (all but White current or former FF racers), and surely they were no threat to FF top dogs Van Diemen, Reynard or Lola said the pundits.

Well, pundits were never more wrong ...

Incredibly, history repeated itself when the sensational Bruns-designed car—which didn't turn a wheel until Oct. 3 at Willow Springs Raceway—debuted at the mid-Oct. SCCA Runoffs, qualified on the pole, and scored a runaway victory, just as the ADF had done in '73. But even then, the English FF constructors had no idea Swift Cars could deliver on its promise of fairly priced production examples.

But this time White, Bruns *et all* had done their homework: Swift *could* deliver and did, to the tune of well over 100 chassis inside of 18 months—breaking the record for an American manufacturer held by Autodynamics (Caldwell) since '70. In the next few years, Swift Cars, Inc. blossomed, too: Bruns produced an FF2000 derivative instantly successful in Canada; Peter Zarcades was added to the ownership group when an S2000 project was launched; and the remarkable Bruns followed through with a winning Formula Atlantic design.

Swift Cars' success came in a form familiar to English constructors but then virtually unique to "gotta do it ourselves" Americans: It subcontracted a lot of the work, employing specialists Wayne Hartman for the fiberglass work, Dale Tholen for the pattern making (oh, those castings were beautiful!), and Marc Bahner for the fabrication of the complex chrome-moly frame.

When the pragmatic Paul White resigned, though, selling his shares to Smith, Swift lost a lot of its production know-how. In '88, Bill Fickling and Jim Chapman, with financial help from Ira Young, took over the assets of the company. A few years later, Swift was acquired by Hiro Matsushita, then soon-to-be-Indy Car driver and heir to a Japanese home electronics (Panasonic) dynasty who is content to let Chapman and Co. run things.

Swift has been a powerful force on the American racing scene since winning the Runoffs in '83—perhaps too powerful, for in part thanks to the wonderful, all-conquering DB-1, the American racing scene no longer includes a healthy Formula Ford.

Talon (GB)

FF1600 chassis around a Metso gearbox using their own castings, the Talon principals were ultimately forced to use a Hewland. The prototype debuted at the FF Festival in '85 but, despite several strong performances in both the U.S. and U.K., sales never took off. The Lewes-based constructor was dissolved by the end of the '86 season.

Taylor Trainer (GB)

These were basically Dulon replicas: Having ceased production, Maxperenco Products (Dulon) apparently produced a few more cars for the late Ian Taylor's then-new racing school.

Technauto (F)

Tecno (I)

Never officially an FF constructor, a couple of the Italian firm Tecno's stunning '69 F3 cars were converted to FF-spec at the factory for Skip Barber by his ace mechanic, Terry Secker. Barber won the SCCA Runoffs with one of these cars in 1970.

Founded by Luciano and Gianfranco Pederzani in '62, the Bologna-based Tecno built some terrific karts and a '68 Formula 3 car so good that 43 examples were sold. Tecno was gone, though, by the end of '73 following the failure of its F1 project.

Tiga (GB)

A firm that really should have made it: As with Crossle, the author confesses a genuine enthusiam for Howden Ganley's well-engineered cars. In 1975, ex-GP drivers Ganley and Tim Schenken founded Tiga Engineering and began production of their first Formula Ford 1600 car: Howden and Tim having bought the assets of MRE, the first Tiga (pronounced "TY-ga") FF76 borrowed heavily from Max Boxtrom's 75F design. The company soon moved from Ganley's shop near Windsor to ex-Fittipaldi workshops at Caversham, near

Another SCCA National win for the Stohr FF2 in '91.

Tidy Talon never gained a claw-hold in the U.S. market.

(ABOVE) Tim Schenken prepares to sample his own (a Tiga FF76) at Bridge-hampton in '76. Opert team driver Tom Davey stands at right. (LEFT) Craig Taylor kindled Tiga's FF1600 flame in '81.

Swift U.K. (GB)

English FF1600/FF2000 racer and businessman Frank Bradley (who attended the Jim Russell Race Drivers School in '69 along with another newcomer to the sport, Danny Sullivan) completed an arrangement late in the '85 racing season to bring the American Swift Cars' David Bruns-designed DB-4 FF2000 chassis to England. The experienced Bradley, who had once for

(ABOVE) By 1990, a year after being sold by Frank Bradley to Brian Holmes, Swift Europe's FF1600 offering had departed completely from David Bruns' original 1983 DB-1 design. (BELOW) The nicely sculpted Swift Europe FB89 FF1600, designed by little-known FF racer Luis Fernando Cruz.

a short time owned Elden, was eventually granted a contract to assemble the cars in the U.K.

Assemble in the U.K. he did, starting in '86, with several design changes made to the 2-liter car by Hugh Moran (who later left for McLaren's F1 team). A few years later, Bradley brought over Bruns' FF1600 design, too. Called the FB88, this was much more extensively "revised" than even the FF2000 machine had been when put into production at the English Swift's Snetterton facility. In 1989, Swift Europe Ltd.'s Luis Fernando Cruz-designed FB89 took the car another full step away from the original Bruns design.

By the time the English Swift won the British FF Festival in 1990, it was a completely autonomous arm: With its production offerings digressing further and further from the American lineup (not always in ways approved by the U.S. principals!), it had become a completely separate entity.

In the early '90s, Swift Europe was a leading challenger in the revitalized British FF scene, making inroads into international markets as well. Interestingly, Bradley sold the company to another motor racing enthusiast and businessman Brian Holmes in '89, only to buy it back in '92, adding a fresh capital impetus.

The wildly advanced '92 SC92F was designed by Mark Bailey who was also involved in Swift's offerings for another popular class, Formula Renault. By then operating from a Chesterfield factory, Swift was looking ahead to a production run of 60 SC93Fs—twice as many as built in any previous year!

Tiga (cont.)

Reading, and added FF2000 and Sports 2000 and eventually Camel Lights sports prototypes to their product mix.

Tiga also did some exotic fabrication work for several F1 teams while Tiga Management Services ran young Andrea de Cesaris in F3.

The watchword at Tiga was always sound engineering but while they were at times dominant in S2000, the various evolutionary models of FF1600 cars followed a roller coaster course.

Into the '80s, Schenken left for America to run an IMSA Porsche team. Ganley retired from the company several years laters. The exotic Rob Edwards-designed S2000 project wound up with Mike Gue's Essex Racing. The FF assets are languishing somewhere ...

Titan (GB)

See expanded entry on page 120.

Totem (GB)

Touraco (GB)

The Touraco was a one-off, home-built in 1977 by Graeme Glew, the Yorkshireman who two years later founded Team Touraco, one of England's most successful-ever racehire companies.

Tsunami (CDN)

A marque that helped launched brilliant Penske Indy Car driver Paul Tracy's career in 1985, the Tsunami he raced to third in the '85 Canadian Runoffs was designed in '82 by Robert McCallum and was one of two built. The cars featured inboard pull-rod suspension at the front and an inboard rocker system at the rear—certainly not your average homebuilts circa '82-'83!

Tuna (USA)

Oklahomans Dave Jackson and Randy Nobles were schoolmates at the University of Tulsa who drag raced and dirt raced together. One day, they decided they wanted to win the SCCA FF National Championship with a homebuilt! Their first attempt was Tuna 1 (the printable version of the anagram forming the name is 'Tulsa Unnamed National Automobile'), a ponderous machine that driver Dave Bradley managed to qualify for the Runoffs in '88. Tuna 2 was a lot closer to the mark—completed in 1990, Bradley won every race he finished with it in 1991—while the T-3 was the only non-Swift in the qualifying top 10 at the '92 Runoffs. Jackson and Nobles may yet realize their dream.

Bob Earl gave the first Tiga FF76 some good rides.

The Tsunami was anything but your average homebuilt

Hot Tuna! Tuna 2 brings home another tin cup in '91.

Ulrich (GB)

An Ulrich was a car raced by Englishman Steve Lincoln in '79, about which, regrettably, the author has no further information.

Titan (GB)

Founded in 1965 by the gregarious Formula 3 driver and team owner Charles Lucas, Titan's first FF was a variant of its lovely Mk3 F3 car. The latter had been built for the '68 season when Lucas, an important customer, got into a feud with Lotus boss Colin Chapman.

'70 Mk6 lovingly restored by Simon Hadfield.

One of the best FFs ever sold in America, the '72-'73 Titan Mk6C.

The Mk8 irreparably damaged Titan's fine reputation.

In 1971, Lucas bowed out of the company which was doing a booming FF engine and chassis sales business, selling the assets to fabricator/engineer R.J. "Roy" Thomas who had served a design apprenticeship with Les Redmond, the brains behind the great '60s Gemini Formula Juniors built by The Chequered Flag.

Thomas was a fabricator who learned about design from Redmond as work progressed on the Gemini Mk3. Much of the work was down in a double lock-up rented by Graham Warner in Shepherd's Bush. Other tenants of the row of garages behind Cliff Davis' car sales yard were Peter Jopp, Tony Settember, the F1 Sirocco team, and Frank Williams.

"The place became a little mecca of motor racing," Thomas recalls, and soon the game everyone in there was playing was 1-liter Formula 3. Thomas and entrant Charles Lucas were soon in the middle of it all, though not for long in Shepherd's Bush, forced to move to more expansive premises in Huntington by the success of the Titan engine business.

Formula Ford must have seemed quite tame; however it soon became profitable and Thomas tightened the focus at Titan on FF when the 1-liter F3 went away. Having built about 12 copies of the F3-based FF Mk4, Titan produced 15 Mk5s, all sold to a single customer, Harvey Snow. The Mk6 bowed in '70 and was a huge success, much credit to superb U.S. importers Fred Opert and Pierre Phillips. Titan built two a week at one point and a total of over 240 over a four-season span which included Mk6A, 6B and 6C derivatives.

The Titan name? "Originally, we were going to call the F3 car a Griffin because Lucas' family crest was a griffin," says Thomas. "But just before we rolled the car out the door, somebody told us there already *was* a Griffin. It just so happened the U.S. Titan rocket was all over the news, and we just couldn't think of anything better. Sometime later we found out that in Greek mythology the Titans took on the Olympian gods and lost ..."

Thomas moved the company to smaller premises in St. Neots in '73 even as its capabilities expanded. Unfortunately, the '74 Mk8 follow up to the beloved Mk6 was simply not a good car. It looked good in pre-season testing in the hands of experienced Derek Lawrence who, it transpired, was simply driving around its problems without complaint, so it was fairly late in the season before all the car's problems were identified. By then, Titan had sold 30 cars; at least 20 customers were given free replacement frames, but the damage was done.

The '75 Mk9, re-labeled the Mk9A when the Mk9B emerged late in year, was a very good car but too little, too late. Titan's design credibility had been damaged in the Mk8 debacle. Momentum lost, it quit the production race car business in '76.

"By then," says Thomas, "the engine side had gone mad—we were out of control." American Lola importer Carl Haas was largely to blame, equipping all his fast-selling T-340 and T-342 FFs with Titan Gold Seal engines.

Thomas sold Titan in the mid '80s, but remained active on the motor racing scene into the '90s.

Van Diemen (GB)

See expanded entry on page 122.

Vaney (B)

One of the few FF manufacturers located in Belgium, the first country outside England to host a Formula Ford race. Vaney FFs were produced in the early '70s at a workshop near the Zolder circuit by Jean-Francois Vaney, a Swiss living in Belgium.

Varo (GB)

Appearing in the results as a Lotus-Varo on occasion, this car—a one-off?—was driven by David Duckitt in several '68 events.

Vector (GB)

Wiet Huidekoper, designer of the '83 Wiet, strikes again, recycling the name Vector which graced his sensational Dutch-built-since-'87 Sports 2000 machines and applying it to a striking new-for-'93 Ford Zeta 1800cc-powered FF.

Vector Racing Cars opened in '92, the principals being Huidekoper himself, engineer Chris Fox, machinist Oz Timms and Diana Thomas. The new FF1800, called the TF-93, is the firm's first production offering and will be offered for sale in the U.S. by renowned FAtl and Indy Car entrant Doug Shierson.

Viking (USA)

Not to be confused with Tore Helle's Len Terry-designed Viking F3 car of '75-'76, Viking FFs were produced in limited number by famed engine tuner Arnie Loyning and college professor Bob Erickson, a fellow Portland, Ore., resident. The two hatched the idea in '76, unveiled a prototype late in '79, and delivered the first customer cars in '82, the year Bob Lobenberg used one to win the Runoffs.

The needle-nosed Vikings were just 30" high at the rollbar, and bridged the engineering and styling gap between David Bruns' ADF and Swift DB-1 designs to which they are often compared. Five were built and sold before Loyning Engine Service became too swamped with engine work to pursue its chassis-building ambitions.

Viroy (GB)

A ponderous one-off built in 1969 by NSU and Volkswagen dealer Roy Adlam (whose wife is Violet, thus "Vi-Roy") and used in a summer of fun on the Continent, competing in the '70 Johnson Wax European Championship.

(ABOVE & LEFT) Wiet Huidekoper's latest, the Vector TF-93, is the first new FF marque in with a Zeta 1800.

'82 Arnie Loyning/Bob Erickson-designed Viking.

Lady racer Kathy Hartman tries a Viking FF in '84.

Van Diemen (GB)

Anthony van Diemen was the 17th century governor general of the Dutch East Indies whose celebrated navigator, Abel J. Tasman, found an island off the southeast coast of what is now called Australia in 1642 and called it "Van Diemen's Land."

Two hundred years later, the portly Dutchman was robbed of his glory as the island was renamed Tasmania and eventually became part of the Australian Commonwealth. Three centuries later, however, van Diemen's name is again celebrated worldwide, though in a context the Dutch politician would never comprehend.

"I suppose it was Ross Ambrose's idea," explains Ralph Firman, the hard-working boss of Van Diemen International Racing Service Ltd. "I had already done my first Formula Ford when he got involved with the company and suggested the name. It was a link between Australia and Britain: We sent all our prisoners there, you know!"

Ambrose, an expatriate Tasmanian F3 driver, lasted only three months as Firman's business partner. Twenty years later, however, the name he thought up has an international reputation that both men could only have dreamed about in the spring of '73.

Both Firman and his hugely successful company (which recently shipped its 2,000th chassis!) have strong ties to Formula Ford. Ralph got involved with motor racing in the early '60s, working on the fleet of school cars operated by brother-in-law Jim Russell. By late '67, "the fleet" consisted almost exclusively of FFs, as Russell was one of the original movers and shakers of the new racing class.

Van Diemen's Chalk Road factory acreage in Feb. '92.

Firman was a superb mechanic/engineer and among his subsequent career highlights were work on the Russell-run Lotus Components FF works team in '69 and his F3/F2 association in '69-'70 with up-and-coming superstar Emerson Fittipaldi. When Lotus decided to run its F2 team in house in '70, Firman left Russell's employ and moved to Cheshunt. But, he says, "six months of back-biting up there was quite enough!" and in June, he opened Ralph Firman Racing Preparations (RFRP) in East Harling.

Among his early customers was another Brazilian, Carlos Pace, whose RFRP Lotus 69 clinched the '70 Forward Trust F3 series. By '71, the year that Lotus shut down Lotus Components and stopped building production race cars, Firman's business had expanded to a staff of four, running F3 cars for Texan Sandy Sheperd and the wealthy Rikki von Opel among others.

Building his own car was a thought which surfaced near the end of the '72 season. An RFRP-run Lotus 69 FF driven by Donald MacLeod won the Scottish Championship and finished fourth in the prestigious British Oxygen series: "MacLeod helped trigger the decision," Firman explains. "My first car was not so much designed as 'built,' taking ideas (*mostly from the Dave Baldwin-designed Lotus 69* -Author) we knew would work and putting them into a chassis with the mechanic's lot in mind."

Firman's short-term partner came up with the name Van Diemen for the first FA73, already completed when he joined the company in April '73, and Canadian David McCullum bought the prototype on the strength of Firman's reputation alone. The second example was the works car, destined for Scotsman MacLeod who gave the wedge-nosed, side radiator-equipped, Scholar-powered machine at a Brands Hatch heat race in June.

By the end of the year, the pale blue FA73 had won the British Oxygen series and FF Festival, had finished second in the STP Championship, and had earned its driver the prestigious Grovewood Award.

In Nov. '73, the updated RF74 emerged from Van Diemen International's old pair of Nissen huts located near the Snetterton circuit in Norwich, by which time 15 FA73s had been sold in four different countries. Firman would sell 35 cars in '74 and 48 in '75, helped by an 18-car order from the Russell School in Canada.

The FF1600 sales freed up capital for Firman to invest heavily in the bankrupt GRD concern near the end of '75—principals of that company included a few of Firman's old Lotus Components acquaintances—which added a new sales dimension (though it ended up being nothing more than a "dabble" in F3, nothing like the major involvement begun in '92).

In '76, the bottom fell out of Firman's FF1600 market. "The RF76 tested well," he says of that troubled year, "but very little else went right." When works driver Derek Daly left for Hawke, RF76 sales plummeted. Firman had to have a fresh offering for the '77 season and to the rescue came Dave Baldwin, a friend from the Lotus 69 days who had recently drawn F1 cars for Ensign and Copersucar. Baldwin went to work mid-summer on the RF77, and the prototype was ready for the Nov. FF Festival at Brands Hatch. A stunningly attractive car, it was entrusted to another old friend of Firman's, driver Don MacLeod, who won his heat,

CONTINUED ON PAGE 124

The RF74 was an updated version of the original FA73.

Chico Serra at Snetterton in the Baldwin-designed RF77.

RF78s to the horizon at the California Russell School.

Racer *magazine founder Paul Pfanner in an RF79.*

Brazilian Roberto Moreno (#19) starred in an RF80.

RF81: The rounded lines were new for '81.

Baldwin gambled in the fall of '83, moving from the conventional RF83 (FAR LEFT) to the advanced but difficult-to-drive RF84 (LEFT). Largely thanks to the late-'83 appearance of the Swift, the gamble failed.

Van Diemen (cont.)

CONTINUED FROM PAGE 122

quarter-final and semi-final only to spin away second place in the very wet final.

The point was made and Firman sold 55 RF77s and 79 of the lightly updated RF78s, at which time Baldwin went from free-lancer to full-time employee.

In the decades since, Van Diemen has only rarely been beaten to the unofficial annual FF sales' title and has never come up dry of championship titles: Every year since '77, someone somewhere won a FF1600 crown using a Baldwin-designed Van Diemen, which is a truly remarkable record. True, the number of FF manufacturers has greatly declined with the class having been on the wane worldwide since the mid-'80s. Nonetheless, Van Diemen claims a whopping 70 percent market share, Formula Fords just part of a range which has expanded to include everything from one-design Formula First machines to Multisports sports racers and an exciting new F3 car.

As well as all those, Van Diemen would also produce in '92 Subaru-powered sports racers for former World Champion Keke Rosberg, more Formula Forwards for BHL, over 40 Formula Vauxhall Juniors, some Mitsubishi-powered FForward-based machines for Japan, and several examples of a Formula Renault chassis—not to mention a significant number of its new monoshock FF2000 and FF1600 machines.

"We do tend to keep busy around here," says the wry Derek Wild, the ex-Team Lotus, GRD and Modus factory boss who, like Baldwin, has been loyal to Van Diemen for nearly two decades. Wilds helped manage Van Diemen's '80s expansion out of the WWII-era Quonset huts into a pair of modern brick buildings on the same Chalk Road site opposite the Snetterton circuit.

Today, much of Van Diemen's lifeblood is one-design formulae, like BHL's FFirst, FForward and Multisports. While appreciative of the business opportunity, the fact of it distresses racing enthusiast Firman: "We've always believed in open competition among manufacturers. That's why Formula Ford was so good for so long," he notes.

"One-design formulae, he goes on, "are a much more difficult proposition than people think: Obviously, you don't sell a new design every year. And, while the parts business looks attractive from the outside, every year the pirates get more brave."

Van Diemen was one of the first to unveil a Ford Zeta 1800cc-powered machine in '92, and is corporately quite optimistic about FF's future. This is noteworthy, because surely no one has played a more significant part in shaping the 1600cc formula's past than Ralph Firman, and no other manufacturer more important overall to its global success than Firman's company, Van Diemen.

Governor Anthony van Diemen would be proud.

Similarities to the Swift were obvious in the RF85.

The RF87 got advanced pushrod front suspension.

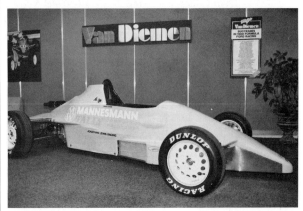

The sleek and slippery RF89.

RF90 FF shares the auto show stand with an FRen.

Vista (GB)

An *Autosport* ad in the Jan. 27, 1972, issue touts the first FF produced by the Asquith Brothers (Engineering) Ltd. of Dewesbury, Yorkshire. It was called the Vista (which apparently stood for 'Victory In Seventy Two Assured') and type-numbered "111."

Weber State (USA)

Project manger Jeffrey Hess and several of his fellow students at Weber State College in Ogden, Utah, presented a 90 percent complete FF machine to the school of engineering at the end of May, 1991. It was designed and built—from scratch—entirely by college students and was anything but a cobbled-together homebrew, featuring complex pushrod front and rear suspension and a simple, handsome fiberglass body.

Wiet (GB)

Sometimes called Chinells after the shop where they were produced, the Wiet W16/83 FFs were designed by then-28-year-old Dutchman Wiet Huidekoper, an ex-Fokker engineer who had been Jan Lammers' mechanic in FF. The prototype was first shown at the '82 FF Festival and Chris Ringrose showed well in '83, but only two cars were built before the obviously skilled Huidekoper was snatched up by first Royale (for assistance in reworking the RP33) and then Reynard (to design its '85 FF1600 and 2000 range).

Wimhurst (GB)

In between designing FFs for Palliser's Hugh Dibley and Nomad's Mark Konig and Ian Heath, and building FFs for McGregor's Kees van der Grint, ex-Brabham and -Lola designer Len Wimhurst built a few FFs in the middle '70s which bore his own name.

Winkelmann (GB)

See Nomad and Palliser.

Wren (AUS)

Australian Bill Reynolds, based in Melbourne, began producing a Formula Ford car in 1969. Four examples had reportedly been made by early 1970.

Xpit (CDN)

The Xpit (pronouced "Speet") was a low-volume FF produced in Ontario, Canada, by Siegrist Enterprises, a Formula 4 chassis specialist. The designer of the wedge-shaped, side radiator-equipped, mid-'70s Xpit Mk6 FF was Eric Siegrist, who previously produced the Kelly Vees and Sadler Formula Juniors.

Autosport ad for the VISTA in '72.

Tidy Wiet (aka Chinell) set Huidekoper on his way ...

'76 Wimhurst FF had a Brabham and Palliser lineage.

Zegler (A)

Zeus (GB)

The first FF built by Peter and Doug Sneller was a heavily modified ex-Tom Wood Royale RP21. In 1980, they built their first Zeus ZR1/2 which remained in production for several years. In '89, the Sneller brothers built all the cars for the BRDC/John Watson Silverstone School where they were called SC1s.

Zeus ZR1 of the middle '80s.

Zink Z-10s on Dover's NASCAR oval.

Zink (USA)

Zink Manufacturing was founded in Charlotte, N.C., by Ed Zink, an extremely practical "hands-on" design engineer, and Super Vee star Harry Ingle. Builders of some of America's best Vees for many years, Zink produced its first Formula Ford—called the Z-10—in 1973. These exceptionally sturdy, well-balanced cars were produced in significant numbers through to the end of the decade, with Citation Engineering's Steve Lathrop handling sales and in-the-field development of the cars from Indiana, and production manager Steve Freeman keeping things moving back at the Charlotte factory.

In Oct. '78, Ingle sold the assets of Zink Manufacturing to Floridian Allen Weatherby who moved the company to Jacksonville. There, he drew up plans to produce a significantly revised and re-bodied Z-10 called the Mk22. This was tested by Super Vee star Tom Bagley in Florida before the start of the '79 season, but made very little impression in the very difficult FF sales arena.

Lathrop, meanwhile, went his own way, calling upon Ed Zink in designing the splendid '79 Citation-Zink Z-16. He also offered Z-16 style update kits called Z-10Cs to existing Z-10 owners. *See Citation.*

Nelson Ledges '76, the first FF race this book's author ever reported on. The winner? Dave Weitzenhof's Zink Z-10.

POSTSCRIPT: One of Formula Ford's greatest attractions was the battle waged among designers with markedly different priorities. (ABOVE) Volume-manufactured John Crossle/Leslie Drysdale-penned Crossle 30F (Marty Loft) vs. limited production David Bruns-designed ADF (Tom Wiechmann). (BELOW) Mighty Van Diemen (Michael Roe) tries to fend off upstart PRS (Bernard Devaney). It all came out in the wash, but doing the laundry sure was fun ...

8

Drivers

Formula Ford was born a drivers' class and enjoyed a long, healthy life as a drivers' class—a thesis that strikes an odd chord coming as it does right after a 60-some-odd page chapter detailing FF chassis in a book entitled *Anatomy and Development of Formula Ford Race Cars*. But there is no doubt: The drivers who participated in FF racing over the last 25 years—and there have been thousands—are the bottom line in the FF story.

The formula's myriad of technical details, after all, were but foils for the talents of the many great drivers who passed right on through, driven by desire, determination and ego, leaving memories for the rest of us to sort and catalog and worry about.

With Formula Ford around for a quarter-century now, several generations of racing car drivers have gone through, and it is a common thread in an otherwise wildly diverse collection of backgrounds. For instance: Indy Car team owner Floyd "Chip" Ganassi and World Champion F1 driver Ayrton Senna have little in common as racing personalities. But they reached FF1600 at about the same time, and their determination was similarly awesome (Chip's wrapped with a little more warmth than the portrait of Senna painted by the journalists who spent time with the intense young Brazilian at the start of his career).

Senna and Ganassi were terrific FF drivers who passed right through, Ayrton en route to the F1 World Championship, Chip on his way to becoming an Indy Car team owner. Today they have little in common but, as fiercely determined, winning FF drivers, they are bound together in the motor sports fabric.

For years—before it became as ridiculously expensive as all the other entry level racing classes—For-mula Ford people were so *interesting*: Young drivers, designers, and mechanics, not yet hardened or cynical; and not yet bored by media people asking the same questions over and over. Idealistic, even naive. Hopeful. Enthusiastic. (All except the engine tuners who had in common the fact they were all old at a very young age!)

As a winnowing-out battleground from which only a few dreams ever survived, FF racing was harshly demanding of individuals. There was always a lot of pushing and leaning and blocking, much of it with serious consequences. Which makes the number of enduring friendships that began here quite astounding.

On the pages that follow is a glimpse at some of the best talent Formula Ford racing turned up over the past 25 years: Not a complete list, but a reasonable selection of drivers who realized their dreams of Formula 1 or Indy Car racing. These are the chosen from among the herd—the deserving and lucky few who finally escaped the wings to appear on center stage.

The drivers in this photo gallery are by no means the only stars to emerge from FF1600. But they are the really good ones who got us all talking.

Two of the greatest champions to emerge from the FF1600 ranks: (LEFT, ABOVE) Ayrton Senna raced a Van Diemen RF81 in 1981; (LEFT) Emerson Fittipaldi ran a Merlyn Mk11A—briefly—in 1969.

You are invulnerable

Formula Ford launched a new, aggressive style of American (race car) driving—a way of thinking that seems to overcome even the most rational of men when they get behind the wheel. It goes something like this:

1. You are invulnerable once strapped inside your 930 lb. racer.
2. If you win the race, Colin Chapman will immediately select you for a Formula 1 drive.
3. Anything goes on the first lap.
4. If the car feels stable, you're not going fast enough.
5. If you can get your nose inside him, you can pass him.
6. Anything goes on the last lap.

     - **Tom Davey**, *SportsCar* magazine, Oct. '78

Fast cousin (son of Mario's brother Aldo) John Andretti.

Michael Andretti: Skip Barber School to Indy to Monaco.

No brakes! Michael A. off-roading at Summit Point.

A younger Andretti, Jeff.

'85 champ Scott Atchison.

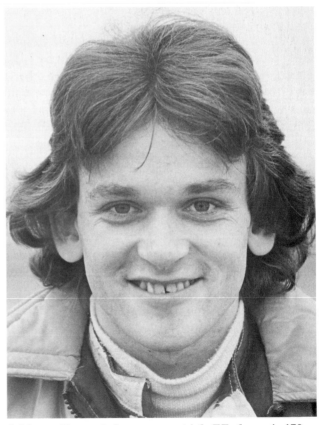

Irishman Kenny Acheson was a triple FF champ in '78.

Julian Bailey's star potential showed in early '80s FF.

The first American FF champ, Skip Barber.

(FAR LEFT) '80s FF star Julian Bailey. (LEFT) '60s FF star Skip Barber.

'82-'84 FF standout Eric Bachelart.

Modern JRRDS star Jon Beekhuis.

The late Stefan Bellof, an FF grad.

'80 RAC British champ Raul Boesel.

Claude Bourgoignie—first FF star?

Geoff Brabham did an FF stint.

Mark Blundell: '84 rookie became '85 Esso FF champion became F1 regular.

Future F1 star Thierry Boutsen was part of the Continental FF crowd in '80.

The great Tony Brise was killed in an airplane crash.

World class inspiration: Brise and mentor Graham Hill.

Tony Brise at speed in his '71 Elden PH8.

Indy regular Scott Brayton.

Irish star Tommy Byrne.

Martin Brundle skipped FF1600 but raced FF2000.

California ex-FF racer Kevin Cogan.

Eddie Cheever's FF stay was brief.

Jim Crawford once raced an Alexis.

Derek Daly, a mid '70s FF star who rose rapidly to F1.

Irish ace Martin Donnelly, Crossle-mounted in '81.

Indy Car man Dominic Dobson.

The great Emerson Fittipaldi, who contributed so much to FF folklore.

"Double Egg" Eje Elgh.

Divina Galica raced an FF.

Works Palliser FF driver Bob Evans.

Dennis Firestone: SoCal FF star gone to Indy.

SCCA star Chip Ganassi.

Bertrand Gachot shot to prominence in '85, winning the RAC British FF title.   *Indy polewinner Roberto Guerrero.*

Canadian Indy Car star Scott Goodyear paid his FF dues.   *Mauricio Gugelmin followed Senna as RAC British champ.*

A smiling Mika Hakkinen in '89.

Dean Hall starred in FF before graduating to Indy Cars.

Damon Hill (at left) storms off the line at Brands.

FF to F1, the brave Johnny Herbert has seen it all.

Damon Hill: works Williams-Renault F1 driver in '93.

James Hunt: leased Russell-Alexis to World Champion!

Stefan Johannson stopped at FF on his rapid rise to F1.

Pete Halsmer.

Howdy Holmes.

Even for the elite, the climb to the top can be treacherous.

Davy Jones debuted with a PRS in his mid teens.

Rupert Keegan's dad bought Hawke.

Mid-'70s FF star David Kennedy.

Phil Krueger finally escaped FF.

Geoff Lees won the top three British FF series in '75.

Brilliant Finn J.J. Lehto rose to prominence in FF.

Before he was "J.J.," he was FF hopeful Jyrki Jarvilehto, a young Finn trying to carve out a name for himself in a Van Diemen.

Dutchman Jan Lammers.

Arie Luyendyk in the '70s.

Flying Dutchmen: Jan Lammers and Arie Luijenduijk (who Americanized his surname).

Nigel Mansell: In '77, a World Champ in the making.

Mansell '77: (ABOVE) Javelin; (BELOW) Crossle 32F.

Brazilian Roberto Moreno was terrific in British FF, racing for Van Diemen and (BELOW) Royale.

Dr. Jonathan Palmer, prominent in British FF for years.

Hiro Matsushita's Swift was a familiar SoCal sight.

Stars of three different generations of American FF racing (L to R): Eddie Miller, John Paul Jr., and Hiro Matsushita.

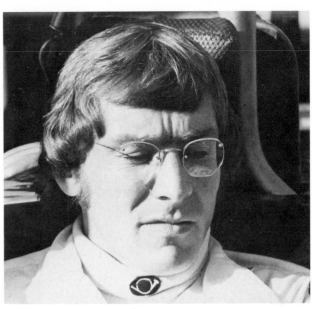

Aussie FF star Larry Perkins raced a Brabham in F1.

Tom Pryce gained stardom in FF, lost his life in F1.

Lola driver Tom Pryce was a '71 British FF frontrunner.

SCCA NEDiv sensation Ed Pimm.

Ted Prappas raced Jim Russell FFs.

Mexican FF ace Hector Rebaque.

Willy T. Ribbs was the '77 Star of Tomorrow champ.

Sideways Swede Bertil Roos.   *Huub Rothengatter.*   *Jody Scheckter shot through FF to GP-racing stardom.*

Tim Schenken was FF racing's first champion in '68.   *The brilliant Michael Schumacher was discovered in FF.*

Danny Sullivan: An Indy Car racing star with FF roots.

Ayrton Senna was a Van Diemen FF hotshoe in '81.

Senna made short work of Formula Ford ...

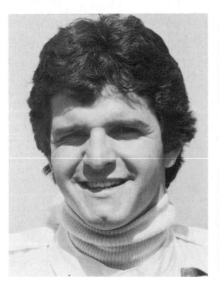

Chico Serra: another fast Brazilian.

The late Gordon Smiley, '70s hero.

Kiwi Mike Thackwell made an impact.

Teenaged Paul Tracy was the '85 Canadian champ.

Belgian Didier Theys now races Indy Cars.

Belgian Eric van de Poele.

American Dennis Vitolo.

FF champ Jim Vasser Jr.'s career holds much promise.

Vitolo tries FF1600's big brother FF2000 at Snetterton.

The late, great Gilles Villeneuve spent little time in FF.

Gilles' younger brother, Jacques..

Dave Walker: works Lotus FF to works Lotus F1.

(LEFT & BELOW) Van Diemen driver Andy Wallace would emerge a sports car racing hero.

Englishman Derek Warwick was in FF's mid '70s elite.

Karl Wendlinger rose rapidly through the ranks.

James Weaver was sideways sensational in FF!

South African lady FF racing star Desire Wilson.

... And other big names

Senna argues a point with Toleman F2 and F1 designer Rory Byrne, the South African who penned Royale's RP21 and 24.

The brilliant Adrian Reynard chats pre-race with FF driver-at-the-time James Weaver.

Van Diemen's proprietor Ralph Firman, a tremendous FF enthusiast.

The designer of all Van Diemen FFs since '76, Dave Baldwin.

The great F1 designer Patrick Head played a part in FF via the Delta.

Veteran U.S. Van Diemen/ Tiga importer Mike Gue.

Journalist Jeremy Shaw reviews Elden history with the English firm's founders, Peter and Brian Hampsheir.

Gary Anderson: Anson FF to Benetton F1.

Tiga's Howden Ganley was one of the best engineers ever in FF.

Royale's boss for well over a decade, Alan Cornock today runs Fulmar.

Clive Hayward, one of the Merlyn principals, still hard at work in '92.

Skip Barber (talking to '80s student John Andretti) is now America's most famous race driving instructor.

Citation Engineering wizard Steve Lathrop (at left) with Dave and Sherrie Weitzenhof.

(LEFT) Hawke's David Lazenby, with the late Jim Clark in '63 and (ABOVE) with wife Jane in '92.

9

Champions

The roster of champions that follows, like this book itself, focuses on FF1600 racing in two countries, the U.S. and United Kingdom, which combine to represent about 80 percent of the formula's history. There was a time in the planning stages of this minor tome that the author fantacized about offering the world's most comprehensive list of Formula Ford 1600 Championship results—no less than a *complete* list of series champions plus at minimum the names of the top three finishers.

But as with racing, dreams sometimes take a back seat to reality. Space became a primary consideration. And results were a lot harder to come by than anticipated: Various clashes and back-biting between organizing groups in Canada, for instance, meant no one would provide a list! And the successful EFDA is now so entrenched with Vauxhall, apparently, that supplying a list of its FF champions was too low on its priority list to get done—even an old acquaintanceship with Dan Partel failed to get this scribe past his assistant.

The author continues to dream.

Meanwhile, there are hundreds of names to celebrate in the list of championships conducted since 1967 in just the two countries noted. Celebrate we shall.

For much of the information contained in the pages that follow, the author is indebted to Jeremy Shaw: On the hard disk of this fine journalist's computer lives a veritable mound of motor racing statistics.

Additional info was gleaned from several sources including Nick Brittan's excellent *The Formula Ford Book*. Special thanks to *Autosport*'s Marcus Pye and to both Bill King and archivist Harry Handley of the SCCA. May all find this list useful.

(LEFT, ABOVE) Enrique Mansilla and Ayrton Senna duel at Mallory Park in 1981. (LEFT) The great American FF champion Bruce MacInnes in '76, Ted Wenz pushing and Seymour at the controls.

Enduring American FF champion Dave Weitzenhof.

Raul Boesel in '81.

The late, great Ian Taylor.

Formula Ford fun in England: Rupert Keegan hangs it out in a Hawke.

United Kingdom

First Formula Ford Race: Brands Hatch, July 2, 1967

1968	Guards FF Championship	Tim Schenken	Merlyn Mk11/11A
1968	King's Cup Scottish FF Ch.	Dave Walker	Russell-Alexis 14
1968	Lotus FF Championship	Bob Ellice	Lotus 51A
1969	Les Leston FF Championship	Dave Walker	Lotus 61
1969	Guards FF Championship	Bryan Sharp	Merlyn Mk11/11A
1969	Tate of Leeds FF Ch.	Ken Bailey	Alexis Mk15
1969	King's Cup Scottish FF Ch.	Tom Walkinshaw	Hawke DL2
1969	Irish FF Championship	Craw. Harkness	Lotus 61
1970	Les Leston FF Championship	Colin Vandervell	Merlyn, Crossle
1970	Townsend Thoresen FF Ch.	Bob Evans	Palliser WDF2
1970	Guards FF Championship	Peter Lamplough	Palliser WDF2
1970	Tate of Leeds FF Championship	Derek Lawrence	Titan Mk6
1970	Town. Thor. Castle Combe FF	Andy Rouse	Dulon LD4C/LD9
1970	King's Cup Scottish FF Ch.	Damien Magee	Crossle 16F
1970	Scottish FF Championship	Graham Cuthbert	Lotus 69
1971	BOC FF Championship	Bernard Vermilio	Merlyn Mk20
1971	Townsend Thoresen FF Ch.	Tony Brise	Elden, Merlyn
1971	Town. Thor. Castle Combe FF	M. Campbell-Cole	Merlyn Mk11A
1971	Tate of Leeds FF Championship	Ken Bailey	Titan Mk6
1971	King's Cup Scottish FF Ch.	Neil Ginn	Lotus 69F
1972	BOC FF Championship	Ian Taylor	Dulon LD9
1972	*Daily Express* FF Championship	Ian Taylor	Dulon LD9
1972	Sunbeam Electric FF Ch.	Syd Fox	Hawke DL9/DL10
1972	Townsend Thoresen FF Ch.	Bob Arnott	Merlyn Mk20
1972	BRSCC (SW) Centre FF Ch.	Buzz Buzaglo	Elden Mk8/Mk10
1972	Tate of Leeds FF Championship	Ken Bailey	Titan Mk6
1972	Scottish FF Championship	Don MacLeod	Dulon LD9
1972	Irish FF Championship	Jay Pollock	Crossle 20F
1973	BOC Golden Helmet FF Ch.	Donald MacLeod	Merlyn, Van Diem.
1973	STP FF Championship	Derek Lawrence	Dulon Mp15
1973	Wella for Men FF Championship	Ted Wentz	Elden PH10/10B
1973	Townsend Thoresen FF Champ.	Frank Hopper	Royale RP16
1973	TEAC FF Championship	Peter White	Palliser WDF2
1973	BRSCC (SW) Centre FF Champ.	Clive Power	Dulon Mp15
1973	Nor. Clubs FF Ch./Tate Trophy	Peter Harrington	Cougar 73F
1973	Rothmans Scottish FF Champ.	Graham Cuthbert	Lotus , Van Diem.
1974	Wella for Men FF Champ.	Richard Morgan	Ray, Royale, Cros.
1974	BOC Golden Helmet FF Ch.	Syd Fox	Hawke DL11
1974	STP FF Championship	Patrick Neve	Lola T-340
1974	Townsend Thoresen FF Champ.	Roy Klomfass	Hawke DL11
1974	BRSCC (SW) Centre FF Champ.	Roger Orgee	Dulon Mp15
1974	TEAC FF Championship	Don Smith	Merlyn Mk20A
1974	Tate of Leeds FF Championship	Pete Clark	Crossle 25F
1974	BARC (Yorks) Centre FF Ch.	Mick Starkey	Merlyn Mk20A
1974	Scottish FF Championship	Kenny Gray	Van Diemen RF74
1975	National Organs FF1600 Ch.	Geoff Lees	Royale RP21
1975	Brush Fusegear FF1600 Ch.	Geoff Lees	Royale RP21
1975	British Air Ferries FF1600 Ch.	Geoff Lees	Royale RP21
1975	Townsend Thoresen FF1600 Ch.	Tiff Needell	Crossle 25F
1975	BRSCC (SW) Centre FF Ch.	Terry Richards	Merlyn Mk11A
1975	Tate of Leeds FF Championship	Kelvin Hesketh	Crossle 30F
1975	BARC (Yorks) Centre FF Ch.	Mick Starkey	Merlyn Mk20A
1976	B. Hunter Crane Hire Scottish FF	Stuart Lawson	Hawke DL12
1975	Welsh FF Championship	Tony Broster	Dulon Mp15
1975	ShellSPORT Irish FF Champ.	Derek Daly	Crossle 30F
1975	Northern Ireland FF Champ.	Trevor Templeton	Lotus 69F
1976	RAC FF1600 Championship	David Kennedy	Crossle 30F
1976	Townsend Thoresen FF1600 Ch.	David Kennedy	Crossle 3F
1976	Brush Fusegear FF1600 Champ.	Jim Walsh	Royale RP21
1976	DJM Records FF1600 Champ.	Rod Bremner	Crossle 30F
1976	Dunlop 'Star of Tomorrow'	Sean Walker	Royale RP21
1976	TEAC FF1600 Championship	Tony Halliwell	Merlyn Mk11A
1976	Tate Trophy for FF1600	Peter Harrington	Lotus 69F
1976	BRSCC (SW) Centre FF1600	David Toye	Royale RP21
1976	BARC Northern FF1600 Champ.	Mick Starkey	Merlyn Mk20A
1976	Marchant & Cox FF1600 Champ.	Tony Halliwell	Merlyn Mk11A
1976	Scottish FF1600 Championship	Stuart Lawson	Hawke DL15
1976	Bannville House N. Ireland FF	Trevor Templeton	Crossle 30F
1977	RAC FF1600 Championship	Trevor van Rooyen	Royale RP24
1977	Townsend Thoresen FF1600	Chico Serra	Van Diemen RF77
1977	Brush Fusegear FF1600 Champ.	Nigel Mansell	Javelin, Crossle
1977	BARC FF1600 Championship	David Leslie	Royale RP24
1977	Dunlop 'Star of Tomorrow'	Willy T. Ribbs	Royale 16A/21/24
1977	Kent Messenger FF1600 Champ.	Tony Halliwell	Hawke, Cross.,V D
1977	BRSCC (N) Centre/Tate Trophy	Cameron Binnie	Royale RP21
1977	BARC Northern FF1600 Champ.	Cameron Binnie	Royale RP21
1977	NSCC N. Eng./Coaker Trophy	Mick Starkey	Merlyn Mk20A
1977	Lydden/Marchant & Cox Trophy	Paul Sleeman	Crossle 25F
1977	TEAC FF1600 Championship	Paul Sleeman	Crossle,Rostron
1977	BRSCC (SW) Centre FF1600	David Wheeler	Royale RP21A
1977	Longridge FF1600 Championship	Alan Stringer	Crossle 30F
1977	Edinburgh Flying Srvc. Scottish	Stuart Lawson	Hawke DL17
1977	Castrol Irish FF1600 Champ.	Joey Greenan	Royale RP24
1977	J.E. Coulter N. Ireland FF Trophy	Kenneth Acheson	Crossle 32F
1978	RAC British FF1600 Champ.	Kenneth Acheson	Royale RP24
1978	Townsend Thoresen FF1600 Ch.	Kenneth Acheson	Royale RP24
1978	Esso FF1600 Championship	Peter Morgan	Lola T-540
1978	Philips Car Radio FF1600 Champ.	Kenneth Acheson	Royale RP24/26
1978	Dunlop 'Star of Tomorrow' FF1600	Rob Zurrer	Crossle, PRS
1978	Kent Messenger FF1600 Champ.	Terry Gray	Royale RP21/24

The fury of a Formula Ford could always be counted upon to get spectators on their feet!

1978	BRSCC Northern Centre FF1600	Cameron Binnie	Van Diemen RF78
1978	BARC Northern FF1600 Champ.	Dave Manners	Hawke DL19
1978	NSCC N. of Eng./Coaker Trophy	Bernard Hunter	Van Diemen RF78
1978	Kirby's of Louth Cadwell FF1600	Dave Manners	Hawke, PRS
1978	Marchant & Cox Lydden Hill FF	Paul Sleeman	Rostron CT78
1978	BRSCC (SW) Centre FF1600	Mike Wallaker	Jomic
1978	Longridge Challenge for FF1600	Alan Stringer	Crossle 30F
1978	Canonmills Tyre Centre Scottish	Cameron Binnie	Van Diemen RF78
1978	Texaco N. Ireland FF1600 Champ.	Colin Lees	Crossle 32F
1979	RAC British FF1600 Championship	David Sears	Royale RP26
1979	Townsend Thoresen FF1600	Terry Gray	Van Diemen RF79
1979	Esso FF1600 Championship	Jim Walsh	Royale RP26
1979	P&O Normandy Ferries FF1600	David Sears	Royale RP26
1979	Dunlop 'Star of Tomorrow' FF	Guy Dormehl	Van Diemen RF79
1979	Kent Messenger FF1600 Champ.	David Griffin	Van Diemen RF79
1979	Ross & Haines BRSCC (SW) FF	Geoffrey Davies	Crossle 32F
1979	BRSCC Northern Centre FF1600	Rick Whyman	Royale RP26
1979	Kirby's of Louth N. of Eng. FF	Dave Manners	PRS RH01
1979	Marchant & Cox Trophy for FF	Wil Arif	Crossle 35F
1979	Shell Scottish FF1600 Champ.	Stuart Lawson	PRS RH01
1979	Wilkes Business Forms FF1600	Tony Trevor	PRS RH01/RH02
1979	Carlton & Bullen Pre-'74 FF1600	Simon Davey	Dulon Mp15
1979	Irish Nationwide FF1600 Champ.	Arnie Black	Crossle 32F
1979	Northern Ireland FF1600 Champ.	Arnie Black	Crossle 32F
1980	RAC British FF1600 Championship	Tommy Byrne	Van Diemen RF80
1980	Townsend Thoresen FF1600	Roberto Moreno	Van Diemen RF80
1980	Esso FF1600 Championship	Jim Walsh	Royale RP26
1980	P&O Ferries FF1600 Champ.	Tommy Byrne	Van Diemen RF80
1980	Dunlop 'Star of Tomorrow' FF	Tim Lee-Davey	Tiga FF79
1980	Kentagon Championship for FF	Peter Argetsinger	Royale RP26
1980	Cars & Car Conversions FF1600	John Booth	Van Diemen RF80
1980	Laidlaws of Edinburgh N. British	Keith Wickham	Van Diemen RF79
1980	Wilkes Business Forms FF	Glenn Bosch	McGregor FF1
1980	Bernard Hunter Crane Hire FF	Eric Horsfield	Tiga FF79
1980	Earle of Chip'ham Castle Combe	Steve Lincoln	Royale RP26
1980	Shell Scottish Championship	Tom Brown	Van Diemen
1980	Marchant & Cox FF1600 Champ.	Trevor Stiles	Ray 80F
1980	All-Irish FF1600 Challenge	Maurice Dunn	Van Diemen RF79
1980	Northern Ireland FF1600 Champ.	Colin Lees	Crossle 40F
1980	Pre-'74 FF1600 Championship	Andy Wallace	Hawke DL11
1981	RAC British FF1600 Championship	Ayrton Senna	Van Diemen RF81
1981	Townsend Thoresen FF1600	Ayrton Senna	Van Diemen RF81
1981	P&O Ferries FF1600 Champ.	Enrique Mansilla	Van Diemen RF81
1981	Esso FF1600 Championship	John Village	Royale RP29
1981	Dunlop-Autosport 'Star of Tom'row'	Phil Kempe	Royale RP26
1981	BARC Junior FF1600 Champ.	Mark Peters	Lola T-540E
1981	Cars & Car Conversions FF1600	Tom Wood	Van Diemen RF81
1981	Kentagon FF1600 Championship	Robert Gibbs	Van Diemen RF81
1981	Bernard Hunter Crane Hire FF	Walter Warwick	Van Diem., Reynard

1981	Earle of Chippenham FF1600	Bob Higgins	Martlet DM3/4
1981	Marchant & Cox FF1600 Champ.	John Oxborrow	Ray 80F
1981	Wilkes Business Forms FF1600	Greg Atkinson	Royale, Agent
1981	Shell Super Oil Scottish FF1600	Tom Brown	Van Diemen
1981	Pre-'74 FF1600 Championship	Simon Davey	Dulon Mp15
1981	Irish Nationwide FF1600 Champ.	Pat Duffy	Van Diemen RF81
1982	RAC British FF1600 Championship	Mauricio Gugelmin	Van Dlemen RF82
1982	Townsend Thoresen FF1600	Julian Bailey	Lola, Van Diemen
1982	Esso FF1600 Championship	Rick Morris	Royale RP31M
1982	P&O Ferries FF1600 Champ.	Gianfranco Cane	Van Diemen RF82
1982	Dunlop-Autosport 'Star of Tom'row'	John Penfold	Van Diemen RF81
1982	BP 'Superfind' Junior FF1600	Mark Newby	Royale, Van Diem.
1982	Bernard Hunter Crane Hire FF	Walter Warwick	Reynard FF82
1982	Birmingham Post & Mail FF1600	Mark Peters	Royale, Lola
1982	'Champion of Brands' FF1600	Andy Ackerley	Ray 81/82F
1982	'Champion of Mallory' FF1600	Don Hardman	Royale RP26/31M
1982	'Champion of Oulton' FF1600	Richard Peacock	Crossle 25F/50F
1982	'Champion of Snetterton' FF1600	Simon Davey	Van Diem. RF78/79
1982	Castle Combe FF1600 Champ.	Bob Higgins	Martlet DM4
1982	Marchant & Cox FF1600 Champ.	Colin Stancombe	Royale RP26
1982	750 Motor Club FF1600 Series	John Bosch	Van Diemen RF82
1982	Marlboro Scottish FF1600 Champ.	Tom Brown	Van Diemen RF80
1982	Irish Nationwide FF1600 Champ.		
1982	Pre-'74 FF1600 Championship	Steve Bradley	Van Diemen FA73
1983	RAC British FF1600 Championship	A. Gilbert-Scott	Lola T-642E
1983	Townsend Thoresen FF1600	A. Gilbert-Scott	Lola T-642E
1983	Esso FF1600 Championship	M. Sandro Sala	Van Diem., Reynard
1983	P&O Ferries FF1600 Champ.	Peter Hardman	Van Diemen RF83
1983	Dunlop-Autosport 'Star of Tom'row'	Perry McCarthy	Van Diemen RF83
1983	BP 'Superfind' Junior FF1600	Graham de Zille	Lola T-642E
1983	Bernard Hunter Crane Hire FF	John Booth	Van Diemen RF83
1983	Birmingham Post & Mail FF1600	John Booth	Van Diemen RF83
1983	John Player 'Champion of Brands'	Karl Jones	Ray 80F/82F
1983	'Champion of Oulton' FF1600	John Booth	Van Diemen RF83
1983	'Champion of Snetterton' FF1600	Simon Davey	Van Diemen RF81
1983	Castle Combe FF1600 Champ.	Bob Higgins	Royale RP29A
1983	Marchant & Cox FF1600 Champ.	Paul Sleeman	Rostron, PRS
1983	750 Motor Club FF1600 Challenge	Alex Postan	Van Diemen, Ray
1983	Marlboro Scottish FF1600 Champ.	Tom Brown	Van Diemen, Rotor
1983	Hubert Mitchell Scottish Junior FF	Cliff Harper	Hawke DL15
1983	Irish Nationwide FF1600 Champ.	Anthony Murray	Crossle 40F
1983	STP Northern Ireland FF1600	Anthony Murray	Crossle 40F
1983	Pre-'74 FF1600 Championship	Paul Sleeman	Rostron CT3
1984	RAC British FF1600 Championship	Dave Coyne	Van Diemen RF84
1984	Townsend Thoresen FF1600	Dave Coyne	Van Diemen RF84
1984	Esso FF1600 Championship	Alvaro Buzaid	Reynard 84FF
1984	P&O Ferries FF1600 Champ.	Pete Townsend	Lola, Reynard
1984	Dunlop-Autosport 'Star of Tom'row'	Jonathan Bancroft	Van Diem., Rey.
1984	BP 'Superfind' Junior FF1600	Jonathan Bancroft	Van Diem., Rey.

*John Village (Van Diemen)
and Dr. Jonathan Palmer
(Hawke) spar in '78.*

United Kingdom (cont.)

1984	Bernard Hunter Crane Hire FF	John Booth	Van Diemen RF84
1984	John Player Spl 'Champ of Brands'	Chris Ringrose	Ray 80/82F
1984	'Champion of Oulton' FF1600	John Booth	Van Diem., Rey.
1984	'Champion of Snetterton' FF1600	Mark Blundell	Lola, Van Diemen
1984	'Star of Mallory' FF1600 Series	Don Hardman	Royale RP36
1984	Castle Combe FF1600 Champ.	Martin Cooper	Royale, Reynard
1984	Towerton Garage Lydden FF1600	Dennis Humphries	Van Diemen RF80
1984	750 Motor Club FF1600 Series	Nick Owen	Van Dlemen RF82
1984	Scottish FF1600 Championship	Tom Brown	Crossle 55F
1984	Ford of Ireland FF1600 Champ.	Vivion Daly	Reynard 84FF
1984	Motorvox Irish FF1600 Champ.	Vivion Daly	Reynard 84FF
1984	BARC 1974-1978 FF1600 Series	John Wardle	PRS RH01
1984	Pre-'74 FF1600 Championship	Jeff Gresswell	Merlyn Mk24S
1985	RAC British FF1600 Championship	Bertrand Gachot	Van Diemen RF85
1985	Esso FF1600 Championship	Mark Blundell	Van Diemen RF85
1985	Dunlop-*Autosport* 'Star of Tom'row'	Jason Elliott	Van Diemen RF85
1985	Townsend Thoresen Junior FF	Adrian Willmott	Van Diemen RF85
1985	John Player Spl 'Champ of Brands'	Colin Stancombe	Lola T-640/642E
1985	'Champion of Oulton' FF1600	Chris Latham	Reynard 84FF
1985	'Champion of Snetterton' FF1600	Simon Davey	Van Diemen RF82
1985	Unigas 'Star of Mallory' FF1600	Richard Dean	Reynard, Van D.
1985	Steve Llewellyn Castle Combe FF	Howard Lester	Reynard 83FF
1985	Bernard Hunter Crane Hire FF1600	Don Hardman	Royale RP36
1985	750 Motor Club FF1600 Series	Antonio Armelin	Reynard
1985	Lydden Hill FF1600 Championship	Steve Brown	PRS 81F
1985	Pre-'74 FF1600 Championship	Bob Berridge	Lotus 69
1985	BARC 1974-1978 FF1600 Series	Jeff Gresswell	Merlyn Mk29
1985	Formula E Championship	Alister Lane	Van Diemen RF80
1985	Scottish FF1600 Championship	Cameron Binnie	Van Diemen
1986	RAC Townsend Thoresen British	Jason Elliott	Van Diemen RF86
1986	Esso FF1600 Championship	Jason Elliott	Van Diemen RF86
1986	Dunlop-*Autosport* 'Star of Tom'row'	Paul Warwick	Van Diemen RF86
1986	Townsend Thoresen Junior FF	Paul Warwick	Van Diemen RF86
1986	John Player Spl 'Champ of Brands'	Len Bull	Van Diemen 84/86
1986	'Champion of Oulton' FF1600	Scott Stringfellow	Van Diemen RF86
1986	'Champion of Snetterton' FF1600	Marcus Koch	Van Diemen RF84
1986	Unigas 'Star of Mallory' FF1600	Scott Stringfellow	Van Diemen RF86
1986	Steve Llewellyn Castle Combe FF	Robert Davies	Van Diemen RF84
1986	Lydden Hill FF1600 Championship	Derek Pullman	Van Diemen RF80
1986	Donington FF1600 Championship	John Booth	Van Diemen RF86
1986	Bernard Hunter Crane Hire FF1600	Bob Berridge	Reynard 84FF
1986	750 Motor Club FF1600 Series	Derek Pullman	Van Diemen RF80
1986	London Motor Fleet Formula E	Richard Peacock	Crossle 30F
1986	Shell Oils '74-'78 FF1600 Series	Douglas League	Van Diemen RF78
1986	DAF Trucks Pre-'74 FF1600	Chris Whittingham	Dulopn Mp15
1986	Scottish FF1600 Championship	Cameron Binnie	Van Diemen

1987	RAC Owen Brown British FF1600	Eddie Irvine	Van Diemen RF87
1987	Esso FF1600 Championship	Eddie Irvine	Van Diemen RF87
1987	Dunlop-*Autosport* 'Star of Tom'row'	Derek Higgins	Ray, Van Diemen
1987	Townsend Thoresen Junior FF	Derek Higgins	Ray, Van Diemen
1987	P&O Ferries 'Champion of Brands'	A. Guye-Johnson	Quest FF87
1987	P&O Ferries 'Champion of Oulton'	Miles Johnston	Van Diemen RF87
1987	P&O Ferries 'Champ of Snetterton'	Luis Cruz	Van Diemen RF87
1987	Unigas 'Star of Mallory' FF1600	Tim Sugden	Van Diemen RF87
1987	Bernard Hunter Crane Hire FF1600	Colin Verity	Van Diemen RF82
1987	Castle Combe FF1600 Champ.	David Llewellyn	Van Diemen RF86
1987	Lydden Hill FF1600 Championship	Derek Pullman	Van Diemen RF80
1987	London Motor Fleet Formula E	Nick Hammerton	Van Diemen RF80
1987	Shell Oils '74-'78 FF1600 Series	Mike Gardner	Van Diemen RF78
1987	DAF Trucks Pre-'74 FF1600	David Porter	Elden Mk10C
1987	Scottish FF1600 Championship	Harvey Gillanders	Van Diemen
1987	STP Northern Irish Championship	Jonathan McGall	Mondiale M87S
1987	Motorvox Irish FF1600 Champ.	Bernard Dolan	Mondiale M87S
1988	RAC British FF1600 Championship	Derek Higgins	Van Diemen RF88
1988	Esso FF1600 Championship	Derek Higgins	Van Diemen RF88
1988	Dunlop-*Autosport* 'Star of Tom'row'	Kurt Luby	Van Diemen RF88
1988	P&O European Ferries Junior FF	Kurt Luby	Van Diemen RF88
1988	P&O Ferries 'Champion of Brands'	Chris Creswell	Van Diemen RF88
1988	P&O Ferries 'Champion of Oulton'	Chris Creswell	Van Diemen RF88
1988	P&O Ferries 'Champion of Cadwell'	Bob Bailey	Van Diemen RF87
1988	P&O Ferries 'Champ of Snetterton'	Mark Woodweiss	Van Diemen RF88
1988	Everyman 'Star of Mallory' FF1600	Stuart Kestenbaum	Reynard 87FF
1988	RG Racewear Castle Combe FF	Gavin Wlls	Van Diemen RF86
1988	Lydden Hill FF1600 Championship	Chris Pullman	Quest FF86
1988	Lond. Mtr. Fleet/*Mot. News* For. E	Peter Eccleston	Crossle 25F
1988	Minister Racing Eng. Pre-'85 FF	Steve Parker	Van Diemen RF84
1988	Intercon Computers '74-'78 FF	John Wardle	Van Diemen RF78
1988	DAF Trucks Pre-'74 FF1600	Peter Hancock	Merlyn Mk20A/25H
1988	Scottish FF1600 Championship	Cameron Binnie	Van Diemen RF86
1988	Irish FF1600 Championship	Vivion Daly	Reynard 88FF
1989	LuK RAC British FF1600 Champ.	Bernard Dolan	Reynard 89FF
1989	Esso FF1600 Championship	Niko Palhares	Van Diemen RF89
1989	Dunlop-*Autosport* 'Star of Tom'row'	David Coulthard	Van Diemen RF89
1989	P&O European Ferries Junior FF	David Coulthard	Van Diemen RF89
1989	P&O European 'Champ of Brands'	Chris Goodwin	Van Diemen RF89
1989	P&O Ferries 'Champion of Oulton'	Miles Johnston	Van Dlemen RF89
1989	P&O Ferries 'Champ of Cadwell'	Colin Verity	Swift FB4
1989	P&O Ferries 'Champ of Snetterton'	Ian McArdell	Van Diemen RF88
1989	Everyman 'Star of Mallory' FF1600	Mark Bryan	Van Diemen RF89
1989	RG Racewear Castle Combe FF	Gavin Wlls	Van Diemen RF89
1989	Lydden Hill FF1600 Championship	Chris Pullman	Quest FF86
1989	Lond. Mtr Fleet/*Mot. News* For. E	Nick Hammerton	Van Diemen RF80
1989	Minister Racing Eng. Pre-'85 FF	Andrew Colson	Ray 84F
1989	BARC '74-'78 FF1600 Series	John Wardle	Van Diemen RF78
1989	Hawk Raceware Pre-'74 FF1600	Billy Burke	Merlyn Mk20A
1989	Scottish FF1600 Championship	Colin Harper	Van Diemen

SCCA Runoffs 1980: Winner Bob Lobenberg (ADF) battles Dave Weitzenhof (Citation).

1990	LuK RAC British FF1600 Champ.	Michael Vergers	Van Diemen RF90
1990	Motorcraft FF1600 Championship	Gareth Rees	Reynard 90FF
1990	Dunlop-*Autosport* 'Star of Tom'row'	Warren Hughes	Van Diemen RF90
1990	P&O Ferries Junior FF1600	Warren Hughes	Van Diemen RF90
1990	HEAT 'Champion of Brands' FF	David Germain	Van Diem., Swift
1990	'Champion of Oulton' FF1600	Peter Kay	Reynard 90FF
1990	'Champion of Cadwell' FF1600	Colin Verity	Swift FB4
1990	HEAT 'Champion of Snetterton' FF	George Cubitt	Van DIemen RF90
1990	Everyman 'Star of Mallory' FF1600	Mark Bryan	Van Diemen RF90
1990	Square Grip Castle Combe FF	Nigel Jenkins	Reynard 89FF
1990	Lydden Hill FF1600 Championship	Peter Thurston	Jamun M89
1990	Brands Hatch FF1600 Winter Ser.	Michael Edgar	Van Diemen RF90
1990	Lond. Mtr Fleet/*Mot. News* For. E	Roger Eccleston	Crossle 25F
1990	Minister Racing Eng. Pre-'85 FF	Peter Bell	Ray 83F
1990	BARC '74-'78 FF1600 Series	Barry Pomfret	Royale RP26
1990	Hawk Racewear Pre-'74 FF1600	Bernard Horwood	Rostron CT3
1990	Scottish FF1600 Championship	Cameron Binnie	Reynard
1990	Irish FF1600 Championship		
1991	Motorcraft Open FF1600 Champ.	Marc Goossens	Van Diemen RF91
1991	Dunlop-*Autosport* 'Star of Tom'row'	Dino Morelli	Reynard 91FF
1991	HEAT 'Champion of Brands' FF	Chris Hall	Jamun M91
1991	'Champion of Oulton' FF1600	Peter Kay	Reynard 90FF
1991	'Champion of Cadwell' FF1600	Mal Davison	Reynard 91FF
1991	'Champion of Snetterton' FF1600	Carl Jarvis	Van Diemen RF91
1991	Everyman 'Star of Mallory' FF1600	Alister Lane	Van Diemen RF86
1991	Square Grip Castle Combe FF	Nigel Jenkins	Reynard 90FF
1991	BARC (L&HCC) Lydden Champ.	Len Bull	Jamun M90
1991	Brands Hatch FF Winter Series	Chris Hall	Jamun M91
1991	Dedicated Micros Formula E	Austin Kinsella	Van Diemen RF79
1991	BRSCC/Minister Pre-'85 FF1600	Steve Parker	Van Diemen RF84
1991	Midtherm Flue '74-'80 FF1600	Nigel Greensall	Royale RP26
1991	Go Ahead Van Hire Pre-'74 FF	Stuart Kestenbaum	Rostron CT3
1991	Scottish FF1600 Championship	Cameron Binnie	Reynard
1991	Irish FF1600 Championship		

United States

First Formula Ford Race: Willow Springs, March 25-26, 1969

1969	SCCA National Champion	Skip Barber	Caldwell D9
1969	SCCA Northeast Division FF	Skip Barber	Caldwell D9
1969	SCCA Southeast Division FF	Roger Chastain	Lotus 61
1969	SCCA Central Division FF	James Clark	Caldwell D9
1969	SCCA Midwest Division FF	Eddie Miller	Merlyn Mk11A
1969	SCCA Southwest Division FF	Stephen Louden	Merlyn Mk11A
1969	SCCA Southern Pacific Div. FF	Herb Brownell	Caldwell D9
1969	SCCA Northern Pacific Div. FF	Gary Johnson	Merlyn Mk11A
1970	SCCA National Champion	Skip Barber	Tecno
1970	SCCA Northeast Division FF	Roger Barr	Crossle 16F
1970	SCCA Southeast Division FF	Skip Barber	Caldwell, Tecno
1970	SCCA Central Division FF	Jim Harrell	Titan Mk6
1970	SCCA Midwest Division FF	Eddie Miller	Merlyn Mk11A
1970	SCCA Southwest Division FF	Steve Louden	Merlyn Mk11A
1970	SCCA Southern Pacific Div. FF	Ron Dykes	Lola T-200
1970	SCCA Northern Pacific Div. FF	Gary Johnson	Merlyn Mk11A
1971	SCCA National Champion	Jim Harrell	Titan Mk6A
1971	SCCA Northeast Division FF	Fred Stevenson	Lotus 69
1971	SCCA Southeast Division FF	Jack Baldwin	March 719
1971	SCCA Central Division FF	Jim Harrell	Titan Mk6A
1971	SCCA Midwest Division FF	Gordon Smiley	Merlyn Mk20A
1971	SCCA Southwest Division FF	John Hancock	Merlyn Mk20A
1971	SCCA Southern Pacific Div. FF	Bob Williams	Titan Mk6A
1971	SCCA Northern Pacific Div. FF	Bob Blackwood	Winkelmann WDF2
1972	SCCA National Champion	Eddie Miller	Hawke DL2B
1972	SCCA Northeast Division FF	Bruce MacInnes	Winkelmann WDF2
1972	SCCA Southeast Division FF	Jack Baldwin	March 719
1972	SCCA Central Division FF	Tom Klausler	Titan Mk6A
1972	SCCA Midwest Division FF	J. Robert Young	Hawke DL10
1972	SCCA Southwest Division FF	Terry Cearley	Merlyn Mk20A
1972	SCCA Southern Pacific Div. FF	Ron Dykes	Merlyn Mk20A
1972	SCCA Northern Pacific Div. FF	Boyd Pearce	Titan Mk6A
1973	SCCA National Champion	Bob Earl	ADF Mk II
1973	SCCA Northeast Division FF	Chris Gleason	Titan Mk6B
1973	SCCA Southeast Division FF	Bob Rodamer	Titan Mk6B
1973	SCCA Central Division FF	Vince Muzzin	Crossle 25F
1973	SCCA Midwest Division FF	Tim Cooper	Merlyn Mk20A
1973	SCCA Southwest Division FF	Rick Houston	Merlyn Mk20A
1973	SCCA Southern Pacific Div. FF	Johnny Kastner	Merlyn Mk24
1973	SCCA Northern Pacific Div. FF	Marty Loft	Titan Mk6B

(LEFT) Standing starts are the way it's done in the U.K.

Runoffs heroes: SCCA National Champs Jackson Yonge and (FAR RIGHT) Bob Lobenberg

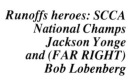

United States (cont.)

1974 SCCA National Champion	Eddie Miller	Lola T-340
1974 SCCA Northeast Division FF	Dan Torpy	Lola T-202
1974 SCCA Southeast Division FF	Jack Baldwin	Royale RP16
1974 SCCA Central Division FF	Vince Muzzin	Lola T-340
1974 SCCA Midwest Division FF	Eddie Miller	Lola T-340
1974 SCCA Southwest Division FF	Bob Ferstl	Titan Mk6C
1974 SCCA Southern Pacific Div. FF	Dennis Firestone	Titan Mk6B
1974 SCCA Northern Pacific Div. FF	Marty Loft	Titan Mk6B
1975 SCCA National Champion	Tom Wiechmann	ADF Mk II
1975 SCCA Northeast Division FF	Bruce MacInnes	Zink Z-10
1975 SCCA Southeast Division FF	Bill McDill	Royale RP16A
1975 SCCA Central Division FF	Tim Evans	Zink Z-10
1975 SCCA Midwest Division FF	Bob Richardson	Lola T-340
1975 SCCA Southwest Division FF	John Stiles	ADF Mk II
1975 SCCA Southern Pacific Div. FF	Richard Shirey	ADF Mk II
1975 SCCA Northern Pacific Div. FF	Marty Loft	Crossle 30F
1976 SCCA National Champion	Dennis Firestone	Crossle 30F
1976 AFFA Pro Formula Ford Champ.	Bruce MacInnes	Zink Z-10
1976 SCCA Northeast Division FF	Bruce MacInnes	Zink Z-10
1976 SCCA Southeast Division FF	R.B. Haynes	Zink Z-10
1976 SCCA Central Division FF	Gary Hackbarth	Lola T-342
1976 SCCA Midwest Division FF	William Henderson	Crossle 30F
1976 SCCA Southwest Division FF	John Stiles	ADF Mk II
1976 SCCA Southern Pacific Div. FF	Dennis Firestone	Crossle 30F
1976 SCCA Northern Pacific Div. FF	Billy Scyphers	Lola T-342
1977 SCCA National Champion	Dave Weitzenhof	Zink Z-10
1977 SCCA Northeast Division FF	Tom Davey	Crossle 32F
1977 SCCA Southeast Division FF	Steve Shelton	Lola T-342
1977 SCCA Central Division FF	Gary Hackbarth	Lola T-440
1977 SCCA Midwest Division FF	Bob Richardson	Lola T-440
1977 SCCA Southwest Division FF	Greg Atwell	Crossle 30F
1977 SCCA Southern Pacific Div. FF	Dennis Firestone	Crossle 32F
1977 SCCA Northern Pacific Div. FF	David Bruns	ADF Mk II
1978 SCCA National Champion	David Loring	Eagle DGF
1978 SCCA Northeast Division FF	Peter Kuhn	Van Diemen RF78
1978 SCCA Southeast Division FF	Rollin Butler	Zink Z-10
1978 SCCA Central Division FF	Gary Hackbarth	Dulon Mp19
1978 SCCA Midwest Division FF	Bob Richardson	Crossle 32F
1978 SCCA Southwest Division FF	Greg Atwell	Merlyn Mk30
1978 SCCA Southern Pacific Div. FF	David Loring	Eagle DGF
1978 SCCA Northern Pacific Div. FF	Bob Lobenberg	Crossle 32F
1979 SCCA National Champion	Dave Weitzenhof	Zink Z-10
1979 SCCA Northeast Division FF	Ed Pimm	Hawke, PRS
1979 SCCA Southeast Division FF	Mike Yoder	Lola T-540

1979 SCCA Central Division FF	Craig Taylor	Tiga FFA79
1979 SCCA Midwest Division FF	Jocko Cunningham	Lola T-540
1979 SCCA Southwest Division FF	Greg Atwell	Merlyn Mk30
1979 SCCA Southern Pacific Div. FF	Rogelio Rodriguez	Crossle 35F
1979 SCCA Northern Pacific Div. FF	Bob Lobenberg	ADF MkII
1980 SCCA National Champion	Bob Lobenberg	ADFG Mk II
1980 SCCA Northeast Division FF	Chip Ganassi	Crossle 40F
1980 SCCA Southeast Division FF	John Paul Jr.	Van Diemen RF80
1980 SCCA Central Division FF	Gary Hackbarth	Lola T-540
1980 SCCA Midwest Division FF	Ted Dillon (tie)	Lola T-540
	Terry McKenna	Lola T-540
1980 SCCA Southwest Division FF	Walter Stewart	Crossle 40F
1980 SCCA Southern Pacific Div. FF	Dave Gott	Crossle 35F
1980 SCCA Northern Pacific Div. FF	Norm Hunter	PRS RH02
1981 SCCA National Champion	Dave Weitzenhof	Citation Z-16
1981 AFFA Pro Formula Ford	Dave Weitzenhof	Citation Z-16
1981 SCCA Northeast Division FF	Mike Andretti	Lola, Scandia, VanD
1981 SCCA Southeast Division FF	Jackson Yonge	Crossle 35F
1981 SCCA Central Division FF	Craig Taylor	Tiga FFA78
1981 SCCA Midwest Division FF	Danny Edwards	Lola T-540
1981 SCCA Southwest Division FF	Paul Barnhart Jr.	Lola T-540
1981 SCCA Southern Pacific Div. FF	Dave Gott	Crossle
1981 SCCA Northern Pacific Div. FF	Bob Lobenberg	ADF Mk II
1982 SCCA National Champion	Bob Lobenberg	Viking 82
1982 SCCA Northeast Division FF	Chip Robinson	Van Diemen RF82
1982 SCCA Southeast Division FF	Jackson Yonge	PRS 82F
1982 SCCA Central Division FF	Steve Ice	Lola T-540
1982 SCCA Midwest Division FF	Danny Edwards	Lola T-540
1982 SCCA Southwest Division FF	Kim Campbell	Van Diemen RF82
1982 SCCA Southern Pacific Div. FF	R.K. Smith	Crossle 32F
1982 SCCA Northern Pacific Div. FF	John Stephanus	Viking
1983 SCCA National Champion	R.K. Smith	Swift DB-1
1983 SCCA Northeast Division FF	Scott McKee	Van Diemen RF83
1983 SCCA Southeast Division FF	Jackson Yonge	Reynard FF83
1983 SCCA Central Division FF	Tony Kester (tie)	Crossle
	Rick Gonzales	Lola
1983 SCCA Midwest Division FF	John Dekker	Lola T-640
1983 SCCA Southwest Division FF	Kim Campbell	Van Diemen RF83
1983 SCCA Southern Pacific Div. FF	Mike van Kralingen	
1983 SCCA Northern Pacific Div. FF	Richard Maier	Reynard FF83
1984 SCCA National Champion	Jackson Yonge	Reynard FF84
1984 SCCA Southeast Division FF	Jackson Yonge	Reynard FF84
1984 SCCA Southern Pacific Div. FF	Cary Bren	Swift DB-1

1984 NOTE: SCCA Northeast Division, Central Division, Midwest Division, Southwest Division and Northern Pacific Div. results not available from the SCCA.

First family of American motor racing (left to right), FFordsters on the right: Aldo, Mario, Michael and John Andretti in '87.

1985 SCCA National Champion	Scott Atchison	Swift DB-1
1985 SCCA Northeast Division FF	NA	
1985 SCCA Southeast Division FF	NA	
1985 SCCA Central Division FF	NA	
1985 SCCA Midwest Division FF	NA	
1985 SCCA Southwest Division FF	NA	
1985 SCCA Southern Pacific Div. FF	NA	
1985 SCCA Northern Pacific Div. FF	NA	
1986 SCCA National Champion	Jim Vasser Jr.	Swift DB-1
1986 SCCA Northeast Division FF	Richard Bahmer	Swift DB-1
1986 SCCA Southeast Division FF	R.B. Haynes	Reynard
1986 SCCA Central Division FF	Dwight Woodbridge	Swift DB-1
1986 SCCA Midwest Division FF	Mike Snow	Swift DB-1
1986 SCCA Southwest Division FF	Duane May	Swift DB-1
1986 SCCA Southern Pacific Div. FF	Richard Wakefield	Swift DB-1
1986 SCCA Northern Pacific Div. FF	Jim Vasser Jr.	Swift DB-1
1987 SCCA National Champion	Dave Weitzenhod	Citation Z-16
1987 SCCA Northeast Division FF	Freddy Rhemrev	Swift DB-1
1987 SCCA Southeast Division FF	William Adeimy	Swift DB-1
1987 SCCA Central Division FF	Dave Weitzenhof	Citation Centurion
1987 SCCA Midwest Division FF	Brian Williams	Citation Centurion
1987 SCCA Southwest Division FF	Craig Taylor	Swift DB-1
1987 SCCA Southern Pacific Div. FF	Brian Ongais	Swift DB-1
1987 SCCA Northern Pacific Div. FF	Mitch Thiemann	Swift DB-1
1988 SCCA National Champion	Kenny Hendrick	Swift DB-1
1988 SCCA Northeast Division FF	Chris Fahan	Swift DB-1
1988 SCCA Southeast Division FF	William Adeimy	Swift DB-1
1988 SCCA Central Division FF	Jim Render	Swift DB-1
1988 SCCA Midwest Division FF	Chris Sundstrum	Swift DB-1
1988 SCCA Southwest Division FF	Craig Taylot	Swift DB-1
1988 SCCA Southern Pacific Div. FF	Ken Hendrick	Swift DB-1
1988 SCCA Northern Pacific Div. FF	Bill Shawhan	Swift DB-1
1989 SCCA National Champion	Richard Bahmer	Swift DB-1
1989 SCCA Northeast Division FF	Chris Fahan	Swift DB-1
1989 SCCA Southeast Division FF	Rich Bahmer	Swift DB-1
1989 SCCA Central Division FF	Scott Rubenzer	Citation 89FF
1989 SCCA Midwest Division FF	Brian Williams	Citation 89FF
1989 SCCA Rocky Mtn Div FF		
1989 SCCA Southwest Division FF	Troy Talamantez	Swift DB-1
1989 SCCA Southern Pacific Div. FF	Danny Hill Jr.	Swift DB-1
1989 SCCA Northern Pacific Div. FF	Stan Townes	Swift DB-1
1990 SCCA National Champion	Tony Kester	Reynard FF88X
1990 SCCA Northeast Division FF	Bill Shearer	Swift DB-1
1990 SCCA Southeast Division FF	Ward Begley	Swift DB-1
1990 SCCA Central Division FF	Scott Rubenzer	Citation
1990 SCCA Midwest Division FF	Trey Jorski	Swift DB-1
1990 SCCA Rocky Mtn Div FF		

1990 SCCA Southwest Division FF	Monty Thompson	Swift DB-1
1990 SCCA Southern Pacific Div. FF	John Marconi	Swift DB-1
1990 SCCA Northern Pacific Div. FF	Stan Townes	Swift DB-1
1991 SCCA National Champion	Richard Schroebel	Swift DB-1
1991 SCCA Northeast Division FF	Bill Shearer	Swift DB-1
1991 SCCA Southeast Division FF	J.J. Carlin	Swift DB-1
1991 SCCA Central Division FF	Bruce May	Swift DB-1
1991 SCCA Midwest Division FF	Dave Bradley	Tuna 2
1991 SCCA Rocky Mtn Div FF		
1991 SCCA Southwest Division FF	Mike Sauce	Swift DB-1
1991 SCCA Southern Pacific Div. FF	Dave Gott	Swift DB-1
1991 SCCA Northern Pacific Div. FF	Stan Townes	Swift DB-1
1992 SCCA National Champion	C.T. Hancock	Swift DB-1
1992 SCCA Northeast Division FF	Bill Shearer	Swift DB-1
1992 SCCA Southeast Division FF	Kurt Stueber	Swift DB-1
1992 SCCA Central Division FF	Bill Wiedner	Swift DB-1
1992 SCCA Midwest Division FF	Dave Bradley	Tuna 2
1992 SCCA Rocky Mtn Div FF		
1992 SCCA Southwest Division FF	Mike Sauce	Swift DB-1
1992 SCCA Southern Pacific Div. FF	Gim Chin	Swift DB-1
1992 SCCA Northern Pacific Div. FF	Stan Townes	Swift DB-1

Europe

First Formula Ford Race: Zolder, Belgium, April 21, 1968

1969	Ford European Cortina Cup	Gerry Birrell	Crossle 16F
1970	Johnson's Wax Euro. FF	C. Bourgoignie	Lotus 61
1971	Johnsons Wax Euro. FF	Mo Harness	Lotus 69F
1979	Townsend Thoresen Euro FF1600	John Village	Royale RP26
1980	Townsend Thoresen Euro F1600	Bo Martinsson	Royale RP26
1981	Townsend Thoresen Euro F1600	Cor Euser	Royale RP29
1982	Townsend Thoresen Euro F1600	Volker Weidler	Van Diemen RF82
1982	Central Region Euroseries FF	Volker Weidler	Van Diemen RF82
1983	Townsend Thoresen Euro F1600	Gerrit van Kouwen	Lola T-642E
1983	Central Region Euroseries FF	Roland Minder	Van Diemen RF83
1984	Energy Release FF Euroseries	Gerrit van Kouwen	Van Diemen RF83
1984	Energy Release Central Reg. FF	Hans Furrer	Van Diemen RF84
1984	Energy Release Channel Reg. FF	Dave Coyne	Van Diemen RF84
1984	Nordic FF1600 Championship	Javi Haavisto	Van Diemen RF84
1987	Bridgestone FF1600 Euroseries	Svend Hansen	Van Diemen RF86
1988	Euroseries FF1600 Championship	Mika Salo	Swift FB88

*Australia action in '79:
Robyn Hamilton (#71 Elfin)
battles Wally Storey.*

Other Nations

Australia

1970 Australian FF1600 Championship	Richard Knight	
1971 Australian FF1600 Championship	Larry Perkins	
1972 Australian FF1600 Championship	Bob Skelton	
1973 Australian FF1600 Championship	John Leffler	
1974 Australian FF1600 Championship	Terry Perkins	
1975 Australian FF1600 Championship	Paul Bernasconi	
1976 Australian FF1600 Championship	Richard Carter	
1984 Australian 'Driver to Europe' FF	Ron Barnacle	Royale RP31

Austria

1971 Austrian FF1600 Championship	Hanno Maurer-Stroh	
1972 Austrian FF1600 Championship	Gerhard Irsa	
1973 Austrian FF1600 Championship	Dieter Karl Anton	
1974 Austrian FF1600 Championship	Dieter Karl Anton	
1975 Austrian FF1600 Championship	Franz Kaiser	
1976 Austrian FF1600 Championship	Franz Kaiser	
1981 Austrian International FF Cup	Hermann Bischoff	PRS 81F
1981 Austrian OSK National FF Ch.	Hermann Bischoff	PRS 81F
1984 Austrian FF1600 Championship	Franz Theuermann	Reynard 84FF

Belgium

1969 Belgium FF1600 Championship	Claude Bourgoignie	
1970 Belgium FF1600 Championship	Claude Bourgoignie	
1971 Belgium FF1600 Championship	Francois Polak	
1972 Belgium FF1600 Championship	Claude Crespin	
1973 (no championship)		
1974 (no championship)		
1975 Belgium FF1600 Championship	Jean-Francois Vaney	
1976 Belgium FF1600 Championship	Claude Crespin	
1981 Benelux FF1600 Champ.	Cor Euser	Royale RP29
1982 Benelux Reg. FF1600 Euroseries	Gerrit van Kouwen	Van Diemen RF82
1983 Benelux Reg. FF1600 Euroseries	Gerrit van Kouwen	Van Diemen RF83
1984 Energy Rel. Franco-Benlx. Reg.	Harald Huysman	Reynard 84FF
1984 Belgian FF1600 Championship	Eric Bachelart	Rondeau M584
1987 Belgian FF1600 Championship	Patrick DeWulf	Van Diemen RF87
1988 Belgian FF1600 Championship	Andre van Hoof	Van Diemen RF88

Brazil

1971 Brazilian FF Championship	Francisco Lameirao	
1972 Brazilian FF Championship	Marcos DeMoraes	
1973 Brazilian FF Championship	Alex Ribeiro	
1974 Brazilian FF Championship	Marcos DeMoraes	
1975 Brazilian FF Championship	Marcos DeMoraes	
1976 Brazilian FF Championship	J. P. Chateaubriand	
1977 Brazilian FF Championship	Artur Bragantini	
1978 Brazilian FF Championship	Amadeo Ferri	
1979 Brazilian FF Championship	Artur Bragantini	
1980 Brazilian FF Championship	Artur Bragantini	
1981 Brazilian FF Championship	Egon Herzfeldt	
1982 Brazilian FF Championship	Egon Herzfeldt	
1983 Brazilian FF Championship	Joao Ferreira	
1984 Brazilian FF Championship	Luis Silveira	
1985 Brazilian FF Championship	Serge Buchrieser	
1986 Brazilian FF Championship	Jefferson Elias	
1987 Brazilian FF Championship	Gil de Ferran	
1988 Brazilian FF Championship	Djalma Fogaca	
1989 Brazilian FF Championship	Antonio Neto	
1990 Brazilian FF Championship	Paulo Garcia	
1991 Brazilian FF Championship	Walter Garcia	
1992 Brazilian FF Championship	Norio Matsubara	

Canada

1972 Bulova FF1600 Championship	Danny Burritt	Titan Mk6
1973 Canadian FF1600 Championship	Dr. David Morris	
1974 Canadian FF1600 Championship	Luke de Sadeleer	
1975 Canadian FF1600 Championship	John Scratch	Ferret
1976 Canadian FF1600 Championship	John Scratch	Ferret
1982 Walter Wolf FF1600 Challenge	Scott Goodyear	Van Diemen RF82
1991 Esso Protec F1600 Championship	Stephen Adams	Reynard 89F
1992 Esso Protec F1600 Championship	Stephen Adams	Reynard 89F

Denmark

1970 Danish FF1600 Championship	Tom Belso	
1971 Danish FF1600 Championship	Jorgen Herlevsen	
1972 Danish FF1600 Championship	Dan Schilling	
1973 Danish FF1600 Championship	Jac Nelleman	
1974 Danish FF1600 Championship	Henrik Spellerberg	
1975 Danish FF1600 Championship	John Nielsen	
1976 Danish FF1600 Championship	Soeren Aggerholm	
1981 Danish FF1600 Championship	Kim Dupont	Van Diemen RF80
1987 Danish FF1600 Championship	Svend Hansen	Van Diemen RF85
1988 Danish FF1600 Championship	Henrik Jacobsen	Van Diemen RF85

Finland

1984 Finnish FF1600 Championship	Javi Haavisto	Van Diemen RF84
1987 Finnish FF1600 Championship	Mika Hakkinen	Reynard 86FF
1988 Finnish FF1600 Championship	Mika Salo	Swift FB88

France

1984 French FF1600 Championship	J.-Ph. Grand	Rondeau M584
1985 French FF1600 Championship	Philippe Gache	Rondeau M584
1986 French FF1600 Championship	J. Goudchaux	Van Diemen RF86

France finally adopted Formula Ford in the mid '80s. Here the great French champion Maurice Trintignant tries a Rondeau.

1987	French FF1600 Championship	Laurent Daumet	Reynard 86FF
1988	French FF1600 Championship	Eric Helary	Reynard 88FF
1989	French FF1600 Championship	William David	Van Diemen RF89
1990	French FF1600 Championship	J.-C. Boullion	Van Diemen RF90
1991	French FF1600 Championship	Franck Guibbert	Van Diemen RF91

Germany

1981	German ONS FF1600 Champ.	Stefan Bellof	PRS 81F
1981	German Nat'l Trophy FF1600	Mario Bauer	Royale RP29
1983	German Silver Lion FF Trophy	Gerrit van Kouwen	Van Diemen RF83
1984	German ONS FF1600 Cup	Uwe Schafer	Van Diemen RF84
1984	German Silver Lion FF Trophy	Hans Furrer	Van Diemen RF84
1987	German FF1600 Championship	Ellen Lohr	Van Diemen RF87
1988	German FF1600 Championship	Meik Wagner	Van Diemen RF88

Holland

1970	Dutch FF1600 Championship	Huub Vermuelen	
1971	Dutch FF1600 Championship	Huub Vermuelen	
1972	Dutch FF1600 Championship	Roelof Wunderink	
1973	Dutch FF1600 Championship	Roelof Wunderink	
1974	Dutch FF1600 Championship	Boy Hayje	
1975	Dutch FF1600 Championship	Jim Vermeulen	
1976	Dutch FF1600 Championship	M. Bleekemolen	
1981	Netherlands FF1600 Champ.	Cor Euser	Royale RP29
1984	Netherlands FF1600 Champ.	Maarten Bottelier	Lola
1986	Netherlands FF1600 Champ.	Jaap Bokhoeven	Reynard 86FF
1987	Netherlands FF1600 Champ.	Piet Bouwmeister	Mondiale M86S
1988	Netherlands FF1600 Champ.	Frank Eglem	Van Diemen RF88

Italy

1970	Italian FF1600 Championship	Biagio Cammarone
1971	Italian FF1600 Championship	Fernando Spreafico
1972	Italian FF1600 Championship	Gaudenzio Mantova
1973	Italian FF1600 Championship	Luigi Castiglione
1974	Italian FF1600 Championship	Orazio Ragaiolo
1975	Italian FF1600 Championship	Luigi Castiglione

New Zealand

1984	Motorcraft NZ FF1600 Champ.	Steve Richards	Titan Mk6
1991	New Zealand FF1600 Champ.	Garry Croft	
1992	ICI/Autocolour Int'l FF Challenge	Garry Croft	Swift

Portugal

1970	Portuguese FF Championship	Ernesto Neves	Lotus 61M
1971	Portuguese FF Championship	Ernesto Neves	Lotus 69
1972	Portuguese FF Championship	Ernesto Neves	Lotus 69
1973-1984 NO PORTUGUESE CHAMPIONSHIPS			

1985	Portuguese FF1600 Champ.	Antonio Simoes	Van Diemen RF85
1986	Portuguese FF1600 Champ.	Pedro Chaves	Van Diemen RF85
1987	Portuguese FF1600 Champ.	Pedro Faria	Van Diemen RF87
1988	Portuguese FF1600 Champ.	D. Castro Santos	Van Diemen RF87
1989	Portuguese FF1600 Champ.	Pedro Lamy	Van Diemen RF87
1990	Portuguese FF1600 Champ.	Pedro Couceiro	Van Diemen RF90
1991	Portuguese FF1600 Champ.	Manuel Giao	Van Diemen RF90
1992	Portuguese FF1600 Champ.	Fredrico Viegas	Swift SC92

Spain

1987	Spanish FF1600 Championship	Antonio Albacete	Van Diemen RF86
1988	Spanish FF1600 Championship	Jordi Gene	Van Diemen RF88

Sweden

1970	Scandinavian Cup	Gregor Kronegard	
1971	Swedish FF Cup	Bengt Gilhorn	
1972	Danish-Swedish Cup	Hakan Alriksson	
1973	Swedish National FF Champ.	John Erik Johansson	
1974	Swedish National FF Champ.	Mats Nygren	
1975	Swedish National FF Champ.	Ronnie Petterson	
1976	Swedish National FF Champ.	Bo Martinsson	
1981	Scandinavian FF1600 Champ.	Jesper Villumsen	PRS 80F
1981	Swedish FF1600 Championship	Lennart Sundahl	Van Diemen RF80
1982	Scand. Reg. Euroseries FF1600	Jens Andersen	
1983	Scand. Reg. Euroseries FF1600	Jens Andersen	
1984	Energy Release Scand. Reg. FF	Javi Haavisto	Van Diemen RF84
1987	Scandinavian FF1600 Champ.	Mika Hakkinen	Reynard 86FF
1987	Swedish FF1600 Championship	Mika Hakkinen	Reynard 86FF
1988	Scandinavian FF1600 Champ.	Mika Salo	Swift FB88
1988	Swedish FF1600 Championship	Peter Aslund	Reynard 88FF

Switzerland

1981	Swiss FF1600 Championship	Heini Jeker	Van Diemen RF81
1982	Swiss FF1600 Championship	Benoit Morand	LCR P12
1984	Swiss FF1600 Championship	Antonio Mangia	Van Diemen RF84

Another kind of champion

David Baldwin has garnered no titles for his driving prowess. However, there can be little doubt he has won more FF championships than any man alive: The well-educated Englishman has designed every Van Diemen Formula Ford built since the RF77 and before that, as an employee of Lotus Components, he did the top-selling Lotus 69 (which coincidentally inspired the first Van Diemen FA73). Van Diemen having been the FF sales leader for nearly two decades now, Baldwin has thus given more shape to the class than anyone else—by a very large margin. He is a champion in the truest sense of the word.

Baldwin is clearly the perfect man for the design job at Van Diemen, well grounded in the essentials of "productionization." In '65, the 24-year-old answered an ad in *The Times* and wound up working for Lotus Components in Cheshunt as a junior design engineer working on everything from F3 cars to the first Lotus 51 FF to Lotus-Cortina sedans. When Components was closed down in '71, he followed its boss, Mike Warner, to GRD, then went to McLaren where he assisted on an Indianapolis car. In '72, he joined Team Lotus, participating in the development of the World Championship-winning 72.

Fledgling team owner Mo Nunn, an acquaintance from his Lotus F3 days, asked Baldwin to design an F1 car in '74 which emerged as the Ensign 176, a greatly admired machine produced on a minuscule budget. Baldwin started the 177, then went to work for another old friend, Emerson Fittipaldi, producing the Copersucar FA5.

"To succeed in F1, you have to be 100 percent committed," Baldwin now observes. "Unfortunately, in the mid '70s, my wife became ill and I simply could not continue to make than kind of commitment."

He was a free-lancer, working from home on projects like the Panther Lima sports car, when Ralph Firman called with the job of reviving Van Diemen's fortunes. Baldwin was given a design brief bounded by the need for economical mass production, but nonetheless came up with a terrific car: The RF77 not only turned Van Diemen around but propelled it to the top of the FF heap where it has remained for 15 years.

Personable and polite, Baldwin took well over an hour out of his day during a crucial Feb. '92 period (he was then hard at work on pre-season development of a complicated F3 machine) to review Van Diemen FF design history with the author—a fascinating and very eye-opening interview.

AUTHOR Did you design the Lotus 61?

DAVID BALDWIN No, I was a project engineer at Lotus Components then, but basically the 61 was the same chassis as the 51 which was not mine. The 61 was a 51 with a wedge shape body that was an image thing.

The 59 and 69 range of Formula 3 and Formula 2 cars *were* mine. After that, Lotus Components finished—they didn't want a racing car company in the public group. I then did a bit of contract work for McLaren, working on an Indy Car.

AUTHOR A brief association with Jo Marquart at GRD followed, did it not?

BALDWIN Yes. Mike Warner (ex-boss of Lotus Components) was there and Marquart was there. I didn't stay very long; I was only there a few weeks (and left) a bit disenchanted.

Mike's got a lot of energy and he's very good. But, (GRD) didn't come off in its entirety.

After that, I went to Team Lotus for a while—it was the year when Fittipaldi won the World Championship, '72. I left Lotus and went directly to Ensign where I designed the 176. It took me 12 months to draw that car. We were very hard up there; we even drew our own Aeroquip fittings because we couldn't afford to get them from the States!

I couldn't do that again: It just went on and on and on, seven days a week and, although you can do that in your twenties and early thirties, you certainly can't do it when you're much older than that—or I couldn't anyway.

AUTHOR So the Ensign came first and then the Fittipaldi?

BALDWIN Yes. With the Fittipaldi, I made one or two basic errors of judgement and it wasn't a good car. That's what it comes down to. I went down to Sao Paulo for six months, and we got the project off the ground, but it just wasn't a good car and I left shortly afterwards.

I was self-employed then for a while. I did a road car chassis for a little firm called Panther. Arch Motors built the chassis; I don't know if you've heard of Arch Motors?

AUTHOR You can't have been around Formula Ford without hearing about Arch Motors!

BALDWIN They built the chassis. And after a time, the firm got into financial troubles, I believe, and was taken over by ... who's the Korean chap? And I believe the chassis is now made in Taiwan or something like that.

AUTHOR It's still essentially your design?

BALDWIN I believe so. Anyway, I'd stayed in contact with Ralph all those years, I knew exactly what was going on with his company. I think that took me up to about '79 or '80.

AUTHOR But your first Van Diemen was the RF77 ...

BALDWIN Ah, but I wasn't working for Van Diemen full time then. That didn't happen until '79-'80.

AUTHOR Regarding the RF77, you had Ralph's RF76 platform to start from and that, like all the early Van Diemen's, was based on your Lotus 69 design, correct? Wasn't the 69 FF a spaceframe version of what had been a monocoque Lotus?

BALDWIN No. The Lotus 59 and 69 were spaceframe cars. The F2 versions of the 69 had a monocoque piece in the middle which had the fuel cell and the driver.

I saw a 69 for sale in *Autosport* a few weeks ago for something like £60-70,000—an absolutely incredible price!

AUTHOR All cars with Lotus badges are much more valuable now than they were in their day—which can be said of a few of your Van Diemen models in Club Ford racing, too!

Can you recall your objectives with the RF77? They were certainly good-looking cars.

BALDWIN At the time, Ralph was still looking at the school car market as far as I can remember—indeed, that was a reasonable portion of Ralph's business. So he wanted a car that was fairly tough and robust, and one that a reasonable number of shapes and sizes could climb in to.

That was it! It was fairly simple; you could bolt it together quite easily. It was easy enough for Van Diemen to make the parts—wishbones and the like, although I don't think they attempted the chassis at that time.

AUTHOR Right. Until a few years ago, Arch did all your chassis, correct?

BALDWIN They did. Arch and there was another company, ex-Arch staff, who made them for us.

Nowadays all the chassis are alloy steel—we went to a chrome-moly chassis effective with the RF88. In the old days, we used mild steel tubing but FF cars today are similar to the Grand Prix cars of about 15 years ago from the technical point of view. The quality had to improve as the cars got more complicated.

AUTHOR Race driver school considerations played some part in your FF design thinking until about '85, right? Ralph says the '85 car was the first one he let you do without school restraints hanging over your drafting table.

BALDWIN Well, certainly the '84 wasn't a good school car. But the racing school had fallen off in demand a little bit by then and we'd gotten some competition there as well.

The RF85 was very, very much done on the lines of the American Swift. In hindsight, we shouldn't have done that, but we'd seen this car in the States which, apart from going very well, was a very attractive car. And we'd had a look and decided, "Right, we'd better do something very, very similar."

We sold a lot of them, though in my opinion, it wasn't as good a car as the Swift itself. The RF86, though, was a very good car—that's possibly one of the favorite Van Diemens in Europe anyway. A very driveable car. Up until possibly two years ago, people were begging us for '86 cars, second hand ones, whenever they came in.

For a driver coming in to Formula Ford, it just happened to be one of those nice, easy, friendly cars to drive.

AUTHOR That "driveability" is what I remember most about the 77-series—I don't know if you called them that, but the cars based on your first Van Diemen chassis. Do you remember taking sort of a survey of the market before you set to work on the RF77 in '76?

BALDWIN We did. There was the Crossle, which had a good form in the States. We just had a look round and decided which way to go. And that was it really.

AUTHOR So there was no attempt to build a milestone car, to come up with a "sales angle" to distinguish your car?

BALDWIN We hung the engine and gearbox in very simply, with just a couple of bolts on the crossbeam and a couple of bolts up front. But we realized pretty soon afterwards that that was a little bit flexible, so we had to stick a couple of tie rods down the bottom.

AUTHOR That was a change for '78?

BALDWIN Yes, '78 or '79: There was definitely a little bit of movement down there. I can't remember much else about those cars, though. In the schools, they lasted a relatively long time.

AUTHOR Was the next big change the move to front radiators?

BALDWIN The early '80s cars were all along similar lines, weren't they? The big change for us was, of course, the 84—a totally different chassis.

We started again in '85. The '86 was a nice friendly little car; the '87—I think went to pushrods that year—wasn't. Again, always a similar number sold but the RF87 wasn't quite such an easy car to drive.

And then, there was the new configuration chassis for 1990 which now, of course, is in its third year.

RF84 (at right) was a huge change from the RF83 (left).

AUTHOR The major development for this year ('92) is the monoshock.

BALDWIN We did that as a test bed for our new F3 because, after committing ourselves to a big project like that, we wanted to see how the system worked. So we built a monoshock 1600—and it went much better than we expected! We planned to do it as a sales pitch in 1600, as something for the following year, and we were hoping for a tenth or two. But the thing went half-a-second quicker. We were very pleased with that, so we jumped right in.

AUTHOR What about aerodynamics?

BALDWIN Well, it's coming into FF more and more. One didn't appreciate it—and couldn't afford to appreciate it too much!—

years ago. But as things progress ... The engines are fairly static, now; your tires are all of one make; and you've got to somehow justify a new car each year. Aerodynamics is an area that has to be looked into. The regulations make it difficult to make big strides, but I'm sure there are still some to make. It's a question of how much time and money you've got to look into it.

AUTHOR If you'd been given a free hand in '83 to design a FF as Swift's David Bruns was given a relatively free hand that year, how would your car have compared to his? Is that at all a fair question?

BALDWIN I don't know, to be honest with you. We hadn't seen the Swift at all when I designed the RF84, of course, and the Swift was a lot nicer car, no two ways about it. It was the wrong time for us to build a bad car, the year the Swift came out with a good one.

We have a Pre-'85 championship over here and, oddly enough, the RF84 is very sought after for it. We built a lot of them that year. It was a nasty car to drive; it wasn't easy. But it was competitive in the right hands—not what you'd call a good customer car at all.

Back to your question: I don't know. I can't imagine why (my "no-restraints") car would have been like the Swift because Dave Bruns and I had totally different thoughts.

I've met Dave Bruns and he's very clear thinking. Prior to that Swift, he had designed other Formula Fords also.

AUTHOR Two others, one a homebuilt, the second the ADF ...

BALDWIN ... which was a very good car as well, if I'm correct.

AUTHOR But far beyond the realm of reality, price wise.

BALDWIN I've never seen one at all. But I was told it was a good car. I should think, obviously, he has straightline speed among his priorities. It's obviously paid off because you've got some very fast circuits over there. The long straights that you have in the States you don't have, by and large, over here.

As a company, basically, we're in business building racing cars to make a profit to survive. We have no sponsorship or anything and you must look at it always from that point of view.

AUTHOR You have to walk a very thin line between cost-effectiveness and competitiveness.

BALDWIN When we build a brand-new car or introduce a brand new concept, we like it to run for three years. That's our ideal situation. But you have to have a number of updates every year however good the car is. Two reasons, really: One, you need to generate new interest. You've got to sell cars, so there's got to be something a bit different to the old car. Second, you get a bit of pirating within two or three months—there are people with nose shell molds by then, there's little tricks for wishbones, all sorts of things. So there's one element to bringing out a new model and there's another one to try and stop the pirating.

Cost-effectiveness is a major part of the design process for us. One of the reasons we've survived, I think, is because what-

ever era of car you look at, we've discussed things beforehand with our suppliers. We don't just open a catalog and say, "Right, let's have six of those." It might be six months delivery on that one. It might cost twice as much as the one below it for some reason. This one they make 10,000 a year; that one they make 100,000, and the one they produce 100,000 of has to be cheaper.

AUTHOR You seem to be challenged by that in ways other designers might not be. Others talk of having a clean sheet of paper and an unlimited budget ...

BALDWIN It's nice to be in a position to do that, but you can't when you do production racing cars. Because all that does is give the next person along the line a headache—in our case, Angie who does all the buying.

From the design point of view, for sure, all this (careful component and material shopping) is a little bit boring and you sometimes end up with things that look a little bit crude. But at the end of the day, if the car doesn't work out properly, you're not going to be here long, are you?

You've got the top end of "Formula Ford engineering" as I call it with the Swifts of America. As I say, they're just super cars and Dave Bruns is just a superb designer. But we'd like to think we're super competitive and winning, and we can build economically too.

Still, from time to time, definitely, we're going to be knocked by people like Bruns who look upon things with a slightly narrower vision. Nothing we can do about it.

AUTHOR Yours is the art of successful compromise.

BALDWIN Well, David Bruns obviously struck a pretty good compromise, no two ways about it. Still, take our '90 car: We had to come up with a new image and we did. I'd like to say that's got a good chassis, although there are areas where possibly it does fall down because we have to get drivers of all size into it. Still, I'm pleased.

The objectives haven't changed in 25 years: A low-powered car like a Formula Ford needs to be kept as light and free of encumbrances as possible, really. You've got 100hp if you're lucky, and you just can't afford to scrub off that power. We all have the same brief; but as I said (Van Diemen) goes at it from the direction that we are in a business to make a profit to survive. And that, really, serves to keep us on our toes.

The RF86 is a Baldwin—and customer—favorite.

Acknowledgements

In the course of a 20-year association with *any* particular endeavor, one picks up many things. What yours truly, this book's author, has collected from Formula Ford are debts—not the financial kind (though there are still some apparently permanent charges on my credit card harkening back to a pair of FF crashes), but a more important kind: This book is a partial payment, but I'm in so deep now, words will never get me out.

I'm in hock for memories. I've enjoyed—no *loved*—Formula Ford racing from the day I saw a pack of them leaping over the ridge between the road course and the oval at an SCCA regional race at Thompson, Conn. In 20 years of wrenching on and writing about these cars, I've ridden a roller coaster over a mountain of thrills, and I can never pay back all the great drivers and mechanics and car builders and importers and component suppliers and engine tuners and tire makers and even other journalists, come to think of it, for what was a particularly wild and enjoyable ride.

So before I run out of pages, let me write checks.

First, this book is dedicated to my best half Betsy and our two little ones Bethany and Jared who accommodated several months of late nights at the computer without understanding why the book never seemed to get done. (Thank you, sweeties. Let's vacation!)

A second dedication is to Paul Pfanner who built the spectacular new *Racer* magazine on the fumes from a thousand FF races. Though *Racer* brings him million$ in the years to come, I know he will not forget his roots. (Thank you, Paul, for making this book happen.)

And more ...

All the great FF memories that are only touched upon in this book would never have been possible without:

• **John Herne**: My first race driver friend and my best race driver friend, and we did get to England, didn't we!

• **Brian Goodwin**: The best FF driver I ever watched, but choosing a "real" career over a racing career got

Best in the business: Carl Haas.

The best of times (1976): MacInnes leads Evans, McKnight and Davey.

you Cindy, three great kids and a life without regrets—remember that! (Meanwhile, I'll remember Summit Point in the rain when you lapped everyone but Chip Ganassi ... and remain in awe.)

• **Bruce MacInnes**: Probably the most fun I ever had was living hand-to-mouth in the back of a station wagon the year you won everything, and looking back, most of the fun was interviewing you!

• **Dave Weitzenhof**: You taught me more about the important technicalities of FF racing than anyone, and in the process showed me the enormous commitment required to be a champion. **Sherrie**, meanwhile, fed me more than anyone (see "living hand-to-mouth", above) and was a more reliable source of race data than anyone I've ever met. Thank you both!

• **Tom Davey**: If advertising is the art of convincing innocents that black is not only white but absolutely essential to our well-being so we run out and buy it today, then you, Tom, are the greatest advertising genius who ever lived.

• **Gordon Kirby**: The first real journalist I ever sat toe-to-toe with over a beer, you talked a lot about the Unsers and Andrettis, but your best stories were about FFs (and I know *you* haven't forgotten *your* roots).

• **Jeremy Shaw**: The only other Indy Car correspondent today who sees the FF kids and the great FF races they participated in behind that methanol curtain—and the only Indy Car correspondent who owns a Mallock.

• **Quentin Spurring**: The most capable editor/publisher/owner in the motorsports business—operating at a level far higher than FF racing, your Q•Editions is a model for doing things right. **Jane Spurring**, meanwhile, knows more about American politics than this book's author, and thank you both for the warm hospitality.

• **David Aronson** and **Gordon Medenica**: Medenica Motor Racing—geez, now that really was a great time had by all, if only in hindsight. Now that you're both frighteningly successful, I'm pleased to know you won't forget your FF roots either.

• **Chris Wallach** and **Norm Marx**: You could enjoy life again once you'd shed the Autodynamics and Fast Company yokes, yet for a couple of years you put up with a poorly paid but big-mouthed employee who was just learning the ropes anyway. Thank you for the opportunities!

• **Scott Harvey, Gordon Smiley, Tom Stewart** and **Jules Williams**: Four I miss—often and a lot.

• The English car constructors, past and present, and especially **Mike Blanchet, Alan Cornock, Ralph Firman, Howden Ganley, Clive Hayward, Vic Hollman, David Lazenby, Adrian Reynard, Tim Schenken**, and **Roy Thomas**.

• The chassis importers, past and present, especially **Bob Cavanaugh, Ken Deeter, Bill Fickling, Mike Gue, Carl Haas, Hugh Kleinpeter, Fred Opert, Pierre Phillips, Dick Scott**, and **Doug Shierson**.

• The folks building FFs in America, past and present, especially **David Bruns, Dan Gurney, Steve Lathrop, John Ward,** and **Paul White**.

Paul Pfanner and Peter Hampshire.

Lola driver Brian Goodwin (at left) listens to David Loring (right) in '74.

• The hundreds of SCCA drivers who made the FF racing great, especially **Carl Anderson, Greg Atwell, Rollin Butler, Bob Earl, Tim Evans, Dennis Firestone, Chip Ganassi, R.B. Haynes, William Henderson, Scott Holmes, Bob Kawash, Nick Kozlov, Peter Kuhn, Kip Laughlin, Bob Lobenberg, David Loring, Dan Marvin, Eddie Miller, Barry Pigot, Ed Pimm, Chip Robinson, Steve Shelton, R.K. Smith** and **Craig Taylor.**

• The American engine tuners who always went out of their way for the press, whether they had time or not (and they never did), especially **Jay Ivey, Fran Larkin, Arnie Loyning, Joe Stimola** and **Ted Wenz.**

• The racing school proprietors and instructors, past and present, and especially **Skip Barber, Bob Butte, Geoffrey Clarke, Jacques Couture, Jim Russell, Richard Spenard** and **Mark Wolocatiuk.**

• **Bob Tullius**: The great Jaguar driver and team owner, one of my first employers, hated Formula Ford with a passion but knew a real racer when he saw one and one day hired Chip Robinson.

• **To all of you**: Thanks for everything. Drive fast.

Dan Marvin: Formula Atlantic inspiration, but that's another story!

The "Van Diemen Twins," Peter Kuhn and Tom Davey.

Now, that's a concept

Let me conclude with a story—actually it's more of a concept—put forth by SCCA Northeast Division FF racer Tom Davey in 1976. Tom's idea was a Lloyd's of London Trophy Dash, a one-lap Formula Ford race with A $10,000 winner-take-all purse featuring an inverted grid and a standing start.

"The winner," Davey explained, "would be the first car/driver combination to cross the finish line. All those old-fashioned notions about having to have body-work/wheels/suspension and the like in place at the conclusion would be waived.

"What do you think?"

If you see the humor in that but at the same time hunger to watch—or better yet, to participate in—such an event, then you are a true Formula Ford worthy. Whatever FF's future, it's certain that you (like me) will never forget its past.

Davey was always on the prowl for a new advertising angle.

Bibliography

Books

A-Z of Formula Racing Cars
by David Hodges
Edited and with contributions by Mike Lawrence
©1990 by Bay View Books Ltd., 13a Bridgeland St.,
    Bideford, Devon EX39 2QE, England

Drive It! The Complete Book of Formula Ford
by Phillip Bingham
A FOULIS Motoring Book
©1984 Haynes Publishing Group, Sparkford, Yeovil,
    Somerset BA22 7JJ, England

Encyclopedia of Motor Sport, The
Edited by G.N. Georgano
©1971 Rainbird Reference Books Ltd.
Pub. by The Viking Press, Inc., 625 Madison Ave.,
    New York, N.Y. 10022

Formula Ford: A 20-Year World Success Story
Edited by Simon North
©1977 Brands Hatch Publications, Fawkham,
    Dartford, Kent DA3 8NG, England

Formula Ford Book, The
by Nick Brittan
©1977 Patrick Stephens Limited, Bar Hill,
    Cambridge CB8 8EL, England

*Pace Motor Racing Directory 1981: Mike Kettlewell's
Guide to British Motor Racing, The*
©1981 Kettlewell Transport Information Trade Srvcs.,
    The Mill House, Station Road, Eastville, Boston,
    Lincolnshire PE22 8LS, England

Periodicals

Autosport
    Haymarket Specialist Motoring Publications Ltd.,
    60 Waldegrave Road, Teddington,
    MiddlesexTW11 8LG, England

Motoring News
    Standard House, Bonhill Street,
    London EC2A 4DA, England

On Track
    OT Publishing Inc., 17165 Newhope St., Unit M,
    Fountain Valley, CA 92708, U.S.A.

Racer
    Racer Communications, Inc., 1371 E. Warner Ave.,
    Suite E, Tustin, CA 92680, U.S.A.

SportsCar
    Pfanner Comm., Inc., 1371 E. Warner Ave.,
    Suite E, Tustin, CA 92680, U.S.A.

Photographers

KEY: ALL = All photos on page, T = Top, M = Middle, B = Bottom, L = Left, R = Right, UM = Upper Middle, LM = Lower Middle

Photographers

Many thanks to Jacqui Weston, Jeff Bloxham and the rest of the staff at Autosport Photographic for their invaluable assistance!

KEY: ALL = All photos on page, T = Top, M = Middle, B = Bottom, L = Left, R = Right, UM = Upper Middle, LM = Lower Middle

Index

Photographs indicated in *bold italic*

Wiechmann, Tom, 52, 54, 74, *127*
Wiet, 125, *125*
Wild, Derek, 124
Wilken, Fred, 87
Williams, Frank, 26-27, *26*, 29, 77, 120
Williams, Ian, 115
Williams, Jules, 32-34, 74, 164
Williamson, Roger, 73
Willis, Ian, 72
Willis, Keith, 72
Willment, John, 103
Willow Springs Int'l Raceway, 33, *33*, 35, 74, 97, 116
Wilson, Desire, *147*
Wilson, Rob, 73
Wittane, Randy, 81
Wimhurst, 125, *125*
Wimhurst, Len, 39, 102, 106-107, 110, 125
Winfield School, 102
Winkelmann, 36, 38, *40*, 50, 106, 125

Winkelmann, Bob, 107
Winstanley, David, 72
Wolocatiuk, Mark, 165
Wood, Tom, 125
Woodhead, Bill, 79
Wooler, C.T., 38
Wren, 125
Wright, Brad, 95
Wyer, John, 86, 103

-X-

Xpit, 125

-Y-

Yonge, Jackson, 55, *156*
Youlden, Tony, 78

Young, David, 103
Young, Ira, 116
Young, Stephen, 103

-Z-

Zagk, 67
Zarcades, Peter, 116
Zegler, 125
Zeus, 125, *126*
Zink, 38, 43, 50, 52, *53*, 55, 81, 126, *126*, *150*, *163*
Zink, Ed, 50, 81, 126
Zink Manufacturing, 81, 126
Zolder, 28, 121

Addendum

As was mentioned in the introduction to Chapter 7, the chassis encyclopedia section of this book will probably *never* be finalized, and so the author sends these words via his publisher to the reader humbly, knowing that questions remain. Case in point: Right in the middle of the frantic, 24-hour-long galley proof stage of this edition's printing schedule, a fax arrived from Tim Schenken, Manager-Motor Racing of CAMS (the Confederation of Australian Motor Sport) containing information he in turn had obtained from the Murrumbeena, Victoria-based Formula Ford Association Inc.

It was by then too late to undertake major surgery on chapters 6, 7 and 9, but the information was simply too interesting to file away. And so we pounced upon this 60 sq. in. hole!

Add to Chapter 6:

Thwarted in their biggest export market, the U.S., by the Swift's sales success in the '80s and by waning FF1600 interest in SCCA Nationals, the remaining English constructors stepped up their marketing activities in other arenas. That has had a dramatic effect on the FF scene in several nations, not the least of which is Australia: "In recent years, because of aggressive marketing by Van Diemen and Swift Europe in Australia and the considerable level of success achieved by the former—with a consequent sales response from competitors—local FF constructors have experienced great difficulty in attracting interest in their designs," explains a bulletin from the Australian Formula Ford Association accompanying an updated list of 'Driver to Europe' FF champions."

While there has been a minor renaissance in the American FF cottage industry in the early '90s, the giants still lord over the rest of the world.

Add to Chapter 7:

Elfin (cont.)
In recent years, the Elfin factory has produced new designs, several of which have been raced at the local level in Australia. Elfin 600 and 620 models are now collectors items and are attracting renewed interest as historic racers.

Elwyn (cont.)
Elwyn Bickley assisted countryman David Mawer with the construction of his FF in '74 and commenced building FFs in his own name in '74. Bickley competed in his own cars in the late '70s, but the marque's most notable success was Warwick Rooklyn's winning the Australian Championship in '86.

Galloway (AUS)
Harry Galloway began building Formula Fords in Sydney in the mid '70s, and ultimately produced three cars, one of which won the Australian Championship in '83, driven by Bruce Connolly.

Mawer (AUS)
David Mawer, a sheet-metal fabricator from Sydney, produced a one-off FF in 1973 with assistance from Harry Galloway and Elwyn Bickley. This famed machine won two Australian FF series driven by Paul Bernasconi ('75) and Russell Nordern ('79).

Add to Chapter 9:

Australia

1970	Australia 'Driver to Europe' FF	Richard Knight	Elfin 600
1971	Australia 'Driver to Europe' FF	Larry Perkins	Elfin 600
1972	Australia 'Driver to Europe' FF	Bob Skelton	Bowin P4A
1973	Australia 'Driver to Europe' FF	John Leffler	Bowin P6F
1974	Australia 'Driver to Europe' FF	Terry Perkins	Elfin 620B
1975	Australia 'Driver to Europe' FF	Paul Bernasconi	Mawer
1976	Australia 'Driver to Europe' FF	Richard Carter	Birrana F73
1977	Australia 'Driver to Europe' FF	John Smith	Bowin P4A
1978	Australia 'Driver to Europe' FF	John Wright	Bowin P4A
1979	Australia 'Driver to Europe' FF	Russell Nordern	Mawer
1980	Australia 'Driver to Europe' FF	Stephen Brook	Lola
1981	Australia 'Driver to Europe' FF	Phillip Revell	Lola T-440
1982	Australia 'Driver to Europe' FF	Jeff Summers	Elfin 620B
1983	Australia 'Driver to Europe' FF	Bruce Connolly	Galloway
1984	Australia 'Driver to Europe' FF	Ron Barnacle	Royale RP31
1985	Australia 'Driver to Europe' FF	Tomas Mezera	Reynard
1986	Australia 'Driver to Europe' FF	Warwick Rooklyn	Elwyn
1987	Australia 'Driver to Europe' FF	Peter Verheyen	Van Diemen RF86
1988	Australia 'Driver to Europe' FF	David Roberts	Van Diemen RF88
1989	Australia 'Driver to Europe' FF	Mark Larkham	Van Diemen RF89
1990	Australia 'Driver to Europe' FF	Russell Ingall	Van Diemen RF90
1991	Australia 'Driver to Europe' FF	Troy Dunstan	Van Diemen RF91
1992	Australia 'Driver to Europe' FF	C. McConville	Van Diemen RF92

Information please

Do you have information to add to the next edition, or facts to contribute to the storehouse of Formula Ford 1600/2000 knowledge/Southern California branch? If so, please take a minute to write or fax the publisher at the address printed in the front of this book, or the author directly at:

Nickless Communications
9201 Heatherton Circle
Huntington Beach, CA 92646-2321, U.S.A.
(714) 965-1549 fax

Thank you!